International Trade, Growth, and Development

T0305347

International trade, growth, and development

Essays by Pranab Bardhan

Blackwell
Publishing

350 Main Street, Malden, MA 02148-5018, USA
108 Cowley Road, Oxford OX4 1JF, UK
550 Swanston Street, Carlton, Victoria 3053, Australia
Kurfürstendamm 57, 10707 Berlin, Germany

First published 2003 by Blackwell Publishing Ltd

Library of Congress Cataloging-in-Publication Data

Bardhan, Pranab K.
International trade, growth, and development : essays / by Pranab Bardhan.
p. cm.
Includes bibliographical references and index.
ISBN 978-1-4051-0140-0
1. International trade.   2. Economic development.   I. Title.

HF1379 .B364 2003
338.9—dc21
2002026254

A catalogue record for this title is available from the British Library.

Set in 10/12.5pt Galliard
by Graphicraft Limited, Hong Kong

For further information on
Blackwell Publishing, visit our website:
http://www.blackwellpublishing.com

FSC
Mixed Sources
Product group from well-managed
forests and other controlled sources
Cert no. SGS-COC-2953
www.fsc.org
© 1996 Forest Stewardship Council

Contents

Preface

The literature on international trade, growth, and development is huge. We do not pretend to even attempt to cover this large literature in any systematic fashion. Instead, this book contains essays, written over three decades, focusing on some of the relatively neglected issues. For example, we deal with the effect of credit market imperfection on the pattern of international specialization, the allocational and distributional implications of localized technical progress, differential learning and different modes of transfer of technology, the equilibrium properties of vintage capital growth models (particularly their implications for international productivity differences brought about by differences in endogenously determined rates of obsolescence of capital), and so on. In the last part of the book we also report several large-scale and yet intensive field surveys in India in which I was involved, which bear on the crucial terms and conditions of contracts in informal factor markets in the rural sector. These contribute to the empirical building blocks that provide microfoundations to a theory of rural development, an area where, as in much of the rest of economics, the theory tends to run far ahead of the slow and tedious but necessary empirical work. So this book straddles a wide range of issues in economic development, both theoretical and empirical, relating to economic agents both at the micro level and the aggregative economy.

A few of the essays were originally published many years back, but I like to think that some of them are on topics that are still relatively neglected. Some readers may be of the opinion that they deserve neglect, but it is part of an aging economist's vanity to think otherwise. In the Introduction to each part I try to briefly put the essays in the context of the more recent literature, when the latter exists.

Exactly half of the 18 chapters in this book are coauthored. My accomplices have been Ashok Rudra (in Chapters 13, 14, 17, and 18), Kenneth Kletzer (Chapters 1, 3, and 8), Harvey Lapan (Chapter 2), and Rodrigo Priale (Chapter 9). My pleasure in having worked with these fine scholars is heightened by the possibility of partial blame-sharing.

Pranab Bardhan
Berkeley, California
November 2001

Acknowledgments

The author and publishers gratefully acknowledge the following for permission to reproduce copyright material:

"Credit Markets and Patterns of International Trade" (jointly with K. Kletzer). Reprinted from *Journal of Development Economics*, 27, pp. 57–70, Copyright (1987) with permission from Elsevier Science.

"Localized Technical Progress, Transfer of Technology and Economic Development", (jointly with H. Lapan), *Journal of Economic Theory*, December 1973. Reprinted with permission.

"Quality Variations and the Choice between Foreign and Indigenous Goods or Technology" (jointly with K. Kletzer). Reprinted from *Journal of Development Economics*, 14, pp. 323–330, Copyright (1984), with permission from Elsevier Science.

"Imports, Domestic Production and Transnational Vertical Integration", *Journal of Political Economy*, October 1982. © 1982 by The University of Chicago. All rights reserved.

"Disparity in Wages but not in Returns to Capital between Rich and Poor Countries". Reprinted from *Journal of Development Economics*, 49, pp. 257–270, Copyright (1996), with permission from Elsevier Science.

"On Optimum Subsidy to a Learning Industry: An Aspect of the Theory of Infant Industry Protection", *International Economic Review*, February 1971. © 1971 Blackwell Publishers.

"International Trade Theory in a Vintage Capital Model", *Econometrica*, October 1966. © 1966 The Econometric Society.

"Dynamic Effects of Protection on Productivity" (jointly with K. Kletzer). Reprinted from *Journal of International Economics*, 16, pp. 45–57, Copyright (1984), with permission from Elsevier Science.

"Equilibrium Growth in a Model with Economic Obsolescence of Machines", *Quarterly Journal of Economics*, May 1969. © 1969 by the President and Fellows of Harvard College.

"More on Putty-Clay", *International Economic Review*, February 1973. © (1973) Blackwell Publishers.

"On Estimation of Production Functions from International Cross Section Data", *Economic Journal*, June 1967. © Blackwell Publishers.

"Terms and Conditions of Sharecropping Contracts: An Analysis of Village Survey Data in India" (jointly with A. Rudra), *Journal of Development Studies*, April 1980. Reprinted with permission.

"Terms and Conditions of Labour Contracts in Agriculture: Results of a Survey in West Bengal 1979" (jointly with A. Rudra), *Oxford Bulletin of Economics and Statistics*, February 1981. © 1981 Blackwell Publishers.

"On Measuring Rural Unemployment", *Journal of Development Studies*, April 1978. Reprinted with permission.

"Labor Tying in a Poor Agrarian Economy", *Quarterly Journal of Economics*, August 1983. © 1983 by the President and Fellows of Harvard College.

"Labour Mobility and the Boundaries of the Village Moral Economy" (jointly with A. Rudra), *The Journal of Peasant Studies*. Reprinted with permission.

"Interlinkage of Land, Labor and Credit Relations in Agriculture: An Analysis of village Survey Data in East India" (jointly with A. Rudra), *Economic and Political Weekly*, Annual Number, February 1978. Reprinted with permission.

The publishers apologize for any errors or omissions in the above list and would be grateful to be notified of any corrections that should be incorporated in the next edition or reprint of this book.

Part I

Trade and Development

Introduction

This part of the book deals with some of the constraints faced by poor countries in international trade with, and transfer of technology from, rich countries. While there is a large literature on international credit market imperfections, sovereign risk in debt contracts and their macroeconomic implications, there has been much less research done on the implications of these market imperfections on the pattern of international specialization in micro trade theory. In Chapter 1 we show that even when technology and endowments are identical between countries, and economies of scale are absent (the usual trinity of explanations for international trade), (a) moral hazard considerations in the international credit market under sovereign risk and (b) differences between countries in the domestic institutions of credit contract enforcement under incomplete information may lead to one country facing a higher interest rate or rationed credit compared to another. In such situations the former country may face a comparative disadvantage in producing processed or sophisticated manufactured goods requiring more working capital or credit to cover selling or distribution costs in comparison to bulk primary products. This is a clear example of how the pattern of specialization may depend on institutional features of the economy, which are not emphasized in the theory of international trade.[1]

In a recent paper T. Beck[2] has tried to test a hypothesis derived from a model like that in Chapter 1, that there is a link between financial development of an economy and its structure of international trade. Using a 30-year panel for 65 countries Beck shows that, controlling for country-specific effects and possible reverse causality, financial development exerts a large causal impact on the level of both exports and the trade balance of manufactured goods. One policy implication is that the effect of trade reforms on the level and structure of trade balance may depend on the level of financial development.

Chapters 2, 3, and 4 discuss some aspects of transfer of technology from rich to poor countries, a topic that has in general attracted a lot of attention since these papers were originally written, but not necessarily on the aspects discussed here. In

Chapter 2 we explore a simple model in which a poor country has to choose between indigenous technology with a lot of substitutability between capital and labor, and a foreign technology which is more advanced but available at a rather high capital-intensity (with limited scope for factor substitutability). The latter is due to the localized (in terms of the prevailing factor proportions in the country of origin) nature of technical progress (which happens at a faster rate) in rich countries. We discuss the allocational and distributional implications of a transfer of superior techno-logy that is available only at specific (high, and therefore costly) capital-intensity for a poor country. For example, such a transfer may have an adverse effect on wages in the poor country. In a general-equilibrium extension of the model H. Lapan[3] has demonstrated the possibility that such a transfer may result in a reversal of the trade pattern in a Heckscher–Ohlin model and K. Miyagiwa[4] has discussed its distributional implications in terms of a Ricardo–Viner model.

In Chapter 3 we extend the model of Chapter 2 in a different direction. Suppose the indigenous technology in a poor country produces a product of highly variable quality and the quality of a foreign product is just more dependable. In this case the transfer of technology improves the quality of the product in the sense of a mean-preserving shrink in the distribution of product quality, but at the cost of a highly capital-intensive technique. As in Chapter 2, we discuss the similar allocational and distributional implications of such a transfer. We then introduce an alternative to the adoption of the foreign technique, that of spending resources on domestic quality inspection and output sorting, assuming scale economies in such quality control. As a departure from the usual analysis of choice of techniques, in this model demand conditions and the relationship between price and quality play an important role in determining the optimal selection of production methods.

Chapter 4 focuses on the mode of technology transfer. Suppose a developing country has a choice of importing cars (mode I) from an oligopolistic world market; or producing them at home in a subsidiary (S) of a transnational company, or in a domestic firm under a licensing contract (L) from a transnational which ties the import of components from the latter. If the criterion of host-country national benefit is given by consumer surplus under I or S, and by consumer surplus plus the profits of the domestic firm under L, we compare the benefits from the alternative regimes I, S, or L under different market structure assumptions. While the literature on direct foreign investment is large, there is not too much analysis of the choice problem involving all modes in a unified framework from the welfare perspective of a host country. I. Horstmann and J. Markusen[5] as well as W. Ethier and J. Markusen[6] have studied the choice between S and L from the perspective of the transnational company in the presence of intellectual property rights in the host country. S. Das[7] has extended the analysis to include the option of a joint venture. The models in these three papers are more advanced in terms of the presumed contractual structures underlying transnational companies.

The last two chapters in this part both involve international differences in total factor productivity between rich and poor countries. In Chapter 5 the differences are both exogenous and endogenous, whereas in Chapter 6 they are endogenous. In Chapter 5 we explain the remarkable similarity of rates of return to capital but not in wage rates between rich and poor countries, in terms of particular types of differences in their production functions, in terms of differential learning effects and differential degrees of specialization in the sector producing intermediate inputs and services. We argue that in understanding this asymmetry in international factor prices the usual explanation in terms of greater international mobility of capital relative to labor is not enough.

Chapter 6 introduces a model of learning-by-doing in international trade theory (many years before the reappearance of the idea in the recent endogenous growth literature). Unlike in the case of the topic for other chapters in this part, a large literature has developed on this topic. Chapter 6 provides a formal rationale for an old argument for infant-industry protection: dynamic learning spillovers accruing from production experience measured, say, by cumulated domestic output may call for policy intervention in favor of some firms and industries, producing import substitutes (or new exports). P. Krugman[8] built on this and emphasized the self-reinforcing nature of initial specialization which results from the learning process, as an economy becomes better at producing the same thing; he also stressed how a deliberate policy intervention may be needed to pry the economy loose from an historical "lock-in" with respect to specialization in a slower-growing sector. Of course, trade policy is not the first-best way of resolving this market failure.[9] (A credit market intervention enabling a nascent firm or industry to tide over temporary losses may be more appropriate.) Besides, in a world of imperfect information, the learning function is not common knowledge, and this may create severe problems for policy intervention (including in the credit market) on the part of an imperfectly informed government. On the other hand, as K. Hoff[10] has suggested, the experience gained by each entrant to a new industry may be viewed as an experiment that reveals information about the production function to later entrants; and, in the context of such learning by experimentation, industrial policy can improve on the competitive equilibrium. There is, of course, a time inconsistency problem that afflicts such policies in most countries: once protected, the infant sometimes refuses to grow and face competition, and instead concentrates on lobbying for prolonged protection.

R. Lucas[11] points our attention to another aspect of the learning process which has been ignored in the earlier literature, including in our Chapter 6: for learning, particularly on-the-job learning, to occur in an economy on a sustained basis, it is necessary that workers and managers continue to take on tasks that are new to them, so as to continue to move up the quality ladder in goods. The major formulations that try to capture this in the context of an open economy are those of A. Young[12] and N. Stokey.[13] Stokey has a model of the so-called North–South trade, based on vertical product differentiation and international differences in labor quality; the South produces a low-quality spectrum of goods and the North, a high-quality spectrum. If human capital is acquired through learning-by-doing and so is stimulated by the production of high-quality goods, free trade (as opposed to autarky) will speed up human capital accumulation in the North and slow it down in the South. A similar result is obtained by Young. The country that begins with a technological lead tends to widen the lead over time. One limitation of the Young–Stokey story is the presumption that all imports substitute for domestic production.

But as H. Wan[14] has emphasized, when imported inputs are complementary with domestic production, there may be a lot of scope for learning in the assembly and processing of imported industrial inputs, as the early stages of East Asian industrialization seem to indicate. Trade may be crucial for development in (a) providing the means to import an essential ingredient for a production process that gives the opportunity to continuously upgrade domestic skills, and (b) providing an external market for the output thus produced, which many consumers at home still cannot afford. Of course, one needs an adequate supply of basic skills and education in the labor force to utilize this trade-related learning.

Notes

1. For some examples of increasing attention paid by international economists to institutional issues in recent years, see the symposium on Business and Social Networks in International Trade in the *Journal of International Economics*, June 1999, vol. 48, no. 1.
2. T. Beck, "Financial Development and International Trade: Is There a Link?," World Bank, Working Paper, May 2001.
3. H. Lapan, "The Possibility of Reversing the Trade Pattern with Internationally-Diffused Localized Technical Progress," *Journal of International Economics*, vol. 5, 1975.
4. K. Miyagiwa, "International Transfer of Localized Technology and Factor Income in the Ricardo–Viner Trade Model," *Canadian Journal of Economics*, vol. 21, November 1988.
5. I. J. Horstmann and J. R. Markusen, "Licensing Versus Direct Investment: A Model of Internalization by the Multinational Enterprise," *Canadian Journal of Economics*, vol. 20, 1987.
6. W. J. Ethier and J. R. Markusen, "Multinational Firms, Technology Diffusion and Trade," *Journal of International Economics*, vol. 41, 1996.
7. S. P. Das, "Direct Foreign Investment Versus Licensing," *Review of Development Economics*, vol. 3, 1999.
8. P. Krugman, "The Narrow Moving Band, the Dutch Disease, and the Competitive Consequences of Mrs. Thatcher: Notes of Trade in the Presence of Dynamic Scale Economies," *Journal of Development Economics*, vol. 27, 1987.
9. M. Melitz compares in this context the effectiveness of different trade policy instruments when these are not perfectly flexible over time, in his "When and How Should Infant Industries be Protected?," working paper, Harvard University, 1999.
10. K. Hoff, "Bayesian Learning in a Model of Infant Industries," *Journal of International Economics*, vol. 43, 1997.
11. R. E. Lucas, "Making a Miracle," *Econometrica*, vol. 61, 1993.
12. A. Young, "Learning by Doing and the Dynamic Effects of International Trade," *Quarterly Journal of Economics*, vol. 106, 1991.
13. N. Stokey, "The Volume and Composition of Trade between Rich and Poor Countries", *Review of Economic Studies*, vol. 58, 1991.
14. H. Wan, "Why Trade Matters," unpublished paper, Cornell University, 1996.

Chapter 1

Credit Markets and Patterns of
International Trade*

1. Introduction

The theoretical literature on the so-called North–South trade models often points attention to a general asymmetry of product specialization in rich and poor countries, with the former concentrating on goods which involve a high degree of processing and the latter on relatively unprocessed primary or intermediate products. The origin and preservation of this asymmetry is usually traced to static differences in factor endowments, in the nature of product and process innovations that take place in rich countries and in the cumulative processes of dynamic economies of scale in manufacturing and generalized learning effects of a larger initial capital stock in rich countries [see, for example, Krugman (1981) and Dutt (1986)]. While not denying the importance of these factors, in this paper we shall abstract from them and focus on the contribution of some aspects of credit market imperfections to inter-country differences in patterns of specialization and trade. In particular we show that even when technology and endowments are identical between countries and economies of scale are absent, (a) moral hazard considerations in the international credit market under sovereign risk and (b) differences between countries in the domestic institutions of credit contract enforcement under incomplete information may lead to one country facing a higher interest rate or rationed credit compared to another. This may lead to differences in comparative advantage[1] in processed goods requiring more working capital, marketing costs, or trade finance. We presume that more sophisticated manufactured finished products require more credit to cover selling and distribution costs than primary or intermediate products.

In general, the impact of financial markets on merchandise trade is a relatively unexplored area of trade theory. In the empirical literature on East Asian success stories the link between dynamic comparative advantage and easier financial access has often been emphasized. In the related literature on trade and industrial policy the use in those countries of selective allocation of credit and loan guarantees to achieve targets of trade and industrial restructuring has been cited as more effective than the more standard practice of trade restrictions and exchange control. We do not intend to take up many of the relevant issues here; our limited goal is to attempt an integration of one part of traditional trade theory with the growing theoretical literature on credit markets under imperfect information.

Sections 2 and 3 have the same basic model of the relationship between differential cost (or availability) of credit and comparative advantage, but they differ with respect to the underlying source of credit market imperfection along the lines of (a) and (b) above: in section 2 we have a model of international borrowing with potential repudiation and sovereign immunity, and in section 3 we have differences in *domestic* credit market institutions (particularly in the manner of contract enforcement and form of bankruptcy laws) in the presence of international borrowing and trade.

2. Sovereign Risk and Comparative Advantage in a Simple Trade Model

The impact of international credit market imperfections on the pattern of production and trade can be demonstrated in a simple two-country, two-sector, two-factor general equilibrium model. We adopt the usual Heckscher–Ohlin–Samuelson assumptions and introduce a simple role for international credit transactions. Technology, factor endowments, and consumer preferences are assumed to be identical across countries. In our simple model, the output of one sector is used only as an intermediate good or raw material in the production of the other output, which is consumable. We further assume that the intermediate good must be committed as an input one period before output is available so that working capital is required. For simplicity, inputs of the two domestic factors, labor and land, are used concurrently with the production of output. A credit market allows the cost of current intermediate input to be paid from the next period's revenues.

Technology in both sectors is described by constant returns to scale production functions which are twice-continuously differentiable and concave. The output of the final good is denoted by y, and output of the intermediate by x. The production functions in intensive form are given by

$$y = lf(k_1, x_1) \quad \text{and} \quad x = (1 - l)g(k_2),$$

where k_1 and k_2 are the land-intensities of production in each sector, x_1 is the intermediate good to labor ratio employed in sector 1, and l is the proportion of the labor force employed in sector 1. The total labor force is normalized to equal unity.

We will assume that perfect competition and free trade prevail throughout, there are no factor-intensity reversals, and equilibrium entails an interior solution. For now, assume that working credit is available at a given rate of interest, r. The first-order conditions for a production-side equilibrium are

$$\frac{\delta f(k_1, x_1)}{\delta k_1} = q \cdot g'(k_2),$$

$$\frac{\delta f(k_1, x_1)}{\delta x_1} = (1 + r)q,$$

$$\left(f - k_1 \frac{\delta f}{\delta k_1} - x_1 \frac{\delta f}{\delta x_1} \right) = q(g - k_2 g')$$

and

$$k = lk_1 + (1 - l)k_2,$$

where q is the relative price of good 2 in terms of good 1 and k is the country's aggregate land–labor ratio.

For this system, we first examine the comparative statics for an increase in the opportunity cost of credit to competitive firms. For fixed q, evaluating at an equilibrium with incomplete specialization, we have

$$\begin{bmatrix} dx_1/dr \\ dk_1/dr \\ dk_2/dr \end{bmatrix} = \frac{q}{f_{xx}f_{kk} - (f_{xk})^2} \begin{bmatrix} f_{kk} + \dfrac{x_1 f_{xk}}{k_1 - k_2} \\ -f_{xk} - \dfrac{x_1 f_{xx}}{k_1 - k_2} \\ \dfrac{-x_1}{(k_1 - k_2)g''(k_2)} \end{bmatrix}. \tag{1}$$

If we accept the additional assumption that the marginal productivity of labor and land in sector 1 rises with additional intermediate input, so that

$$-k_1 f_{xk} - x_1 f_{xx} > 0 \quad \text{and} \quad f_{xk} > 0,$$

then

$$\frac{dk_1}{dr} \quad \text{and} \quad \frac{dk_2}{dr} \gtreqqless 0 \quad \text{as} \quad k_1 \gtreqqless k_2.$$

Therefore, with a rise in r the proportion of the labor force employed in sector 2 rises and, consequently, the output of sector 1 falls and output of sector 2 increases. The wage–rentals ratio rises (falls) if sector 2 is relatively land-intensive (labor-intensive).

In this model, with identical factor endowments across borders, the outputs of each country will be identical under free trade if the opportunity costs of credit to firms are the same. Since only one good is consumed, there will be no trade (for a model with many consumables, identical tastes across borders ensures this). If the cost of credit is higher in one country than in the other, then that country will have a comparative advantage in the production of the intermediate good. Therefore, in equilibrium, the country with a credit disadvantage will export the intermediate good and import the final good. In order to explain the differential credit advantage of countries, we now add to the production model a simple moral hazard model of the international credit market under sovereign risk.

Since international borrowing and lending involves different political and legal jurisdictions, there is no external authority to ensure that parties to a contract abide by the terms of that contract ex post. In the presence of sovereign immunity, a debtor country can always elect to repudiate its obligations, so that repayment occurs only if the costs of repudiation exceed the debt-service obligations. Therefore, international loan agreements necessarily and indirectly enforced by penalties which can be credibly imposed in the event of a default. Examples of such penalties often discussed are disruptions of a debtor's commodity trade and moratoria on future foreign lending.[2] In the case of a financial intermediary reneging on foreign obligations, the loss of the discounted stream of future expected profits concurrent with the loss of reputation can comprise an indirect penalty to the owners of the institution.[3] The amount lent is constrained by the extent of the penalties which can be credibly imposed.

We develop an especially tractable model of borrowing with potential repudiation for inclusion in our general equilibrium framework following the non-stochastic model of Eaton and Gersovitz (1981). A debtor country (or, equivalently, intermediary) perceives that it will suffer a loss of size P if it defaults on its obligations. This penalty can be the present discounted value of future income losses. Therefore, an obligation will be repaid whenever

$$(1 + r)b \leqq P, \tag{2}$$

where b is the loan principal and r is the contracted rate of interest. We assume that indifference [i.e., equality in (2)] leads to repayment. Otherwise, the debt is not repaid and a penalty is incurred (which need not actually equal P).

Lenders receive nothing if repudiation takes place, so that they lose the opportunity cost of their loans. Furthermore, they possess incomplete information about the size penalty perceived by borrowers. Their information can be summarized by a distribution over the size penalties which borrowers believe they face. This set-up can be represented directly as an extensive game with incomplete information.[4] We restrict the possible beliefs of creditors to those for which the resulting equilibrium paths always entail repayment. In this model, revising beliefs which give rise to a repayment equilibrium [that is, a loan contract such that $(1 + r)b \leqq P$] can be costly to the lender because a repudiation may result from a movement off the original equilibrium. While learning may occur, asymmetries of information can persist for long periods even though repudiations do not occur.

If a repudiation does result from initial beliefs, then those beliefs will be revised. Furthermore, we could add the assumption that the penalty is a random variable and can change over time. The equilibria which we choose to adopt are characterized by loan contracts satisfying

$$\text{prob}[\tilde{P} \geq (1 + r)b] \cdot (1 - r)b \geq (1 + \rho)b$$

and

$$(1 + r)b \leq P,$$

where $\text{prob}[\tilde{P} \geq (1 + r)b]$ is the probability according to lenders' beliefs that the penalty perceived by borrowers (a random variable, $\tilde{P}$) is greater than the debt-service obligation, $(1 + r)b$, and ρ is the opportunity cost of lending. In this formalization, we have made the inessential assumption that lenders are risk neutral. Further, we may assume that there is free entry in loan contracts so that the first inequality is an equality, while the second may hold strictly.

Since the probability of repayment implied by lenders' beliefs declines with rising debt-service obligations, the supply curve of funds is upward-sloping after a possible initial flat segment (along which, $r = \rho$) and may be backward-bending, eventually. The entire curve lies inside the corresponding L-shaped supply curve in Eaton and Gersovitz (1981). This type of supply curve is identical in shape to those in Kletzer (1984), which are generated from a model with stochastic technology in a game of complete information, and in which the probability of default is positive in equilibrium. We adopt this alternative approach so that repudiation never occurs and no stochastic element need enter the general equilibrium model. The supply curve is depicted in fig. 1.1.

To place this model of international borrowing with potential repudiation into our trade model, we assume that all consumers are identical and possess a wealth-holding motive. All wealth is held in loans extended to either of the two countries. For simplicity, consumers' utility functions can be inter-temporarily separable with a common constant rate of discount, ρ. Firms obtain credit on the domestic market either from the government or through a set of intermediaries, which in turn borrow in the international market. We assume that there is no risk or imperfect information

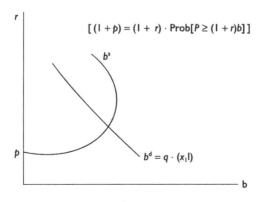

Fig. 1.1

associated with these second-stage loans. Consumers are free to lend to either country, so that their expected return under their beliefs in equilibrium is equal to ρ on assets of either country. Further, we assume that the rate of interest charged to firms on working credit is equal to that paid to creditors.

The demand for working credit is derived from the basic production model. Eqs. (1) imply that the amount of credit demanded, $b = q(x_1 \cdot l)$, is a decreasing function of the interest rate charged ($x_1 \cdot l$ is the total input of good 2 in production of good 1; we also need to assume that the marginal productivity of labor rises with the land employed in sector 1). This curve is depicted in fig. 1, for constant q. The intersection of the supply and demand curves is an equilibrium point for the credit market in the country.

In all respects countries A and B are assumed identical, save for the beliefs of wealth-holders in both countries about the penalty perceived by each country's government or financial intermediaries. For example, the government of B could be believed more likely to possess a shorter horizon, hence greater time rate of discount, than the government of A. While learning by lenders may be possible, it will take time so that reputations can persist. If debtors' perceptions of the penalties they face change over time or the penalty is stochastic, then the supply curves of credit can retain their shapes and relationships, indefinitely. If country B has a worse reputation than A, as represented by a greater probability that each debt-service obligation exceeds the perceived penalty for repayment obligations beyond a certain level, then the supply curve of credit to B will be above that for country A, as depicted in fig. 1.2. Therefore, in the competitive free trade equilibrium, the opportunity cost of working credit in B will exceed that in A, and A will possess a comparative advantage in production of the final good.

In this approach, consumers in both countries are creditors and the government or intermediaries are debtors (firms' obligations are anticipated correctly to be repaid). On net one country will be a borrower and the other a lender; however, consumers face the possibility of a sovereign repudiation by either country. The mechanism which leads to a discrepancy in the opportunity cost of credit is the sovereign immunity of the borrowers. In the next section, we consider an alternative approach in which differences in *domestic* credit market institutions give rise to a pattern of comparative advantage in the presence of sovereign immunity.

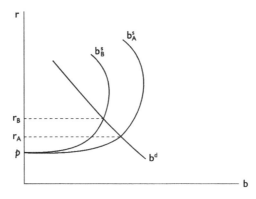

Fig. 1.2

3. Domestic Credit Market Imperfections, Sovereign Immunity, and the Pattern of Trade

International differences between the institutions surrounding domestic contract enforcement with incomplete information can give rise to patterns of comparative advantage in our basic trade model under sovereign immunity. The legal framework of bankruptcy generally differs across countries. In particular, the rights of lenders and of a firm's equity-holders and the manner of dispensing of assets vary internationally. In the presence of sovereign immunity, the best which a foreign lender can expect, in general, is to be treated on an equal footing with domestic lenders in the firm's home legal jurisdiction (in our model, all production by final output producing firms takes place in their home country).

A simple moral hazard model of borrowing by firms is developed in this section, and international differences in the treatment of creditors in the event of bankruptcy are shown to lead to a pattern of comparative advantage.[5] The production model is identical to that of the previous section, except that we assume that each firm in sector 1 faces technological uncertainty. To avoid unnecessary complications, we assume that the random variable in firms' production functions is identically independently distributed and that each country has a (fixed) large number of sector 1 firms, so that invoking the law of large numbers, mean aggregate output and both commodity and factor prices are non-stochastic. We also concentrate on standard debt contracts without explicitly deriving their existence [costly observation of the output realization of firms is an adequate basis for the use of debt contracts with bankruptcy; see Townsend (1978)].

Sector 1 firms produce according to

$$Y = \theta \cdot l \cdot f(k_1, x_1),$$

where θ is a random variable with support $[0, 1]$ and cumulative distribution function $F(\theta)$. The simplifying assumption of multiplicative uncertainty need not be adopted. $F(\theta)$ will be assumed continuously differentiable as necessary. Firm owners declare bankruptcy whenever the current value of the firm is negative, and we assume that the owners lose all their equity in the firm when a bankruptcy is declared. Therefore, under these assumptions, the firm's value is given by

$$V(\theta) = \max\{\pi(\theta) + \beta EV, 0\},$$

where current profit, $\pi(\theta) = \max_{k_1, l}\{\theta \cdot lf(k_1, x_1) - wl - vk_1 \cdot l - (1 + r)qb\}$, EV is the expectation of the value of the firm, v is the rental on land, and β is a discount factor. This definition assumes that land and labor inputs are chosen by the firm after the realization of θ is observed. We have also defined the value for any given current loan contract terms, r and $x_1 \cdot l \equiv b$ (the total amount lent, $x_1 \cdot l$, is fixed, the intermediate input to labor ratio varies with l, of course). In an equilibrium, the expectation of $V(\theta)$ will equal EV, which is the price for which the equity of the firm would sell in a competitive market. Since firm owners, consumers, and ultimate debt-holders are all the same people, the discount factor, β, is the same as consumers' constant time discount factor. Therefore,

$$\beta = 1/(1 + \rho),$$

in equilibrium. Furthermore, we assume individuals are risk-neutral for expositional simplicity only.

In the event of bankruptcy, creditors can, at most, obtain ownership of the firm, including current output. In other events, creditors simply receive the debt-service obligations specified by the contract. The present value of a loan is given by

$$\bar{V} = \beta \left[\int_{\bar{\theta}}^{1} (1 + r)q \cdot b \, dF \right] + \beta \Gamma \int_{0}^{\bar{\theta}} \{(\theta l f(k_1, x_1) - wl - v k_1 \cdot l) + \beta E V\} dF - qb, \quad (3)$$

where

$$\beta \equiv 1/(1 + \rho).$$

The parameter $\bar{\theta}$ is given by

$$\pi(\bar{\theta}) + \beta E V = 0,$$

so that $\int_{\bar{\theta}}^{1} dF$ is the probability of repayment by our assumptions on technology. The first term in (3) is the expected value of debt-repayments, and the second term is the value of the firm gross of the opportunity cost of the debt. The last term is simply the initial value of the loan. The lender can either sell the firm's equity for EV next period or operate the firm attaining a discounted expected stream of net income EV, beginning the next period. The parameter, Γ, represents the costs to creditors of resolving a bankruptcy. The lender loses some of the current value of the firm in the bankruptcy proceedings if Γ is less than unity. Such costs include provisions for some payment to equity holders, costs of litigation, or uncertainties concerning the creditors' priority, for example. This parameter is a simple expositional way to introduce international differences in domestic credit markets.

In the absence of possible bankruptcy, the first-order conditions for expected profit maximization, under our assumptions, are

$$\theta \cdot \frac{\delta f(k_1, x_1)}{\delta k_1} = v \qquad \text{for all } \theta,$$

$$\theta \cdot \left[f(k_1, x_1) - k_1 \frac{\delta f}{\delta k_1} - x_1 \frac{\delta f}{\delta x_1} \right] = w \quad \text{for all } \theta,$$

$$E \cdot \left[\theta \cdot \frac{\delta f(k_1, x_1)}{\delta x_1} \right] = (1 + r)q,$$

where the expectation operator is $\int_{0}^{1} (-) \, dF(\theta)$.

In the presence of possible bankruptcy, the probability of bankruptcy depends upon the interest rate and amount lent. Firms take future expected value as given and maximize

$$\int_{\theta}^{1} \pi(\theta)\, dF,$$

where $\pi(\bar{\theta}) + \beta EV = 0$.

This implies that

$$\frac{d\bar{\theta}}{dr} = \frac{qb}{f(k_1, x_1)}, \tag{4}$$

$$\frac{d\bar{\theta}}{db} = \frac{-(\bar{\theta}\delta f/\delta x - (1 + r)q)}{f(k_1, x_1)}. \tag{5}$$

Since $EV > 0$, both of these are positive, because constant returns to scale implies that

$$\bar{\theta}\frac{\delta f}{\delta x} - (1 + r)q = \pi(\bar{\theta}),$$

which is negative. Furthermore, for constant firm value, the trade-off between r and b is given by

$$\left.\frac{dr}{db}\right|_{V} = \int_{\theta}^{1}\left[\theta\frac{\delta f}{\delta x} - (1 + r)q\right] dF/qb \int_{\theta}^{1} dF.$$

Because of the presence of moral hazard, we need to specify an equilibrium concept carefully. This model has much in common with those in Kletzer (1984) and Gale and Hellwig (1985); therefore, following these, we consider Nash equilibria in loan contracts, which are equivalent to equilibria with non-linear repayment schedules. Contracts that provide zero net value to lenders satisfy

$$\bar{V} = 0,$$

or, from (3),

$$(r - \rho)qb + \Gamma \int_{0}^{\bar{\theta}} (\pi(\theta) + \beta EV)\, dF - (1 - \Gamma) \int_{0}^{\bar{\theta}} (1 + r)qb\, dF = 0. \tag{6}$$

Recall that $(\pi(\theta) + \beta EV) < 0$ for $0 \leq \theta < \bar{\theta}$, so that eq. (6) implies that r is larger than ρ. Eqs. (4), (5), and (6) imply that zero value contracts for the lender display increasing rates of interest with rising principals. An equilibrium loan contract is a contract which provides maximum expected firm value from amongst those contracts

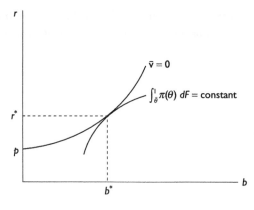

Fig. 1.3

providing zero value to lenders [where the equilibrium expected value of the firm enters into (6)]. A loan market equilibrium is depicted in fig. 1.3.

The amount of intermediate input used per unit of final good output for each realization of θ is lower in this equilibrium with bankruptcy than it would be in the absence of possible bankruptcy in a competitive equilibrium of our model.[6] A reduction in the parameter Γ, representing a different legal framework more adverse for creditors, reduces the value of a previously offered contract to the lender so that the supply curve shifts upwards. Because increasing the interest rate, holding the principal constant, raises the probability of bankruptcy, the slope of the new, lower Γ, supply curve at the same principal amount increases. [This can be readily shown using (6).] At this new possible loan contract, the marginal cost of credit has increased, but the marginal value of credit (since the principal is fixed) is lowered. Therefore, a decrease in Γ will lead to a new equilibrium contract with a lower principal. A reduction in principal, leaving the rate of interest unchanged, leads to an increase in the marginal value of increased credit to the firm. For this model, a reduction in Γ generally leads to a decreasing slope of the shifting supply curve as the interest rate is held constant. Therefore, a reduction in Γ from unity leads to a reduction in the amount lent in equilibrium and, typically, to an increase in the interest rate charged.[7]

The inclusion of this credit market model in our trade model is straightforward because of the assumptions which allow non-random mean relative prices and aggregate outputs and input demands. As in the previous section, we assume that consumers hold assets in either country and that all individuals have the same constant rate of discount, ρ. Either individuals directly lend or hold deposits in intermediaries which lend to firms and honor their obligations with probability one. A foreign loan and a domestic loan receive identical treatment in the home legal jurisdiction of the debtor firm. Sovereign immunity rules out credible contracts subjecting bankruptcies to foreign legal systems.

Equilibrium conditions for the trade model include

$$E\left[\theta \frac{\delta f}{\delta k_1}\right] = q \cdot g'(k_2)$$

and

$$E\left[\theta f(k_1, x_1) - k_1\theta\frac{\delta f}{\delta x_1} - x_1\theta\frac{\delta f}{\delta x_1}\right] = q\{g(k_2) - k_2 g'(k_2)\},$$

where $x_1 \cdot l$ is fixed for all θ. It is easy to show that a reduction in the level of good 2 used as an input in each sector 1 firm leads to an increase in the output of sector 2 and a reduction in factor employment in sector 1 by reducing the expected marginal products of factors in sector 1. Therefore, differences in the legal institutions surrounding contract enforcement between country A and country B represented by asymmetries in the value to lenders of the equity of bankruptcy-declaring debtor firms lead to a pattern of comparative advantage comparable to that found in the previous section. In the previous model, individual firms faced perfectly elastic supply curves of credit. Higher interest rates lead to a reduced aggregate output of sector 1. The model of bankruptcy in this section leads to a standard model of credit-rationing under moral hazard, in which each firm obtains less credit than it would demand at the equilibrium interest rate.[8] Larger amounts of credit would be forthcoming to the firm if its personalized rate of interest (not the market rate of interest; aggregate loan demand can remain constant) increases. A reduction in the quantity of working credit available to the firm in equilibrium leads to a reduction in the output of this industry at a fixed relative price of outputs.

4. Conclusion

We have shown that even with identical technology or endowments between countries comparative costs will differ in a world of credit market imperfection when credit for working capital or trade finance is needed to cover the pre-commitment of inputs before the accrual of output revenues. We have explored in some detail two distinct but complementary types of credit market imperfection under considerations of moral hazard. In section 2 we have a model of international lending under sovereign risk, where poorer reputation of a country results in its facing a higher equilibrium interest rate (updating beliefs about reputations being costly). In section 3 we have differences between countries in domestic credit market institutions (including bankruptcy laws) along with the lack of a global contract enforcement mechanism (so that ex ante changes in jurisdictions are not enforceable, i.e., a Brazilian firm cannot credibly commit itself to a New York bankruptcy court should the eventuality arise). In the model of section 2 the higher interest rate faced by firms in the poorer country drives the latter country away from specializing in sophisticated manufactured products requiring more working capital, selling costs and trade finance; in the model of section 3 the country does not face higher interest rates but tighter credit rationing with a similar production and trade result. Both models are examples of how comparative advantage explicitly depends, unlike in standard trade theory, on institutions (in this case, financial institutions).

Notes

*   The authors are grateful to J. Eaton and J. A. Ocampo for useful comments. Kletzer also acknowledges support from a grant of the National Science Foundation.
1.   Our attention was recently drawn to a paper by Baldwin (1985) which also traces comparative advantage differences to capital market "quality", but in a completely different way. Unlike our model Baldwin's model has no international asset transactions; capital market imperfections take the form of incomplete stock markets, so that it is risk-aversion and differential ability of investors to diversify that lead to differences in trade patterns. We, on the other hand, assume risk-neutrality. In our model it is (a) sovereign immunity and (b) differences in domestic credit contract enforcement institutions with international borrowing and lending that lead to the differential pattern of trade.
2.   The points summarized here are made at length by a number of authors, notably, Eaton and Gersovitz (1981) and Eaton, Gersovitz and Stiglitz (1986).
3.   This approach implies that intermediaries may require positive profits to make the threat to penalize default credible; see Eaton (1985).
4.   This part of the model is identical to the approach taken by Aizenman (1986). The equilibrium is a sequential equilibrium, as defined by Kreps and Wilson (1982).
5.   A possible alternative, not taken here, is to portray institutional differences as differences in the information available to lenders about debtors, as in Kletzer (1984). The comparison between Nash equilibria in loan contracts and price-taking equilibria in that paper and in Gale and Hellwig (1985) could give rise to patterns of comparative advantage between otherwise identical economies.
6.   The comparative statics of this credit market model are similar to those in Gale and Hellwig (1985).
7.   Additional conditions necessary to show that the equilibrium interest rate rises with a drop in Γ are messy and do not provide useful intuition.
8.   See, for example, Jaffee and Russell (1976), Kletzer (1984) and Gale and Hellwig (1985). This contrasts with the adverse selection model of Stiglitz and Weiss (1981) in which firms either receive no loan or the project is fully funded.

References

Aizenman, J., 1986, Country risk, asymmetric information and domestic policies, Working paper no. 1880 (NBER, Cambridge, MA).

Baldwin, R., 1985, Exporting the capital markets: Comparative advantage and capital market imperfection, Mimeo. (Economics Department, MIT, Cambridge, MA).

Dutt, A., 1986, Vertical trading and uneven development, Journal of Development Economics 20, no. 2.

Eaton, J., 1985, Lending with costly enforcement of repayment and potential fraud, Working paper no. 1697 (NBER, Cambridge, MA).

Eaton, J. and M. Gersovitz, 1981, Debt with potential repudiation: Theoretical and empirical analysis, Review of Economic Studies 48.

Eaton, J., M. Gersovitz and J. Stiglitz, 1986, The pure theory of country risk, European Economic Review 30, no. 3.

Gale, D. and M. Hellwig, 1985, Incentive-compatible debt contracts: The one-period problem, Review of Economic Studies 52.

Jaffee, D. and T. Russell, 1976, Imperfect information, uncertainty and credit rationing, Quarterly Journal of Economics 90.

Kletzer, K.M., 1984, Asymmetries of information and LDC borrowing with sovereign risk, Economic Journal 94, June.

Kreps, D.M. and R. Wilson, 1982, Sequential equilibria, Econometrica 50, no. 4.

Krugman, P., 1981, Trade, accumulation and uneven development, Journal of Development Economics 8, no. 2.

Stiglitz, J. and A. Weiss, 1981, Credit-rationing in markets with imperfect information, American Economic Review 71, June.

Townsend, R., 1978, Optimal contracts and competitive markets with costly state verifications, Journal of Economic Theory 21.

Chapter 2

Localized Technical Progress and Transfer of Technology and Economic Development

In much of neoclassical growth theory technical progress is represented as a uniform shrinking of the unit isoquant toward the origin. In much of the development literature, however, it is emphasized that technical advances applicable to the factor-proportions of capital-rich developed countries are hardly of any use in improving techniques of low capital-intensity in less developed countries; taking transport technology as an example, the improvements in modern jet aircraft technology do not particularly help raising the productivity of rickshaw-pullers in the streets of Calcutta or Hong Kong. In a recent paper Atkinson and Stiglitz (1969) have introduced the concept of localized technical progress to capture this phenomenon of improvements in technical knowledge being specific to particular processes. Although most of their formal analysis refers to the extreme case of technical progress being completely localized to one technique, they have also mentioned the more general possibility of spillover of improvements to some other techniques near enough to the currently used factor proportions. If knowledge acquired through learning or research activity is localized, they have correctly argued that the history of the economy is important in determining its current characteristics and that planning of present activities cannot be made independently of their long run consequences. In this respect localized technical knowledge has the same characteristics as "putty–clay" capital.

In this paper we intend to pursue some of these implications further and apply them to the problems of borrowing foreign technology in a developing economy. Transfer of technology from developed to developing economies has been a relatively unexplored area both in theoretical and empirical research. Only in very recent years has some analytical attention been paid to direct and indirect costs of such

transfer. A long-standing issue has been the problem of appropriate factor proportions; to quote from a popular text in economic development [Kindleberger, 1956,
p. 249], the question is

> whether countries at early stages of development, with capital scarce and often with labor
> abundant, should take advantage of the modern technology developed by advanced count-
> ries, where capital is abundant and labor scarce, or whether they should devise a technology
> of their own or use production methods which are obsolete in countries abroad.

The problem, therefore, is to decide whether the gains in production due to the
increased efficiency of advanced technology ("localized" to the prevailing factor
proportions of the advanced country) outweigh the costs necessitated by the high
level of capital-intensity in a capital-scarce country.
  We shall explore a rather simple model in which the developing nation must
choose between production in which capital and labor are substitutable, or an
alternative method which is more efficient, but which is available only at a particular
capital–labor ratio (hereafter, a technique will be defined by its capital–labor ratio).
We shall find:

(i)   The "advanced" technique is, as may be expected, more likely to be employed
      the greater is its efficiency (vis-a-vis technology available in the developing
      country), and the smaller is the difference between the capital–labor ratio used
      in this technique and the capital–labor ratio of the developing nation.
(ii) At most two techniques will be employed at once.
(iii) The adoption of the more advanced, capital-intensive technique tends to sup-
      press wages in the developing country.
(iv) If the wage rate in the developing country exceeds the shadow price of labor,
      the advanced technique may be employed under profit maximization, though
      from society's viewpoint this decision is inefficient. Finally, we shall demon-
      strate how our results can be extended to consider cases in which many
      alternate advanced techniques exist.

  Assume that differences in production functions are due to differences in efficiency
alone, and that the developing nation seeks to maximize total output Q given its
resource limitations:[1]

$$Q = Q_1 + Q_2 = L[\gamma f(k_1) + (1 - \gamma)Af(\bar{k})]; \; A > 1; \tag{1}$$

$$\bar{k} = \text{capital–labor ratio of advanced technique, taken as given;} \tag{2}$$

$$k_1 = \text{capital–labor ratio of backward technique, to be chosen;} \tag{3}$$

$$k = \text{aggregate capital–labor ratio;} \tag{4}$$

$$\gamma = (L_1/L); \; \gamma k_1 + (1 - \gamma)\bar{k} = k. \tag{5}$$

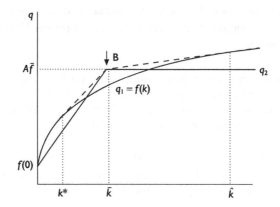

Fig. 2.1 Maximizing output and localized technical progress.

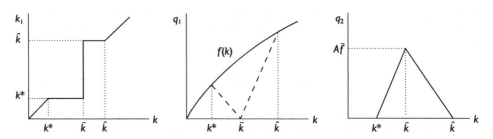

Fig. 2.2 Development and allocation of resources.

Though this problem is readily solvable by mathematical techniques, a simple graphical interpretation exists. In Fig. 2.1, point B represents the advanced technique, whereas the $f(k)$ curve represents the basic production function. To maximize output we seek a line segment through B and tangent to $f(k)$ (assuming such a tangent exists[2]); in general, two such tangents exist – one for $k < \bar{k}$, the other for $k > \bar{k}$ (our interest is for the case $k < \bar{k}$; the other case follows by symmetry). Once these tangents are found, the aggregate production function becomes $f(k)$ for $k \leqslant k^*$; (or $k \geqslant \hat{k}$), and the (dashed) tangent lines for $k \in (k^*, \hat{k})$.

Mathematically, this is equivalent to finding $k^* < \bar{k}$ and $\hat{k} > \bar{k}$ such that

$$A\bar{f} = [f(k_1) - k_1 f'(k_1) + \bar{k} f'(k_1)]; \ k_1 = k^* \quad \text{or} \quad k_1 = \hat{k}. \tag{6}$$

Economically, (6) states that, in order to maximize output and for both sectors to coexist, the opportunity cost of the labor and capital transferred from the backward sector must just equal the output produced in the advanced sector by these resources.[3]

Given the interior tangencies, Fig. 2.2 summarizes how resources should be allocated and where production should occur (q_1 is the per capita output in the backward sector, q_2 the per capita output in the advanced sector). For $k < k^*$, the capital-intensity differences make it unprofitable to employ the advanced technique. However,

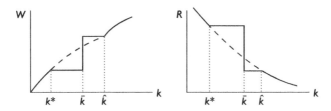

Fig. 2.3   Factor prices, development, and localized technical progress.

increases in k lower the return on capital, until at $k = k^*$, it just becomes worthwhile to start utilizing the advanced technique. Increases in k, for $k \in (k^*, \bar{k})$, leave k_1 unchanged but cause resources to be transferred to the advanced sector, so that γ and q_1 decrease and q_2 increases. Finally, for $k = \bar{k}$, all output is produced in the advanced sector. Similar results hold for $k > \bar{k}$.

An interesting aspect of this problem is the effect of the advanced technique on factor prices. Assuming factors are paid their marginal product,[4] we can readily see either from Fig. 2.1 or Fig. 2.2 how localized technical progress affects factor prices. In particular, for $k < k^*$ factor prices are unaffected since the advanced technique is not used. However, for $k \in (k^*, \bar{k})$, it is apparent that utilization of the advanced technique holds down wages (since $k_1 = k^* < k$), while bolstering the return to capitalists. Furthermore, increases in k, for $k < \bar{k}$, have no impact on factor prices, so that capital accumulation cannot be relied upon to improve the plight of workers. These results are summarized in Fig. 2.3. For $k = \bar{k}$, factor prices are indeterminate;[5] comparable results hold for $k > \bar{k}$.

The above result is analogous to a two-sector world (each sector producing identical goods) in which an increase in efficiency occurs in the capital-intensive sector. In order to maintain coexistence of the two sectors, the return to the factor used intensively in the advanced sector (capital) must rise while the return to the other factor (labor) must fall.

Consequently, though the advanced technique benefits the nation as a whole, workers suffer. Nor does economic development alleviate this problem. This poses a cruel dilemma for planners who must choose between increased output and the seemingly contradictory goal of improving labor's standard of living[6] (assuming no nondistortionary way of redistributing income exists).

Moreover, attempts to mitigate this problem through minimum wage legislation may cause the advanced technique to be adopted, even though its use can lead to greater decreases in output than would normally accompany this second best situation. This may occur because the minimum wage places an artificially high premium on labor, conceivably causing profit-seeking businesses to adopt the more capital-intensive advanced technique, even though this leads to higher levels of unemployment and lower total output (that this result may occur follows from the obvious distortion in the factor market). Whether or not this result occurs depends on the size of the minimum wage; if it is set below the wage rate at which the advanced technique is profitably adopted $[f(k^*) - k^* f'(k^*)]$ then the minimum wage has no impact on the decision concerning adoption of the advanced technique. Comparably, if the

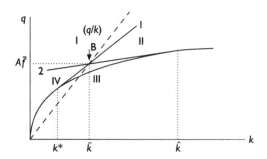

Fig. 2.4 Comparative statics.

minimum wage is set sufficiently high (so that the average product of capital on the basic technique associated with the minimum wage is less than the average product of capital for the advanced technique), then the advanced technique, which will be used, is superior to the alternate basic technique. However, for minimum wages in between these limits, the use of the advanced technique, while privately profitable, is contrary to the interests of the society.

It is worth commenting upon factor prices in the developing country compared to those in the advanced country. Assuming that fixed proportions do not prevail in the advanced country so factors are paid their marginal product there, we readily find

$$f(k^{\star}) - k^{\star}f'(k^{\star}) < \bar{W} = A[\,f(\bar{k}) - \bar{k}f'(\bar{k})\,], \tag{7}$$

$$f'(k^{\star}) > \bar{R} = Af'(\bar{k}). \tag{8}$$

(For $k_1 = \hat{k} > \bar{k}$, these inequalities are reversed.) Thus, as expected, workers in the advanced nation are better off, while capitalists in the developing nation earn the larger rate of return.

In order to see how changes abroad effect the developing economy, we must consider how changes in A or $\bar{k}$ affect the decisions made by these countries. Figure 2.4 greatly facilitates that task. Letting point B represent the initial advanced technique, and the lines 1 and 2 be the tangent lines (with slopes $f'(k^{\star})$ and $f'(\hat{k})$, respectively), it is clear that a change in technique that moves B into area I (above both tangents) causes $k^{\star}$ to decrease and $\hat{k}$ to increase, shifting out the entire production function. Similarly, a movement into region II increases $k^{\star}$ and $\hat{k}$, making the advanced technique more costly to the developing country (though more beneficial to the "over-developed" country), whereas a movement of B into region IV has the opposite result. Finally, a movement of B into region III hurts any borrowing nation (thus, we can say point B dominates region III and is dominated by region I).

What economic interpretation can we give to these results? An increase in A, given $\bar{k}$, moves B into region I, benefiting any borrowing country[7] and causing more resources to be allocated to that advanced technique ($k \in (k^{\star}, \hat{k})$). Comparably, an increase in $\bar{k}$ moves B into region II (since $f'(k^{\star}) > Af'(\bar{k}) > f'(\hat{k})$), hurting the developing economy, though benefiting the over-developed economy. The impact of these changes on the allocation of resources and factor prices is immediately apparent from our prior discussion. Furthermore, all of this could readily be demonstrated mathematically.

The obvious question at this point is how a joint change in A and $\bar{k}$ affects $(k^*, \hat{k})$ and the allocation of resources (assuming only the new technology can be used). From the developing country's perspective, it is clear that an increase in A associated with a decrease in $\bar{k}$ can only be beneficial, since each change alone moves out their production function. However, increases in technology (A) are normally accompanied by increases in capital-intensity $(\bar{k})$ and the net impact of this change on the developing country clearly depends upon the magnitudes of the changes of A and $\bar{k}$. If A increases a "little," and $\bar{k}$ quite a bit, the developing country is hurt (k^* increases); reverse results hold for large increases in A and small increases in $\bar{k}$. One interesting case, often cited in the literature, is when the advanced country has been following a steady-state path, so that (q/k) is fixed (dashed line in Fig. 2.4). As is apparent from the figure, such changes benefit the developing country (though hurting its workers) and the new, advanced technology along this steady-state path dominates all past technology.

Once again, all of this could be demonstrated mathematically. Figure 2.4 tells us that the combination of increases in A and $\bar{k}$ that hold k^* constant imply that the average product of capital on the new technique must be falling; any smaller increase in $\bar{k}$, for given A, means that the new technique benefits the developing nation. Similar interpretations hold for the over-developed country.[8] Clearly the distributional implication of these changes in technology depends upon the impacts of these changes on k^*.

The prior discussion assumed that only one advanced technique could be considered at any time. We shall now investigate how the developing nation should choose among several alternative techniques.

As mentioned earlier, one recurrent theme of the development literature is whether the developing economies should borrow any foreign technology, and if so, should they borrow the most recent technology or technology now obsolete in the developed world? Having investigated the first question, let us now consider the latter question of choosing between obsolete and modern technology.

In order to study this problem we obviously must have knowledge of the type of advanced techniques available to the developing economy. Since presumably these different advanced techniques reflect the historical development of the now-developed nations, our need to know the specifics of these techniques reflects, to a certain extent, the Atkinson-Stiglitz (1969) contention of the past as being instrumental in shaping the present and future. Moreover, in answering the question as to which advanced techniques should be adopted, we concurrently determine whether these developing countries should mirror the development process that took place in other countries, or whether certain steps should be by-passed.

Assume that in addition to the basic production function, the developing economy has n advanced techniques to choose from, each described by an efficiency parameter and a capital-intensity

$$X_i = [A_i, \bar{k}_i]; \quad i = 1, \ldots, n; \quad X_i \in T. \tag{9}$$

For simplicity, arrange T so that $\bar{k}_1 < \bar{k}_2 < \ldots < \bar{k}_n$. As earlier, the developing economy's problem is to decide how to allocate resources in order to maximize output. The nature of this problem makes it clear that, barring singular cases, at most two techniques will be used at once (including backward techniques).

As discussed earlier, to each X_i corresponds a pair $[k_i^*, \hat{k}_i]$. From Fig. 2.4 it is clear that technique j dominates i, if and only if,

$$\bar{k}_j > \bar{k}_i, \quad \text{then} \quad k_j^* \leqslant k_i^*;$$

or

$$\bar{k}_j < \bar{k}_i, \quad \text{then} \quad \hat{k}_j \geqslant \hat{k}_i; \tag{10}$$

or

$$\bar{k}_j = \bar{k}_i, \quad \text{then} \quad A_j > A_i.$$

If j dominates i, then i will never be used, given the availability of j, and the developing economy can exclude X_i from consideration.

Following (10), we form a subset $\bar{T}$ of T such that

$$X_{s_i} \in \bar{T}, \, i = 1, \ldots, r \leqslant n \to \bar{k}_{s_1} < \bar{k}_{s_2} < \ldots < \bar{k}_{s_r}$$

and

$$k_{s_1}^* < k_{s_2}^* < \ldots < k_{s_r}^* \tag{11}$$

and

$$\hat{k}_{s_1} < \hat{k}_{s_2} < \ldots < \hat{k}_{s_r}.$$

Thus, $\bar{T}$ has the property that no technique in it is dominated by any other single technique, and that every technique in T, but not in $\bar{T}$, is dominated by some element of $\bar{T}$. Note that $\bar{T}$ may have only one element, as in the case of steady-state growth abroad, or it may contain all the elements of T. Moreover, the presence of a technique in $\bar{T}$ is no guarantee that that technique will ever be used (with the exception of X_{s_1} and X_{s_r}) since, if $\bar{T}$ contains more than two elements, two elements in $\bar{T}$ may dominate a third one.

The above process greatly simplifies the decision for the developing economy. If there is only one technique in $\bar{T}$, development proceeds as discussed earlier. If $\bar{T}$ contains more than one element, then for $k < k_{s_1}^*$ and $k > \hat{k}_{s_r}$, only the backward technique is used, while for $k \in (k_{s_1}^*, \bar{k}_{s_1})$ a backward technique (with capital-intensity $k_{s_1}^*$) and an advanced technique (X_{s_1}) should be used (similarly for $k \in (\bar{k}_{s_r}, \hat{k}_{s_r})$). Finally, for $k \in (\bar{k}_{s_1}, \bar{k}_{s_r})$, only advanced techniques should be used, and the decision regarding which ones to use is merely a linear-programming problem. Figure 2.5 illustrates the nature of the aggregate production function for several cases.

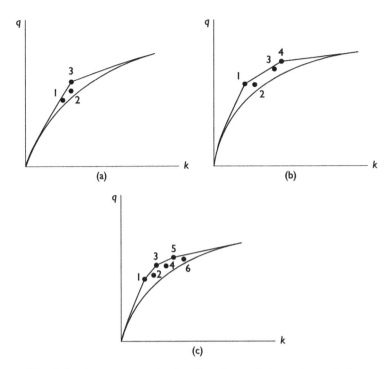

Fig. 2.5 Aggregate production function and alternative techniques.

Thus, without more specific information, we cannot tell whether the developing economy will use only the most modern advanced techniques or whether it will employ techniques now obsolete in the developed world. In addition, even if some of these now obsolete techniques are employed, the developing nation may skip other techniques once used abroad, so that its development process need not mirror that of the advanced world.

Moreover, the impact of localized technical progress on factor prices now may be ambiguous.[9] If there is only one relevant advanced technique, our earlier discussion holds; otherwise, the result depends on the techniques involved. Specifically, for $k \in (k^*_{s_1}, \bar{k}_{s_1})$, the localized technical progress holds down wages, hurting labor. However, when two advanced techniques are used concurrently $(k \in (\bar{k}_{s_1}, \bar{k}_{s_2}))$, it is not possible, without further information, to state how factor prices are affected, except that at least one factor must gain from the localized technical progress (assuming no distortions exist). Similarly, for $k \in (\bar{k}_{s_2}, \hat{k}_{s_2})$, capitalists are hurt by the localized technical progress. Finally, increases in the capital–labor ratio of the developing economy lead to increases in the wage rate and decreases in the rental rate (assuming no change in foreign technology), though this occurs by steps, and not in a continuous manner (that is, the production function is concave, but not strictly concave).

This paper has considered the allocational and distributional implications of localized technical progress for a developing economy. In another paper one of the authors (Lapan, 1972) has discussed the impact of localized technical progress on the pattern of trade in a two-sector, two-country world and has shown that when technology is transferrable between nations only at specific capital-intensities, then a cyclical pattern of trade may occur. It is the authors' belief that further study of the implications of localized technical progress should prove quite fruitful.

Notes

1. If a fixed fraction of the output from the advanced technique must be paid as royalties, then the impact of this on allocational decisions is equivalent to the impact of a decrease in A.

2. Existence of an interior tangency for $k < \bar{k}$ requires: $Af(\bar{k}) < \lim_{k_0 \to 0}[f(k_0) + (\bar{k} - k_0)f'(k_0)]$; if this is not met then all capital should be allocated to the advanced technique. The same condition must be fulfilled as $k_0 \to \infty$ to yield an interior tangency for $k > \bar{k}$; if it is not met, then all labor should be allocated to the advanced sector. The Inada conditions suffice to guarantee existence of these tangencies; uniqueness is guaranteed by $f'' < 0$.

3. The coexistence of these advanced and "backward" (or "craft") firms has been noted in the literature; for example, see Nelson (1968).

4. Since the wage rate is frequently larger in the advanced sector, this assumption may seem implausible. However, these wage differences may be due to: (a) short-run labor market disequilibria; (b) the fact that labor in the advanced sector may embody more human capital; or (c) an effort on the part of the advanced sector, which may be foreign-owned, to mitigate the political resentment of foreign ownership.

5. This discontinuity and nonuniqueness in R raises the possibility, that in a neoclassical growth model in which only capitalists save then: (i) there exists a range of (capitalists') savings rate that yields the same steady-state k and (ii) to some savings rate ($s_k = n/f'$ (k^*)), there corresponds a range of steady-state k ($k \in (k^*, \bar{k})$). Comparably, for optimal growth, two countries may choose the same optimal k, even if discount rates differ.

6. A similar conflict between the interests of wage earners and the desire for capital accumulation is familiar in the development literature. See Sen (1960).

7. The country benefits from an increase in A, but since this decreases k^*, workers in the LDC are hurt, assuming marginal product pricing holds.

8. Throughout we have taken technical progress as Hicks neutral in order to stress the separate roles of efficiency and capital-intensity. Obviously, the analysis can be altered to study Harrod-neutral technical change.

9. When a backward technique is used, factor prices are determined by marginal products in that sector. When two advanced techniques are employed, factor prices are determined by the condition of zero profits; the rental rate on capital equals the slope of the production function at that point, and the wage rate is the q-intercept of this line. Finally, at a vertex, when only one advanced technique is used, factor prices are indeterminate.

References

A.B. Atkinson and J.E. Stiglitz, A new view of technological change, *Economic J.* 79 (1969), 573–578.

C.P. Kindleberger, "Economic Development," McGraw Hill, New York, 1956.

H.E. Lapan, Localized technical progress and the pattern of trade, unpublished, 1972.

R.R. Nelson, A diffusion model of international productivity differences, *Amer. Econ. Rev.* **58** (1968), 1219–1248.

A.K. Sen, "Choice of Techniques: An Aspect of the Theory of Economic Development," Basil Blackwell, Oxford, 1960.

Chapter 3

Quality Variations and the Choice between Foreign and Indigenous Goods or Technology

1. Introduction

In V.S. Naipaul's *An Area of Darkness* one Mrs. Mahindra of New Delhi tells the author about her preference for *imported* varieties of goods in an outburst, marked more for candor than for grammar: "I am craze for foreign, just craze for foreign." Such a craze for foreign goods is, of course, not unknown in industrially more advanced countries: from wine to dress fashions, from fancy cars to art films, from perfume to mineral waters, examples are far too many of imported brands having special customer appeal in these countries. But there is no doubt that this craze is particularly rampant in poor countries, even in the case of varieties of goods for which fairly decent domestic substitutes are available in the market, often at a lower price than the imported variety. In the market for soft drinks, to take a popular example, that the local youths go for the foreign brand cola drink, in preference not merely to fresh coconut juice but to several varieties of local cola drinks (similar in taste as well as in negative nutritional value), is usually attributed to the effects of high-pressure international salesmanship and the undoubted advantages of being able to claim membership of the international Pepsi Generation. But beyond the effects of artificial product differentiation in favor of the foreign variety, there is a genuine problem of quality variability as perceived by the consumer. Even when the local and foreign varieties are regarded as of roughly similar *average* quality, one usually associates a more uneven distribution in the quality of the former ("Yes, I know, the local cola tastes the same, but didn't you know last year someone discovered a fly in the bottle?") and hence is prepared to pay a higher price for the latter.

In this paper we suppose that various production techniques provide similar outputs which differ in their distribution of product quality about a common mean. The optimal selection over techniques is considered when output from a more advanced, foreign, technique which is capital-intensive differs from the output from a poor country's traditional technology by a *mean-preserving shrink* in the distribution of product quality. In our model in section 2 we assume that capital and labor are substitutable in the indigenous technique, but the more advanced technique borrowed from abroad is available at a particular (high) capital–labor ratio. At this capital–labor ratio, the foreign technique produces a more uniform quality of output than the traditional technique, so that it represents a form of localized technical progress. We show the optimal conditions of adoption of the more advanced technique and how it may result in lower wages for local labor.

We then introduce in section 3 an alternative to the adoption of the foreign technique in reducing quality variability, through spending resources on quality inspection and sorting of output produced by the domestic technology. We assume scale economies in quality control, so that the cost of attaining a given level of quality improvement falls with scale of output. The optimal quality improvement expenditure for the indigenous technique and the pattern of choice between this type of quality improvement and the adoption of more advanced capital-intensive techniques are described. As a departure from the usual analysis of choice of techniques, in our model demand conditions, the relationship between price and quality, play an important role in determining the optimal selection of production methods.

2. Quality Improvement and the Choice of Technique

We consider a specific type of quality variation in products: the characteristics of goods, from which consumers derive utility, vary across individual units of the output of each method of production. At the time of purchase, neither the producer nor the consumer knows the relevant attributes of a particular unit, but instead, they share a common perception of the distribution over the characteristics of all output. Demands are derived through the maximization of expected utility for consumers, given these perceptions of the distribution of qualities for the output of each producer.

Although differences in output quality could take the form of arbitrary changes in the distribution over characteristics, we restrict the set of possible production techniques so that the distributions for their outputs differ from one another through a combination of a mean-preserving shrink and an increase in the mean qualities. Rothschild and Stiglitz (1970) prove that a distribution is preferred to its mean-preserving spread under all strictly concave utility functions defined over the random variables. Therefore, the ordinal ranking of the output of different techniques is identical under all concave utility functions. We define a quality improvement as a shrink in the distribution over the characteristics of output, with no decrease in their mean.

Suppose that two distinguishable types of a product are available, for example, that each is produced in a different country. Subject to their budget constraints, consumers maximize expected utility,

$$\mathrm{E}U(x_1, x_2) = \int_{q_2} \int_{q_1} U(x_1 q_1 + x_2 q_2) \, dF_1(q_1) \, dF_2(q_2),$$

where $U(q)$ is a concave, regular utility function, x_1 and x_2 are the quantities of each product type consumed, and q_1 and q_2 are the vectors of attributes of units of each good. The vectors q_1 and q_2 are random variables distributed according to $F_1(q_1)$ and $F_2(q_2)$, respectively. Because $U(q)$ is concave and the $dF_i(q_i)$ are cumulative functions, expected utility is a concave function of x_1 and x_2. If the distribution $F_1(q_1)$ is a mean-preserving spread of $F_2(q_2)$, then the first product type receives a higher price than the latter in a competitive equilibrium.

In this paper, we characterize the optimal choice of a production technique when different methods are associated with different qualities of output. Perfect competition and constant returns to scale in the production of physical quantities of output are assumed.

Suppose that a capital-poor country contemplates the adoption of a capital-intensive, advanced, technique which produces output of more uniform quality than the local technology operated at the same capital–labor ratio. The output of the advanced technique commands a higher price in world markets, but its exclusive use will also reduce national income. We assume that capital and labor are substitutable in the indigenous technology, while the advanced technique operates at a unique capital–labor ratio, equal to k_0.

The country seeks to maximize national income,

$$y = L[\gamma f(k_1) + p(1 - \gamma) f(k_0)],$$

subject to $k = \gamma k_1 + (1 - \gamma) k_0$, where $f(k)$ is the production function for physical output written in intensive form, k_1 is the capital–labor ratio employed in the indigenous technology, k is the aggregate capital–labor ratio, γ is the proportion of the labor force employed in the indigenous sector, and L is the total labor force. The relative price of output of the advanced technique in terms of the local technology's output, p, is greater than unity. Both methods produce the same quantity of output when operated at the same level and capital–labor ratio (k_0).

This problem is formally similar to the choice of techniques problem studied by Lapan and Bardhan (1973). In their model, the capital-intensive technique differs from the indigenous one by a Hicks-neutral technical advance. Improved product quality is equivalent to localized Hicks-neutral technical progress in terms of the value of output produced by a given amount of inputs. All the conclusions of their paper hold for the current model. The first-order conditions can be represented by Fig. 3.1, where the production function for indigenous technology is described by $f(k_1)$, and point A describes the advanced technique. The lines AB and AC are tangent to $f(k_1)$ at k^* and $\hat{k}$, respectively. The frontier formed by $f(k_1)$ and lines AB

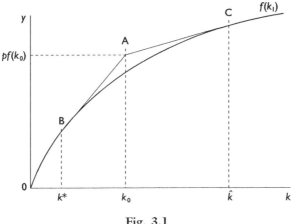

Fig. 3.1

and AC gives the maximum per capita income attainable for each capital–labor ratio. A level of per capita income given by AB is reached by allocating resources between the advanced technique and the indigenous one operated at capital–labor ratio k^*.

The advanced technique should be adopted if $k^* < k < \hat{k}$ and only used exclusively if $k = k_0$. At most two techniques should be employed: for $k^* < k < k_0$, the indigenous technology will be operated at $k_1 = k^*$. Therefore, the advanced technique is more likely to be adopted, the greater, in terms of relative price, its effect on product quality and the smaller the difference between its capital–labor requirement and the country's aggregate capital–labor ratio.

If factors of production are paid their marginal products, the adoption of the advanced technique by a capital-poor country ($k < k_0$) reduces the wage rate and raises the rate of return on capital on account of resource reallocation in favor of the capital-intensive sector, in the same way as in Lapan and Bardhan (1973).

3. Quality Inspection and the Choice of Technique

A probable alternative to improving product quality and increasing the value of output by raising the capital-intensity of production is the inspection and sorting of output. This activity will reduce the amount of tradable output produced by any technique operated at a given level. The cost of improving quality in this way is the amount of tradable output foregone plus any resources expended in the effort.

In this model, the quality inspection process operates at the same capital–labor ratio as production in the indigenous technology. The cost of attaining a given level of quality improvement is assumed to decline with increasing scale of production. The relative price of output increases with increases in a parameter, θ, measuring quality improvement, and this schedule of prices is unaffected by the country's production decisions.

The price of output of the indigenous technique with inspection is given by $p(\theta)$, such that $p'(\theta) > 0$ and $\theta \equiv c - \beta/x_1$, where c is the amount of tradable output foregone (through both rejection of units and the use of capital and labor in the inspection process) per unit of output sold and x_1 is the amount of tradable output produced. The output of the indigenous technique is

$$x_1 = \frac{1}{1 + c} \gamma f(k_1),$$

where we let $L = 1$ throughout.

We assume that the advanced technique produces output which receives a price, p_0, on world markets.

The country seeks to maximize

$$y = \left[\frac{p(\theta)\gamma f(k_1)}{1 + c} + (1 - \gamma)p_0 f(k_0) \right],$$

subject to: $k = \gamma k_1 + (1 - \gamma)k_0$ and $\theta = c - \beta/x_1$. The first-order conditions are (for $\gamma < 1$)

$$\left[p(\theta)f(k_1) + p'(\theta)f(k_1) \cdot \frac{\beta}{x_1} - (1 + c)p_0 f(k_0) \right] \Big/ (1 + c)(k_1 - k_0)$$

$$= \frac{f'(k_1)}{1 + c} \left[p(\theta) + p'(\theta) \cdot \frac{\beta}{x_1} \right],$$

$$p(\theta) = p'(\theta)\left(1 + c - \frac{\beta}{x_1} \right) \quad \text{and} \quad k = \gamma k_1 + (1 - \gamma)k_0.$$

The first condition can be simplified to

$$\frac{f(k_1) - (p_0/p'(\theta)) \cdot f(k_0)}{k_1 - k_0} = f'(k_1).$$

The second condition gives the optimal level of quality improvement for each choice of γ and k_1.

If the optimal choice of $[p(\theta)/(1 + c)]$ exceeds p_0 for $k = k_0$, then the advanced technique should not be adopted for any aggregate capital–labor ratio. In the opposite case, the first-order conditions can be illustrated by Fig. 3.2. The values of θ^* and c^* are the optimal choices of θ and c for each value of k_1. For this model the values of k^* and $\hat{k}$ do not change with k, because $[p(\theta)/p'(\theta)]$ is constant in γ. Using the envelope theorem, this fact is derived as follows:

$$p'(\theta^*)\left(1 + c^* - \frac{\beta}{x_1} \right) = p(\theta^*)$$

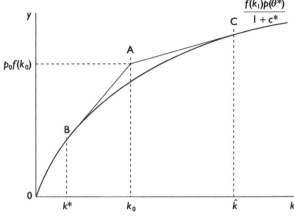

Fig. 3.2

implies that

$$\frac{p_0}{p'(\theta^*)} = \frac{p_0}{p(\theta^*)}\left[1 + c - \frac{\beta}{x_1}\right],$$

so that

$$\frac{d}{d\gamma}\left(\frac{p_0}{p'(\theta^*)}\right) = \left(\frac{p_0}{p(\theta^*)}\right)\left(\frac{\beta}{\gamma x_1}\right) - \frac{p_0\left(1 + c - \dfrac{\beta}{x_1}\right)}{p^2(\theta^*)}\left(p'(\theta^*) \cdot \frac{\beta}{\gamma x_1}\right)$$

$$= \frac{p_0}{p(\theta^*)}\left(\frac{\beta}{\gamma x_1}\right)\left(1 - \frac{p'(\theta^*)}{p(\theta^*)}\left(1 + c - \frac{\beta}{x_1}\right)\right) = 0.$$

Therefore, for an aggregate capital–labor ratio between k^* and k_0, both the advanced technique and the indigenous technology, operated at k^* with an optimal level of quality inspection, will be employed. Wages will be lower and the return to capital higher than if only the indigenous technology were used. For k between k_0 and $\hat{k}$, the indigenous technology is operated at $\hat{k}$ and wages are raised and the return to capital decreased by the adoption of the advanced technique.

4. Conclusion

In this paper, different production techniques are distinguished by both their resource requirements and the quality of their outputs. The optimal choice of production methods depends upon demand conditions, as well as the economy's capital–labor endowment and the technical characteristics of the alternatives. When product quality improvement is possible through the adoption of a foreign, advanced, capital-intensive technique, at most two techniques should be employed and the more closely matched are the capital–labor requirement of the advanced method and the aggregate capital–labor ratio, the greater the extent of adoption. The presence of a competing quality-improving activity using the indigenous technology reduces the range of aggregate capital–labor endowments for which the advanced technique should be employed. We consider quality inspection of units which reduces the amount of tradable output produced by given inputs as its market value increases. Economies of scale, in that the per unit cost of a given quality improvement falls with increasing sectoral output, are included.

A possible extension is to consider a technology in which capital and labor are substitutable under constant returns to scale and quality improvement takes place continuously with increasing capital-intensity. An interpretation is that more auto-mated techniques produce more standardized output, i.e., of less variable quality. The marginal productivity of capital is the partial derivative of the production func-tion with respect to capital plus a term reflecting the marginal increase in the value of output, so that the sector employs a higher capital–labor ratio than it would otherwise.

If both an advanced, capital-intensive technology in which quality improves with increasing capital-intensity and an indigenous technology with quality inspection are available, then at most two techniques should be employed. Each technology should be operated at one capital–labor ratio (different for each technology) and an optimal level of inspection undertaken in the indigenous technique. The first-order condi-tions are straightforward but messy. In general, two types of output will be pro-duced, one by each technique, which are distinguishable by their quality distributions.

Finally, it should be noted that this paper has addressed the problem of technique choice and output quality using a planning approach in which national income is maximized. Quality variations in this model influence the distribution of income via the optimal choice of techniques. It ignores the general problem of distribution of income in turn affecting the pattern of demand and hence the pattern of production. By assuming a shared perception of quality distribution by producers and consumers, the model also abstracts from product differentiation by producer action.

References

Lapan, H. and P. Bardhan, 1973, Localized technical progress and transfer of technology and economic development, Journal of Economic Theory 6, Dec.

Rothschild, M. and J. E. Stiglitz, 1970, Increasing risk I: A definition, Journal of Economic Theory 2, Dec.

Chapter 4

Imports, Domestic Production, and Transnational Vertical Integration: A Theoretical Note*

I

In the international economics literature on transactions in technology or technology-embodying goods with transnational companies, one frequently encounters more of vague generalities and colorful anecdotes and less of serious theoretical analysis. This is no doubt partly because these transactions essentially involve issues in an area where the general body of available economic theory is rather weak – that of the economics of the origin and diffusion of new technology and its integration with a satisfactory theory of oligopoly. The very limited purpose of the present paper is to focus theoretical attention on a specific problem of choice in technology buying from transnational companies and to apply simple partial-equilibrium analysis of a kind familiar in the industrial organization literature on vertical integration.

Suppose a developing country has the choice of: (i) *importing* cars from an oligopolistic world market; or (ii) producing them at home in a domestic firm *licensing* the technology from a transnational company, which also involves buying the necessary intermediate goods, equipment, and parts (we shall call them "components") from that company – the familiar case of licensing with tied purchase of inputs, tied either by restrictive contracts or by the specificity of the licensed technology; or (iii) producing them at home in a *subsidiary* of a transnational company. We shall denote alternative i by I (import), ii by L (licensing), and iii by S (subsidiary) in our subsequent analysis. Alternatives L and S both involve import substitution in a protected market, but, as is usually the case, it is essentially substitution of imports of a finished output by that of inputs, with the domestic production process largely consisting of assembling operations. In the case of S, the import of components involves intrafirm trade, whereas in the case of L it is interfirm. This difference has important implications in our analysis.

In the case of alternatives I and S our criterion of choice is the amount of consumer surplus generated in the domestic market for cars, whereas in the case of L it is this consumer surplus *plus* the profits for the domestic firm. The desirability of each alternative is thus evaluated in terms of total national welfare. For simplification, there is no tax or tariff revenue and all profits of the wholly owned subsidiary in the case of S are remitted abroad. We assume three alternative market structures for considering our choice problem:

a) The country directly imports from a duopolistic world car market if it goes for choice I, but in the case of domestic production under S the home market size is such that it allows the subsidiary of only one transnational company to cater to this market; similarly, in the case of L the licensing firm has a monopoly in the domestic car market. In this alternative the assumed asymmetry in market structure is to capture, though in an extreme form, the fact that import substitution (under either S or L) often increases the degree of monopoly faced by the domestic consumers.

b) We get rid of the asymmetry in market structure and assume monopoly all around. The cases of S and L are the same as in *a*; but in the case of I now consumers buy from a single monopolistic trading company (which imports from the duopolistic world car market).

c) Again, we have symmetry in market structure but now assume Cournot-Nash duopoly all around. In the case of I the country directly imports from a duopolistic world car market, as in *a*. In the case of S, subsidiaries of two transnational companies produce and compete in the domestic market; in the case of L, there are two licensing firms catering to the domestic market, each buying components from only one of two licensor transnationals in the world market.

We start with market structure alternative *a* and have a comparative evaluation of benefits from L and S in Section II, and I and S (or L) in Section III, all under the assumption that production of cars uses labor and components in fixed proportions. At the end of Section III we briefly indicate how the results change when we have instead a Cobb-Douglas production function. We then consider market structure alternatives *b* and *c* in Section IV. Section V summarizes the conclusions and their limitations.

II

In this section we confine ourselves to a comparison of the two alternative forms of import substitution, L and S under market structure alternative *a*. In the case of L the domestic firm licenses technology for producing cars from a particular transnational company and is obliged to buy car components from the latter, either because the contractual agreement frequently[1] stipulates that or because the licensed technology is embodied and rigidly component specific. We ignore license fees or royalties since with tied purchase of components, the price charged for the latter provides enough leverage for the transnational company.

Suppose the domestic market for cars is characterized by the following constant-elasticity demand function:

$$Q = P^{-\eta}, \ \eta > 1, \tag{1}$$

where Q is the amount demanded, P is the price, and η is the (positively defined) price elasticity of demand.

If Q_S and Q_L are the equilibrium quantities of cars produced under S and L, respectively, expressions for total national benefit, our criterion of choice, are:

$$B_S = \int_0^{Q_S} [P(Q) - P(Q_S)]\,dQ = Q^{(\eta-1)/\eta}/(\eta - 1), \tag{2}$$

$$B_L = \int_0^{Q_L} P(Q)\,dQ - C(Q_L), \tag{3}$$

where B_S is the consumer surplus at quantity Q_S under S; B_L is the consumer surplus *plus* producer profits at quantity Q_L under L; and $C(Q_L)$ is the cost function associated with production under L. No part of producer profits under S enters the expression for national benefit, since all of it is assumed to be remitted abroad.

We shall assume that car components, m, are produced abroad by the transnational company at a fixed per-unit cost k. Imported components m and domestic labor l are combined in fixed proportions to produce cars at home, so that

$$Q = \min(m, l). \tag{4}$$

The domestic market equilibrium for Q, characterized by marginal cost equal to marginal revenue, will yield, from equation (1),

$$Q_i = [\eta M_i/(\eta - 1)]^{-\eta}, \quad i = S, L, \tag{5}$$

where M_i is marginal cost for regime i. This means (2) and (3) may be rewritten as

$$B_S = [\eta/(\eta - 1)^2]Q_S \cdot M_S, \tag{6}$$

$$B_L = [(2\eta - 1)/(\eta - 1)^2]Q_L \cdot M_L. \tag{7}$$

Now, under S, the subsidiary of the transnational company maximizes $[P(Q)Q - Wl - km]$ subject to (4), paying domestic labor at the local wage rate W. The cost function in this case is:

$$C_S(Q_S; k, W) = (W + k)Q_S. \tag{8}$$

Computing marginal cost, M_S, from (8) and output, Q_S, from (5), we rewrite (6) as

$$B_S = (\eta - 1)^{-1}[(\eta - 1)/\eta(W + k)]^{\eta-1}. \qquad (9)$$

Let us now take the alternative regime L. If q is the price charged per unit of car components by the transnational company, the cost function of the licensing domestic firm is:

$$C_L(Q_L; q, W) = (W + q)Q_L. \qquad (10)$$

Computing marginal cost M_L from (10) and putting it into (5), one gets $Q_L(q)$. The demand for car components, $m(q)$, can be computed by using Shephard's lemma, so that

$$m(q) = \frac{\partial C_L}{\partial q} = Q_L(q). \qquad (11)$$

The transnational company, which is the licensor, will utilize its monopoly power (derived from the tied purchase of components by the licensee) to fix q at a level which maximizes the former's profit from the sale of components, that is, $(q - k)m(q)$. By solving the first-order condition of the maximum, we get

$$q = (W + \eta k)/(\eta - 1). \qquad (12)$$

Note that the transnational's profit per unit of tied sales of components to the licensee – the gap between q and k – is larger, the more monopolistic is the domestic car market (i.e., the smaller is η, the price elasticity of demand for cars).

Substituting (12) into (10) and (7), we get

$$B_L = [(2\eta - 1)/(\eta - 1)^2][(\eta - 1)/\eta]^{2\eta-1}(W + k)^{1-\eta}. \qquad (13)$$

Having derived the expressions for total national benefit under S and L in (9) and (13), respectively, in terms of the parameters η, W, and k, let us now compare the two regimes:

$$B_L/B_S = \left(2 - \frac{1}{\eta}\right)\left(1 - \frac{1}{\eta}\right)^{\eta-1} \equiv F(\eta). \qquad (14)$$

In Appendix A we prove that $F(\eta)$ is less than unity for all $\eta > 1$. This proves that in our model a subsidiary of a transnational contributes to national benefit of the host country more than a domestic firm licensing the technology (with tied input purchases) from the transnational. This is despite the fact that producer profits of the domestic firm are added to consumer surplus for evaluating the national benefit under licensing, while producer profits of the subsidiary are not so counted. The primary reason behind this result is that the distortion caused by monopoly pricing

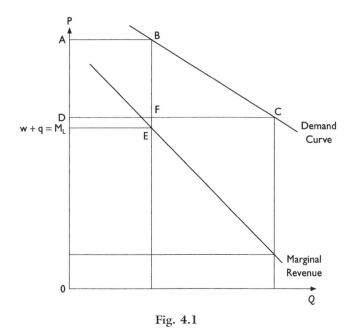

Fig. 4.1

of intermediate goods for downstream producers is avoided by vertical integration by the transnational. So the subsidiary will market cars at a lower price (which generates more consumer surplus) than the licensing domestic firm can, and the *additional* consumer surplus in the former case, indicated by the area $ABCD$ in Fig. 4.1, is large enough to overcompensate for the producer profits, indicated by the rectangle $ABEM_L$ in Fig. 4.1, in the case of licensing. Our result would, of course, be strengthened if we allowed the expression for national benefits to include domestic tax revenue from corporate profits in the subsidiary (subject to the effects of consequent attempts at transfer pricing by the transnational, on which we comment later).

It is interesting to note from Appendix A that $F(\eta)$ is a declining function of η, which indicates that the more competitive the domestic market, the larger is the gap between B_S and B_L. From (12) we also know that $(q - k)$ is a declining function of η. This suggests that a larger η, while it reduces the gap between marginal costs (and price) in regimes S and L, for the same price difference also implies a larger difference in consumer surplus, and the latter outweighs the former.[2]

III

Let us now compare alternatives S and I under the same market structure alternative a. Under I the country imports cars from a duopoly in the world car market. The easiest solution concept to adopt is that of Cournot-Nash. Assume that the two transnational sellers in the world market are identical. Each of them has the following cost function:

$$C_I^i(Q_I^i) = (\bar{W} + k)Q_I^i, \quad i = 1, 2, \tag{15}$$

where Q_I is the equilibrium output[3] of cars in regime I, i denotes the duopolists 1 and 2, and $\bar{W}$ is the wage rate abroad where the cars are produced. Each duopolist maximizes $[P(Q_I^1 + Q_I^2)Q_I^i - C_I^i(Q_I^i)]$, $i = 1, 2$. By symmetry, Q_I^i is exactly half of the total equilibrium output of cars, Q_I. So we get

$$Q_I = [(2\eta - 1)/2\eta(\bar{W} + k)]^\eta. \tag{16}$$

The total benefit, given by consumer surplus, under regime I is:

$$B_I = \int_0^{Q_I} [P(Q) - P(Q_I)]\,dQ = (\eta - 1)^{-1}[(2\eta - 1)/2\eta(\bar{W} + k)]^{\eta - 1}. \tag{17}$$

Comparing B_S and B_I from (9) and (17) we get

$$B_I/B_S = \left[\frac{(2\eta - 1)(W + k)}{2(\eta - 1)(\bar{W} + k)}\right]^{\eta - 1}. \tag{18}$$

Clearly, there are two possibly conflicting forces at work on the ratio of B_I to B_S. If wages were the same here and abroad, it would obviously be better for the consumers in the country to import cars from transnational duopolists than to allow one of them the monopoly power of producing cars in a subsidiary for the domestic market. But usually W, the wage in the developing country, will be much lower than $\bar{W}$, the wage in the car-exporting country.

Let us define $\lambda \equiv (W + k)/(\bar{W} + k) < 1$ and $\eta^* \equiv (2 - \lambda)/2(1 - \lambda) > 1$. It is now clear from (18) that $B_I > B_S$ for $\eta^* > \eta > 1$ and $B_I < B_S$ for $\eta > \eta^* > 1$. The smaller the value of η, that is, the more the monopoly power of the subsidiary in the protected domestic market, the better off the consumers are likely to be in buying instead from the duopolists in the world market.

Let us now compare alternatives L and I. From (14) and (18),

$$B_L/B_I = F(\eta)/D(\eta, \lambda), \tag{19}$$

where $D \equiv [\lambda(2\eta - 1)/2(\eta - 1)]^{\eta - 1}$. In Appendix A we have proved that $F'(\eta) < 0$, $F(1) = 1$, and $F(\infty) = 2e^{-1} > 0$. In Appendix B we prove that, for a given $\lambda < 1$, $D(1, \lambda) = 1$, $D(\infty, \lambda) = 0$, and $D(\eta, \lambda)$ intersects $F(\eta)$ at a unique value of η, say η^{**}, which is larger than η^*. All this is put together in Fig. 4.2. From Fig. 4.2 it is now clear that $B_I > B_L$ for $\eta^{**} > \eta > 1$ and $B_I < B_L$ for $\eta > \eta^{**} > 1$. Again, at small values of η, that is, at high degrees of monopoly power of the licensing firm in the protected domestic market, it is better for the country to import cars from the world

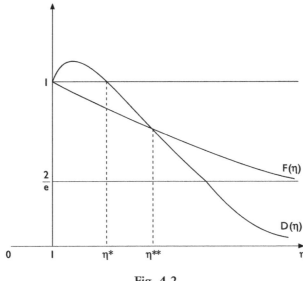

Fig. 4.2

duopoly. Of course, this case is more complicated than the case of S and I in (18), since the criterion of choice is biased in favor of L, when producer profits enter the expression for national benefits, unlike in S or I.

Finally for this section, let us note that in the industrial organization literature on vertical integration it is well known (see, e.g., Schmalensee 1973; Warren-Boulton 1974) that its welfare effects can be quite different between the case of fixed factor proportions and that of variable proportions in the downstream production process. Accordingly, we take the simplest case of variable proportions, Cobb-Douglas functions, in car production and briefly point out how our results on a comparative evaluation of regimes S, L, and I change.

Equation (4) will now have to be replaced by

$$Q = l^a m^{1-a}, \tag{20}$$

where a is the labor elasticity of output in car production. Equations (1), (5), (6), and (7) remain as before. Making appropriate changes in equations (8)–(12) we get:

$$B_L/B_S = \left(2 - \frac{1}{\eta}\right)\left[1 + \frac{1}{(1-a)(\eta-1)}\right]^{-(1-a)(\eta-1)} \equiv G(\eta, a). \tag{21}$$

Note that $G(\eta, 0) = F(\eta)$, which we have already proved in Appendix A to be less than unity. In Appendix C we prove that for $1 > a > 0$, a sufficient condition for $G(\eta, a)$ to be less than unity is $a \leq 0.43$. Appendix C also proves that for $1 > a > 0$, very large values of η ensure $G(\eta, a)$ to be less than unity. In other words, for small values of the labor elasticity of final output (which is not uncommon to assume for developing countries), or when the degree of monopoly power in the domestic market is sufficiently low, the subsidiary of a transnational contributes to national benefit of the host country more than a domestic firm licensing the technology from the transnational. (One gets a reverse result when the labor elasticity of final output is very high; e.g., as $a \to 1$, $G[\eta, a]$ tends to a value larger than unity.) Similarly, we get:

$$B_I/B_S = \left[\left(\frac{W}{\bar{W}}\right)^a (2\eta - 1)/2(\eta - 1)\right]^{\eta-1}. \tag{22}$$

For the general case of $1 > a > 0$, let us define $\hat{\lambda} \equiv (W/\bar{W})^a < 1$ and $\hat{\eta} = (2 - \hat{\lambda})/2(1 - \hat{\lambda}) > 1$. Similar to our results for the fixed-coefficients case, $B_I > B_S$ for $\hat{\eta} > \eta > 1$ and $B_I < B_S$ for $\eta > \hat{\eta} > 1$. Thus if the monopoly power of the subsidiary in the protected domestic market is large (or if labor elasticity of output is extremely low), the consumers are better off buying instead from the duopolists in the world market.

Let us now compare alternatives L and I:

$$B_L/B_I = G(\eta, a)/D(\eta, \hat{\lambda}), \tag{23}$$

where $D(\eta, \hat{\lambda}) = [\hat{\lambda}(2\eta - 1)/2(\eta - 1)]^{\eta-1}$. In Appendix C we show that, for a given $\hat{\lambda} < 1$, $G(1, a) = D(1, \hat{\lambda}) = 1$ and that $D(\eta, \hat{\lambda})$ intersects $G(\eta, a)$ at a unique value of η, say $\bar{\eta}$, under the sufficient condition $a \leq 0.43$. So we can say that, under that condition, $B_I > B_L$ for $\bar{\eta} > \eta > 1$ and $B_I < B_L$ for $\eta > \bar{\eta} > 1$. For η very large $B_I > B_L$ even if the condition on the value of a is not satisfied. In other words, for small values of labor elasticity of final output and a high degree of monopoly power in the domestic market, it is better for the country to import from the world duopoly than to produce domestically in a firm licensing the technology. On the other hand, for a low degree of monopoly power in the domestic market, domestic production under licensing gives more benefits than import.

IV

We now go back to the fixed-proportions case and consider the market structure alternatives b and c as specified in Section I. Since the general analytical framework of the problem is not very different from that in the last two sections, we shall skip the details and briefly present only the results. Let us first take market structure alternative b: B_S and B_L are the same as in Section II, and so the comparison between B_S and B_L is the same as in equation (14). However, B_I is now different, because we have a monopolistic importing firm (which buys cars from a Cournot-Nash duopoly in the world market) selling to the captive domestic market.

Let P_I stand for the price of imported cars. If the two identical Cournot-Nash world market sellers have their cost functions and maximands as in Section III, then with the importing firm maximizing its monopoly profits we have to replace equation (17) by

$$B_I = \int_0^{Q_I} [P(Q) - P_I] dQ \tag{24}$$

$$= (\eta - 1)^{-1}[\eta/(\eta - 1)]^{1-\eta}[(2\eta - 1)/2\eta(\bar{W} + k)]^{\eta-1}.$$

From (9) and (24),

$$B_I/B_S = [1 - (1/2\eta)]^{\eta-1}\lambda^{\eta-1} < 1. \tag{25}$$

From (13) and (24),

$$B_I/B_L = \tilde{D}(\eta, \lambda)/F(\eta), \tag{26}$$

where $\tilde{D}(\eta, \lambda) \equiv [\lambda(2\eta - 1)/2\eta]^{\eta-1}$. Both the numerator and the denominator in (26) are declining in η. But we can prove that, while $\tilde{D}(1, \lambda) = F(1) = 1$, $\tilde{D}(\infty, \lambda) = 0$ whereas $F(\infty)$ is positive and that the slope of $\tilde{D}$ is steeper than that of F as η changes. So there is a unique value of η, below which $B_I > B_L$ and above which $B_I < B_L$.

Let us now take up market structure alternative c, which is somewhat more complicated. We now have duopoly in the world market as well as in domestic production. As in market structure alternative a, the consumers under I directly import from the duopolistic world market, so that B_I is again given by (17). But under S we now have two transnational subsidiaries in domestic production. Using profit maximization under Cournot-Nash duopoly assumptions for each subsidiary, we get

$$B_S = (\eta - 1)^{-1}[(2\eta - 1)/2\eta(W + k)]^{\eta-1}. \tag{27}$$

Under L, we have two domestic firms producing cars and buying components from outside, each tied under its licensing contract to buy them from one of the two transnationals in the world market. We assume that both the domestic duopolists and the transnational duopolists in the world market operate in the Cournot-Nash way. We first work out the reaction function of each domestic duopolist, which then gives us the demand for components from the transnational to which it is tied; that in turn gives us the reaction function of the transnational duopolist, and assuming symmetry we work out:

$$B_L = [(\eta - 1)(4\eta - 1)/4\eta^2(W + k)]^{\eta-1}[(3\eta - 1)/2\eta(\eta - 1)]. \tag{28}$$

Now from (27) and (28)

$$B_S/B_L = [2\eta(2\eta - 1)/(\eta - 1)(4\eta - 1)]^{\eta-1}[2\eta(3\eta - 1)]. \tag{29}$$

It is analytically too cumbersome to prove if the expression in (29) is larger than unity. But for all practical values of η (we have numerically checked up to $\eta = 10$) it is, and as $\eta \to \infty$, it goes to $(2/3)e^{0.75} > 1$. From (17) and (27),

$$B_I/B_S = \lambda^{\eta-1} < 1. \tag{30}$$

From (17) and (28),

$$B_I/B_L = [\lambda 2\eta(2\eta - 1)/(\eta - 1)(4\eta - 1)]^{\eta-1}[2\eta/(3\eta - 1)]. \tag{31}$$

For large values of η, (31) is less than unity so that $B_L > B_I$.

V

Table 4.1 summarizes our results for the fixed-proportions case for the three market structure alternatives. In general, as a form of import substitution licensing by a domestic firm with tied purchase of inputs from a transnational seems to be inferior to the transnational subsidiary in most cases in our model. This is in spite of the fact that in the case of licensing domestic producer profits are included in the national benefit criterion, unlike in the other two alternative regimes.

Transnational vertical integration through the subsidiary seems also to dominate imports in both the symmetrical market structure alternatives b and c and even in the asymmetrical alternative a if the degree of monopoly in the domestic market is low. Licensing seems to dominate imports when the domestic market is not highly monopolized.

Table 4.1
Comparison of Alternative Regimes under Fixed Proportions

	Market Structure Assumption		
Regimes Compared	a	b	c
S and L	$S > L$	$S > L$	$S > L$ (for all practical values of η)
I and S	$I > S$ (for small η) $S > I$ (for large η)	$S > I$ . . .	$S > I$ . . .
I and L	$I > L$ (for small η) $L > I$ (for large η)	$I > L$ (for small η) $L > I$ (for large η)	. . . $L > I$ (for large η)

Note: $->$ implies superior national benefit.

There are, of course, many other considerations, left out in our simplified model, which will influence the choice among the alternative regimes. For example, transnational vertical integration, while it may achieve significant economies of internal organization and information,[4] will usually involve a degree of packaging in the transfer of technology which may inhibit the development of local entrepreneurial and technological capacity. In developing countries licensing and other less packaged forms of technology transfer, by leaving a larger scope for local decision making and for the choice to put the package together for themselves, may contribute to the all-important process of learning by doing and all the externalities it generates.[5]

Our comparative evaluation of regimes S and L is also influenced by our simplifying assumption of absence of taxation. If corporate profits are taxed, this will, on the one hand, raise B_s (and hence reinforce our conclusion of $B_S > B_L$), but, on the other hand, this will induce the transnational to manipulate transfer prices of components in the case of S. Much will, of course, depend on the form (apart from the intercountry variations in rates and exemptions) of taxation; a business expenditure tax or a uniform tax on profits plus imported inputs may reduce the tax incentive for transfer price manipulation.

Our comparison of S and L has also ignored the question of raising finance. The comparison will, of course, be affected if transnational vertical integration is associated with an inflow of additional capital. The importance of this effect is somewhat reduced if, as is not infrequently the case, the subsidiary of a transnational raises much of the capital locally or transnational banks provide finance under both S and L regimes. The question of differential access to finance is particularly important in view of the fact that the financial economies of scale achieved by vertical integration are likely to raise barriers to market entry much more formidable than in the case of licensing firms operating in a protected domestic market.

Another possibly restrictive assumption in our comparative evaluation is that of constant returns to scale, which implies constant marginal costs. We may briefly indicate here how the results change when returns to scale are not constant. If, for example, we rewrite our production function equation (20) as $Q = l^a m^b$, we may recompute the results at the end of Section III and replace equation (21) by

$$B_L/B_S = \left(2 - \frac{1}{\eta}\right)\{1 + [\eta - (a + b) \times (\eta - 1)]/b(\eta - 1)\}^{-b(\eta-1)/[\eta-(a+b)(\eta-1)]}. \quad (32)$$

When $(a + b) = 1$, the constant returns to scale case, the right-hand side of equation (32) is the same as $G(\eta, a)$, which we have proved to be less than unity for $a \leq 0.43$. Since the right-hand side of equation (32) is decreasing in $(a + b)$, it is easy to conclude that $B_S > B_L$, under the same condition on labor elasticity of output, when there are *increasing* returns to scale.

In comparing the alternative regimes we have adopted Cournot-Nash assumptions whenever a duopoly is involved. The crudity of those assumptions is, of course, well known. In general a bargaining-theoretic framework of negotiations in which each side is aware of the benefits its strategies generate for the other party and simultaneously weighs all options in the context of an oligopolistic market for technology would have been a more satisfactory approach, though obviously more difficult, than the one adopted in this paper. Finally, all the usual caveats about the partial equilibrium analysis, the consumer surplus as an index of consumer benefits, insufficient allowance for income distribution effects, etc., clearly apply to the present paper.

Appendix A

$$\left(2 - \frac{1}{\eta}\right)\left(1 - \frac{1}{\eta}\right)^{\eta-1} = \left(\frac{1 + 2x}{1 + x}\right)\left(\frac{x}{1 + x}\right)^x = F(x).$$

when $x = \eta - 1 > 0$. Differentiating in $F(x)$, we get

$$\frac{F'(x)}{F(x)} = \log\left(\frac{x}{1 + x}\right) + \left(\frac{2}{1 + 2x}\right) = \log\left(\frac{1}{1 + y}\right) + \left(\frac{2y}{2 + y}\right) = H(y),$$

when $y = 1/x > 0$. It is easy to check that $H(0) = 0$ and $H'(y) < 0$, hence $H(y) < 0$. Since it is also easy to see that $F(0) = 1$, we can now say that $F(x) < 1$ for $x > 0$. Thus, in equation (14), $F(\eta) < 1$ for $\eta > 1$. Also,

$$\lim_{\eta\to\infty} F(\eta) = 2 \lim_{\eta\to\infty}\left(1 - \frac{1}{\eta}\right)^{\eta} = 2e^{-1} > 0.$$

Appendix B

$$D(\eta, \lambda) = [\lambda(2\eta - 1)/2(\eta - 1)]^{\eta-1}, \text{ where } 1 > \lambda > 0,$$

$$\lim_{\eta\to1} D(\eta, \lambda) = \lim_{x\to0}\left[\lambda\left(1 + \frac{1}{2x}\right)\right]^x, \text{ where } x = \eta - 1,$$

$$= \lim_{x\to0} \exp\left\{x \log\left[\lambda\left(1 + \frac{1}{2x}\right)\right]\right\}$$

$$= \exp\left[\lim_{x\to0} x \log \lambda + \lim_{x\to0} x \log\left(\frac{1}{x}\right)\right]$$

$$= 1,$$

$$\lim_{\eta\to\infty} D(\eta, \lambda) = \lim_{\eta\to\infty} \exp\{(\eta - 1) \log [\lambda(2\eta - 1)/2(\eta - 1)]\}$$

$$= \exp\left\{\lim_{\eta\to\infty} \eta \log\left[\lambda\frac{2 - (1/\eta)}{2 - (2/\eta)}\right]\right\}$$

$$= \exp\left\{\lim_{\eta\to\infty} \eta \lim_{\eta\to\infty} \log\left[\lambda\frac{2 - (1/\eta)}{2 - (2/\eta)}\right]\right\}$$

$$= \exp(-\infty) = 0.$$

Redefine $D(\eta, \lambda)$ as

$$D(x) = \left[\lambda\left(1 + \frac{1}{2x}\right)\right]^x,$$

where $x = \eta - 1 > 0$. Differentiating, we get

$$\frac{D'(x)}{D(x)} = \log \lambda + \log\left(1 + \frac{1}{2x}\right) - \frac{1}{1 + 2x}$$

$$= \log \lambda + \left[\log(1 + y) - \frac{y}{1 + y}\right], \quad \text{where } y = \frac{1}{2x} > 0,$$

$$= \log \lambda + J(y).$$

Since it is easy to check that $J(0) = 0$, $J'(y) > 0$, and $\log \lambda$ is negative, $D(x)$ has a unique maximum. We have already proved in Section III that

$$D(\eta, \lambda) \gtreqless 1 \quad \text{for} \quad \eta \lesseqgtr \eta^*,$$

so it is clear that the unique maximum for $D(\eta, \lambda)$ occurs at a value of η less than η^*. Define

$$T(y) = \frac{D'(x)}{D(x)} - \frac{F'(x)}{F(x)} = \log \lambda + J(y) - H(2y),$$

$$T(0) = \log \lambda < 0,$$

and

$$T'(y) = J'(y) - 2H'(2y) > 0.$$

So there is a unique value of y (and, hence, x) at which $T(y) = 0$; for y greater than this value (x less than this value) $T(y)$ is positive, and for y less than this value (x more than this value) $T(y)$ is negative. So the ratio $D(x)/F(x)$ starts at value one when x is zero, rises, and reaches a unique maximum and then starts declining and reaches the value of one again (at the unique value of x, x^{**}) and goes on declining until it becomes zero as x tends to infinity. In terms of Fig. 4.2 for a given λ both the $D(\eta, \lambda)$ and $F(\eta)$ curves start at value one, and for $\eta > 1$ there is a unique intersection of the two curves at η^{**}.

In the Cobb-Douglas case the $D(\eta, \hat\lambda)$ function behaves exactly the same way as $D(\eta, \lambda)$ for $a > 0$.

Appendix C

From equation (21), write the reciprocal of $G(\eta, a)$ as

$$R(x) = \left(\frac{1 + x}{1 + 2x}\right)\left[1 + \frac{1}{(1 - a)x}\right]^{(1-a)x},$$

where $x = \eta - 1 > 0$. Then $R(0) = 1$, since it is easy to check that $G(1, a) = 1$. Differentiating $R(x)$ and defining $y = 1/x\,(1 - a) > 0$, we get

$$\frac{R'(x)}{(1 - a)R(x)} = \log(1 + y) - \frac{y}{1 + y} - \frac{y^2(1 - a)}{[1 + (1 - a)y][2 + (1 - a)y]} = N(y).$$

It can be checked that $N(0) = 0$ and that $N'(y) > 0$ if $[4a + (1 - a)y\,(1 + 3a) + y^2(1 - a)$ $(3 - 7a) + 3y^3(1 - a)^2(1 - 2a) + (1 - a)^4 y^4] > 0$. This latter condition is satisfied under the sufficient condition that $a \le 3/7 = 0.43$. So, for $a \le 0.43$, $R(x) > 1$ and hence $G(\eta, a) < 1$. We can also show that for $1 > a > 0$, $R(\infty) > 1$, and hence $G(\infty, a) < 1$:

$$\lim_{\eta \to \infty} R = \frac{1}{2} \lim_{\eta \to \infty} \left[1 + \frac{1}{(1 - a)(\eta - 1)}\right]^{(1-a)(\eta-1)}$$

$$= \frac{1}{2} \lim_{\eta \to \infty} \left(1 + \frac{1}{\eta}\right)^{\eta} = \frac{e}{2} > 1.$$

It can also be checked that for $a = 1$, $G(\eta) = 2 - (1/\eta) > 1$.

Let us find out about the value of $B_I/B_L = D(\eta, \hat{\lambda})/G(\eta, a) = D(x)R(x)$ for given $\hat{\lambda}$ and a. Define $V(x) = [D'(x)/D(x)] + [R'(x)/R(x)]$. Under the assumption of $a \le 0.43$ it is easy to check that, analogous to the case of $T(y)$ in Appendix B, there is a unique value of x at which $V = 0$; for x less (more) than this value V is positive (negative). So $D(x)R(x)$ starts at the value of one when x is zero, rises, and reaches a unique maximum and then starts declining and reaches the value of one again (at the unique value of x, say $\bar{x}$) and goes on declining until it becomes zero as x tends to infinity. Thus $B_I \gtreqless B_L$ as $\bar{\eta} \gtreqless \eta$.

It can be checked that for very large η, our assumption of $a \le 0.43$ is not necessary for our result, since as $\eta \to \infty$, R tends to a positive number, whereas D tends to zero (for $a > 0$).

Notes

* Valuable research assistance was provided by Leonard Cheng, Ibrahim Hasan, and Ken Kletzer, and useful comments on an earlier draft by a referee, an editor, and Sanjaya Lall. Thanks are also due to the National Science Foundation for partial research support under grant no. SES-7804022 A01.
1. Stewart (1979) summarizes some of the UNCTAD data on the importance of this stipulation in actual agreements for transfer of technology.
2. A referee has suggested that I consider the case when the licensor transnational uses a two-part tariff, i.e., a fixed charge for the use of the license plus a price for components. It is easy to see that this will reduce our expression for B_L in (13) by the amount of the fixed charge and reinforce our result of $B_S > B_L$.
3. We are, of course, suppressing the output produced by the duopolists for other markets. If the output for other markets is given for our present problem, its inclusion in the duopolists' cost functions does not change our results.
4. For an account of some of these economies of vertical integration, see Williamson (1971). Technical economies arising out of integration of production of components with the assembly of those components are not usually significant; see, on this, Bain (1968, p. 381). Sanjaya Lall has pointed out to me that the auto industry has a rather strong propensity to buy components from independent suppliers than to internalize.

5. Sanjaya Lall in his field work in India on automobile transnationals vis-à-vis local companies has found that there is a very active and dynamic process of learning and technological diffusion in the auto assembly and components industry, which strengthens the case for a licensing as opposed to subsidiary relationship.

References

Bain, Joe S. *Industrial Organization.* New York: Wiley, 1968.

Schmalensee, Richard. "A Note on the Theory of Vertical Integration." *J.P.E.* 81, no. 2, pt. 1 (March/April 1973): 442–49.

Stewart, F. "International Technology Transfer: Issues and Policy Options." Staff Working Paper no. 344, World Bank, July 1979.

Warren-Boulton, Frederick R. "Vertical Control with Variable Proportions." *J.P.E.* 82, no. 4 (July/August 1974): 783–802.

Williamson, Oliver E. "The Vertical Integration of Production: Market Failure Considerations." *A.E.R. Papers and Proc.* 61 (May 1971): 112–23.

Chapter 5

Disparity in Wages but not in Returns to Capital between Rich and Poor Countries

1. Introduction

One of the striking features of the international economy is that while the level of average wage rates (for most categories of labor) in rich countries is many times that in poor countries, their average rates of return to capital seem to be roughly similar or the differences in them relatively very small. The wage disparity between, say, U.S. and South Asia, is so palpably large that any attempt to find corroborative evidence is somewhat redundant. Even for skilled labor the disparity in wages between rich and poor countries is extremely large. For example, the International Comparison Project of Kravis et al. (1982) shows that the average wage rate for skilled blue-collar workers in six Asian developing countries (India, Pakistan, Sri Lanka, the Philippines, Thailand and South Korea) was about 9 percent of that in seven rich countries (U.S., France, Germany, the Netherlands, Belgium, Luxembourg and Denmark); even for professional workers with post-secondary education the figure was about 13 percent. Estimating comparable rates of return to capital between countries is a much trickier exercise, but let us refer to the results of two such heroic exercises. Harberger (1978) found the difference in the rate of return to capital between developed and developing countries very modest: for example the average private after-tax rate of return to capital in the two poorest counties in his sample (Sri Lanka and Thailand) was 8.5 percent in 1969–71, whereas it was 7.6 percent in the richest country in his sample (U.S.). Earlier, on the basis of 1950s data, Minhas (1963) computed the rates of return to capital in manufacturing to be approximately 19–20 percent in India and Japan, and 15–16 percent in Canada, U.K. and U.S.

The easiest explanation of this asymmetry in the pattern of factor prices, which many including Harberger opt for, is that capital is internationally much more mobile than labor. While that is generally true, there is, however, remarkably little movement of return-sensitive private capital between rich and poor countries, certainly compared to the amounts of capital movement among rich and middle-income countries. In fact private capital inflow to the poorest countries of the world has been historically so small (except in a few mineral-rich countries) that we need a better or stronger explanation of the asymmetry. (Recent large increases in private foreign investment in countries like China or Indonesia cannot be used in explaining the long-standing asymmetry.) In most of this paper I shall, therefore, stick to the extreme assumption of international immobility of factors of production familiar from classical international trade theory, and search for explanations of the international asymmetry in factor prices between rich and poor countries under that assumption. Of course these explanations will themselves have a bearing on why capital does not flow from rich to poor countries, and in that context we shall have an occasion to comment on the answer provided by Lucas (1990) to the latter question. (I shall also ignore short-run macroeconomic effects like those following from exchange risk or political risk in poor countries.)

The rest of the paper is organized as follows. In Section 2 we discuss the implications of a particular type of international difference in production functions. In Section 3 we consider the model with sector-specific factors of production. In Section 4 we explore the factor price implications of the average level of human capital in a country through its learning effects and through its ability to speed technological diffusion. In Section 5 we consider the effects of differential degrees of specialization in the sector producing intermediate inputs and services on the pattern of factor prices between a rich and a poor country.

2. Implications of International Difference in Production Functions

Let us start with the old workhorse of international trade theory, the two-by-two Heckscher–Ohlin–Samuelson model (where both goods are produced in positive amounts), with the change that production functions are internationally different, as is likely to be the case between rich and poor countries. In this case, of course, factor price equalization will not hold under free trade, but under certain types of international differences in production function we can get the result that the wage rate will be higher in the rich than in the poor country while the rate of return to capital is the same between the two countries. (For a detailed algebraic and geometric derivation of this result see Bardhan (1965) and Bardhan (1970), pp. 29–38 respectively). The intuitive idea is very simple: The rich country is technologically more advanced than the poor country, but suppose the technological gap is wider in the labor-intensive industry than in the capital-intensive industry. If factor prices between the two trading countries were the same, the labor-intensive commodity would then have been relatively cheap in the rich country. But under free trade, absent transport

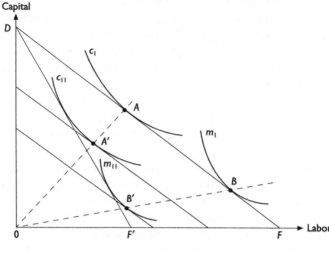

Fig. 5.1

costs, all commodity prices have to be equal between the two countries. So factor prices have to adjust; only by letting labor to be more expensive in the rich country can the market under free trade keep the rich country producing the labor-intensive commodity at the same post-trade price as the other country.

We illustrate this in Fig. 5.1. c_I and m_I are unit isoquants for the capital-intensive good c and labor-intensive good m respectively in the poor country I. c_{II} and m_{II} are the corresponding unit isoquants in the technologically more advanced rich country (for simplification, we have drawn the isoquants only for the case where the production function differences between the countries are Hicks-neutral, but it can easily be checked that our result does not depend on that assumption). Under free trade prices are the same between the two countries; without loss of generality, we take those prices to be unity, so that the unit isoquants for each country lie on a common tangent. The tangents indicate the ratio of the wage rate to the rate of return to capital in the two countries, so the steeper common tangent for the rich country confirms geometrically our intuitive result in the previous paragraph that the rich country has a higher relative wage under free trade.

What about the absolute factor prices? Since OF′ is the price of either good in terms of labor in the rich country and OF the corresponding price in the poor country, taking reciprocals it is clear that the rich country has a higher absolute level of real wage. In the particular case drawn in Fig. 5.1, OD represents the price of either good in terms of capital in *both* countries, and so the real rate of return is the same in both countries. (The steeper tangent can, of course, cut the capital axis above or below D, but all we want to show in Fig. 5.1 is the possibility of its cutting the capital axis at D.)

Note that we get this result of higher real wage but the same rate of return to capital in the rich country under free trade, only for the case when the technological gap is wider in the labor-intensive than in the capital-intensive sector. If the pattern of technological gaps were different (say, the technological gap is uniform in both sectors, or larger in the capital-intensive sector), we cannot get in this model the pattern of factor prices consistent with the observed factor price differences between rich and poor countries. How plausible is the presumption of the technological gap between the rich and the poor country being wider in the labor-intensive sector?

Rigorous quantitative work on sectoral differences in production functions across countries is rather scanty. We can, however, draw some support from the evidence garnered by several people who some years back tried to test what came to be known as "the Hirschman hypothesis". Hirschman (1961) had suggested that the productivity differential between rich and poor countries is likely to be smaller in industries where the operations are largely machine-paced leaving less latitude for human operators. This hypothesis, which is clearly consistent with our empirical presumption above,[1] received some (weak) confirmation in the work of Diaz-Alejandro (1965) comparing Argentina and U.S., of Clague (1967) comparing Peru and U.S., of Healey (1968) comparing India and U.K., and of Gouverneur (1970) comparing Zaire and Belgium.

Apart from the rationale suggested by Hirschman, one can think of at least three other kinds of reasons for the likelihood of the technological gap between rich and poor countries being wider in the labor-intensive sector. First, in a poor country usually the more "modern" sector of the economy is relatively capital-intensive, the technological distance from the industrially advanced country is relatively small with better access to new blueprints and designs, engineers working in this sector in both countries may have roughly similar training, and so on. On the other hand, the labor-intensive sector in the poor country is usually the "residual" sector, the "hold-all" for anybody who could not be absorbed elsewhere; it has a long "tail" of inefficient enterprises peopled with the army of the "disguised" unemployed scrounging for survival. Secondly, the particular sectoral pattern of inter-country technological gap is likely to be perpetuated by the nature of transfer of technology through transnational companies. Problems of private appropriability of benefits of technological improvements are usually more acute on labor-intensive production techniques – as, for example, suggested by Magee (1977), and, hence, transnational companies may be more interested in developing and transferring technology to the more capital-intensive sector. Thirdly, average productivity in an industry may depend on the economic life of its capital stock. If new machines embody new technology, older machines will be scrapped faster in the higher-wage country as the wages eat up the revenues from old machines requiring a larger number of workers to operate them (and faster in the latter's labor-intensive sector[2] than in the capital-intensive sector). This might bring about a larger efficiency gap in labor-intensive industries between rich and poor countries. The appropriate framework for analyzing this problem is the vintage-capital model of international trade, as in Bardhan (1966) and Smith (1976).[3]

3. The Model with Sector-Specific Factors of Production

What happens if we take a Ricardo–Viner model, instead of a Heckscher–Ohlin–Samuelson model, with the non-labor factor (capital or land) specific to a sector? Suppose the production functions of the two goods are given by

$$Q_i = A_i(t) F_i(\bar{K}_i, L_i), \quad i = c, m, \tag{1}$$

where Q_i is output, $A_i(t)$ is a technology parameter changing over time, $\bar{K}_i$ is the amount of specific factor in sector i and L_i is the amount of the mobile factor (labor) used in ith sector. Suppose $\bar{K}_m$ is the stock of capital and $\bar{K}_c$ is the endowment of land.

From the standard calculations of the Ricardo–Viner model under competition, incomplete specialization and constant returns to scale,

$$\hat{P}_i = \alpha_i \hat{W} + (1 - \alpha_i)\hat{R}_i - \hat{A}_i, \quad i = c, m, \tag{2}$$

where $^\wedge$ represents percentage change of a variable,[4] P_i is the unit price of the ith good, α_i is the labor share in ith industry, W is the wage rate and R_i is the rate of return to the specific factor in the ith industry. If we put $\hat{P}_i = 0$ (to get the case where prices are the same between the two countries under free trade), it is possible to have the following pattern of factor prices: $\hat{R}_m = 0$, $\hat{W} = \hat{A}_m/\alpha_m > \hat{A}_m$, and $\hat{R}_c = (\hat{A}_c\alpha_m - \hat{A}_m\alpha_c)/\alpha_m(1 - \alpha_c)$. In other words, in this Ricardo–Viner model it is possible to have under free trade the wage rate higher in the technologically advanced rich country, the rate of return to capital the same between the rich and poor country, and the rental rate on land higher in the poor country if the technological gap between the two countries is sufficiently wider in the industry m that uses capital compared to the industry c that uses land. This is consistent with the pattern of factor prices in some historical data: comparing Egypt with the U.S. at the turn of the century, Hansen (1991) estimates that while wages were much higher in the U.S., the real rate of return on corporate equity was about the same between the two countries, and the rent per acre of agricultural land was much higher in Egypt.

4. Differential Learning

Let us now consider some alternative explanations for the phenomenon of disparity in wage rates but not in returns to capital between rich and poor countries. Lucas (1990) would largely explain it by the influence (including the external effects) of the higher average level of workers' human capital in a rich country. In particular, the latter boosts the marginal product of physical capital in the rich country. But if one goes beyond the aggregative one-sector model of Lucas, our earlier discussion suggests that his explanation is somewhat inadequate. If the external effects of human capital improve the technology level of the rich country in a uniform way in the two sectors of our model in Section 2, one may not still get the factor price result we are looking for, depending on the sectoral pattern of productivity improvement on account of the *internal* effect of human capital (for example, if the internal effect of human capital is uniform in the two sectors, the rate of return to capital will not be equalized between the rich and the poor country). If, however, we reformulate the model on the lines of Bardhan (1970), pp. 27–28, we can generate the factor price result. Following Arrow (1962), Bardhan (1970) had a model with a simple production function of the following form:

$$Q_i = F_i(K_i, H^n L_i), \quad i = c,m, \tag{3}$$

where labor-augmenting technical progress in either sector depends on the cumulated volume of investment in the economy, H, as in Arrow's model, and n is the learning coefficient. This captures the dynamic externalities of investment (assumed sectorally symmetric). For the purpose of Lucas we can reinterpret H as the average level of human capital in the economy. Putting price equal to unit cost we can derive in the standard way:

$$\hat{P}_i = \alpha_i \hat{W} + (1 - \alpha_i)\hat{R} - \alpha_i n \hat{H}, \quad i = c,m, \tag{4}$$

where, as before, α_i is the labor share in ith industry. Putting $\hat{P}_i = 0$ (again to get the case where prices are the same between the two countries under free trade), it is possible to have $\hat{R} = 0$ (the rate of return to capital the same) and the wage rate higher in the country with higher H (i.e. the rich country).

We can obtain a similar result if instead of the Arrow-type learning function we introduce the role of human capital in speeding technological diffusion, following Nelson and Phelps (1966). Suppose we replace the production function in (3) by

$$Q_i = F_i(K_i, A(t)L_i), \quad i = c,m, \tag{5}$$

where

$$A(t) = a\, e^{\lambda[t - g(H)]}, \quad g'(H) < 0,$$

with λ as the rate at which technology advances and g as the time lag between the theoretical availability of a new technology and its adoption. The higher the stock of human capital, H, in a country, the shorter is this time lag. Again, from an equation similar to (4) we can prove that under free trade the wage rate will be higher in the rich country with a larger H, but the rate of return to capital can be the same. Both of the cases in this section are in one way akin to the static model in Section 2, but now the relative advantage of the rich country in the labor-intensive sector is endogenously derived from human capital accumulation or learning which has a bigger impact in the labor-intensive sector on account of being tied in to labor in the production function.

5. Effects of Differential Degrees of Specialization

In the preceding sections of the paper we have focussed on production function differences between countries and their impact on international factor prices. But in a world of pervasive importance of fixed costs and imperfect competition international differences in market sizes and in division of labor may also have a significant effect on factor prices. In the recent growth theory literature productivity in final goods production has been linked with the variety of specialized inputs and services produced in the country. Ethier (1982) and Romer (1990) have formalized this old idea of the wealth of nations being dependent on the extent of division of labor. One frequently observed difference between the production structure of a rich and a poor country is in the extent of specialization in these (non-traded) inputs and services. In this section we shall show that a capital-rich country will generate a higher degree of specialization in the domestic production of these inputs and services and this will have an effect on factor prices: even when production functions are otherwise similar between countries, the rich country will have a higher wage rate and the rate of return to capital in the poor country will be depressed. In building the basic model we start with a formulation first provided by Rodriguez (1996, published in this special issue), although we use it for a somewhat different purpose. Unlike Rodriguez, we stick to our earlier assumptions of international immobility of factors of production and incomplete specialization (we do not explore here the stability dynamics of the equilibrium with incomplete specialization).

Let us suppose, as before, c and m are the two final goods, and capital and labor are the two primary factors of production. But final goods production requires a composite intermediate good S (let this stand for all kinds of produced inputs, supplies, services including infrastructural facilities), which is aggregated, in the Ethier (1982) way, from a whole array of intermediate inputs:

$$S_i = \left[\sum_{j=1}^{N} x_i^{\alpha}(j) \right]^{1/\alpha}, \quad 1 > \alpha > 0, \quad i = c,m, \tag{6}$$

where N is the number of firms producing differentiated intermediate inputs that are imperfect substitutes of one another, and $x_i(j)$ is the amount of the intermediate good j used in the production of the final good i.

Let us, for simplification, assume that the final goods are produced with Cobb–douglas production functions:

$$Q_i = K_i^{a_i} L_i^{b_i} S_i^{c_i}, \quad a_i + b_i + c_i = 1, \quad i = c,m, \tag{7}$$

where Q_i is output of final good i, K_i is capital, L_i is labor and S_i is the composite intermediate good used in the production of i.

Like Rodriguez, we shall assume that each intermediate input is produced under monopolistic competition with a decreasing average cost technology: there is a fixed requirement of one unit of capital, and each unit of $x_i(j)$ requires one additional unit of labor. Given the symmetric way in which the intermediate goods enter in the sub-production function (6), the same quantity $x_i(j) = x_i$ for all j will be produced. Since each firm in the intermediate good sector is small relative to the whole industry, the (absolute value of the) price elasticity of demand for the intermediate good can be computed as $1/(1 - \alpha)$. Since the marginal cost of producing intermediate good

j is equal to the wage rate, W, profit maximization by each monopolistically competitive firm in the intermediate goods sector implies

$$p_j = W/\alpha, \tag{8}$$

where p_j is the price of the intermediate good j.

Solving for S_i, the amount of the composite intermediate good and denoting by E_i the total labor hired by sector i directly (L_i) or indirectly through the use of intermediate goods $(N x_i)$, Eq. (7) can now be rewritten as

$$Q_i = v_i N^{\phi_i} K_i^{a_i} E_i^{1-a_i}, \quad i = c, m, \tag{9}$$

where

$$\phi_i = (1 - \alpha) c_i / \alpha$$

and

$$v_i = [\alpha c_i / b_i]^{c_i} [1 + \alpha c_i / b_i]^{a_i - 1}.$$

Eq. (9) shows how the degree of specialization in the intermediate inputs sector, indexed by N, affects total factor productivity in final goods production.

W_i, the cost of hiring each unit of E_i, i.e. direct plus indirect labor, is not equal to the wage rate W that a laborer gets paid. From the profit maximization conditions in the final goods sectors, using the production function given in Eq. (9), we can get

$$W_i = \gamma_i W, \quad i = c, m, \tag{10}$$

where

$$\gamma_i = (b_i + c_i)/(b_i + \alpha c_i),$$

which is larger than one since $\alpha < 1$. The difference between W_i and W is on account of competitive supply of the primary factors of production and monopolistic competition in intermediate goods supply. (γ_i approaches one, as α approaches one.)

From the equations for factor prices, one can derive the relationship between the relative prices of primary factors and the relative prices of final goods, depending on N, the degree of specialization of the economy, so that

$$\hat{P} = (\phi_c - \phi_m)\hat{N} + (a_c - a_m)\hat{w}, \tag{11}$$

where P is the relative price of m in terms of c, w is the ratio of the wage rate to the rate of return on capital, and, as before, $^\wedge$represents percentage change of a variable. But N is endogenous, it depends on the endowments of capital and labor and on the relative factor price w. N, which is the number of firms producing intermediate inputs, can be obtained from the condition that with free entry the long-run profits in the intermediate goods sector is zero. This condition, along with the condition of full employment of both primary factors, yields, after some manipulation,

$$N = D^{-1}[(b_m c_c - b_c c_m)K + (a_c c_m - a_m c_c)wL],$$ (12)

where

$$D = [(b_m c_c - b_c c_m)(1 - \alpha) + a_c(b_m + \alpha c_m) - a_m(b_c + \alpha c_c)]/(1 - \alpha),$$

and K and L are the endowments of capital and labor in the economy.

Now, if we assume that our sector c uses both capital and intermediate goods more intensively than sector m, i.e. $a_c > a_m$ and $c_c > c_m$ it is easy to work out that $D > 0$. One can then see from (12) that the degree of specialization of the economy, N, increases with the stock of capital, K. But for saying anything definite about the relationship between N and w, we seem to need a stronger factor-intensity condition. If

$$a_c c_m > a_m c_c,$$ (13)

i.e. the capital–intermediate good ratio is larger, in sector c than in sector m, then N and w are positively related. If N and w were negatively related, then from Eq. (11) there could be a non-unique relationship between P and w, which implies that for the same P there could be more than one equilibrium w, an outcome we want to avoid for our present purpose, like much of international trade theory. Condition (13) is, of course, a sufficient, not a necessary, condition for uniqueness of equilibrium.

Now suppose there are two countries I and II, each with its production and price structures described by Eqs. (6) to (13), freely trading their final goods with each other (so that, absent transport costs, their final goods prices are the same). To simplify, we shall assume that both have access to the same technology so that their production functions are identical. The only difference is that one country, country II, has a larger endowment of capital. Then the capital-rich country[5] will in this model have a larger range of specialization in the (non-traded) intermediate goods sector (division of labor being limited by the extent of the market). This will have a differential effect on the pattern of factor prices between the two countries even when final goods prices are equalized by free trade. This is described in Fig. 5.2.

The isoquants c_I and m_I in Fig. 5.2 are, as in Fig. 5.1, unit isoquants for producing c and m in the poor country I, and c_{II} and m_{II} are the corresponding isoquants for the rich country II. But now the unit isoquants of the rich country are nearer the origin, not because the rich country's production functions are superior, but because its degree of specialization in the intermediate goods sector is larger. In Fig. 5.2, in each country the unit cost line of good c is steeper than the unit cost line of good m. This reflects the fact that in Eq. (10), $\gamma_c > \gamma_m$ under our assumption that sector c uses both capital and intermediate goods more intensively than sector m, i.e. $a_c >$

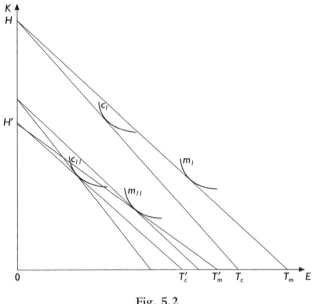

Fig. 5.2

a_m and $c_c > c_m$. The slope of the unit cost line is W_i/R for each country, where R is the rate of return to capital. With production functions internationally identical γ_c and γ_m are same between the two countries, so that if the wage–rentals ratio were the same, for each good the unit cost lines would be parallel for the two countries. But when free trade equalizes commodity prices, i.e. $\dot{P} = 0$ in Eq. (11), the wage–rentals ratio, w, has to change. The new equilibrium unit cost lines are now given by $H'T'_m$ and $H'T'_c$ in Fig. 5.2. We can now read off the absolute factor prices from Fig. 5.2, by looking at the reciprocals of the distances from the origin to the points where the new unit cost lines cut the capital axis (H') and the labor axis (T'_c and T'_m) It is clear that the capital-rich country has both a higher wage rate and a rate of return to capital than the capital-poor country under free trade (without international mobility of the factors of production).

   Intuitively, what is going on is something like this. The rich country has a larger domestic market for non-traded intermediate inputs and services which allows for a larger degree of specialization. This increases the productivity of both labor and capital in final goods production tending to push up both the wage rate and the rate of return to capital. This productivity change has, however, a second effect on factor prices on account of final goods prices being equalized by trade between the rich and the poor country. The productivity change, due to more specialization in the intermediate goods sector, will tend to lower the relative cost (and thus price) of good c which uses intermediate goods more intensively in the rich country. But under free trade final goods prices have to remain equal between the two countries; this is possible if factor prices adjust by lowering the wage–rentals ratio so that the relative cost of the capital-intensive good c is bolstered up. With a lower w, the capital–labor ratio will fall in both final goods sectors, lowering marginal productivity of labor and raising that of capital. So this second effect reinforces the first (positive) effect on the rate of return on capital, but counteracts with the first (positive) effect on the wage rate. In the Cobb–Douglas case discussed here and with the factor-intensity condition (13), the positive effect outweighs the negative effect on the wage rate. A high degree of factor substitutability reduces the need for large factor price adjustments and thus weakens the second (negative) effect. Condition (13) plays a role here because it implies that the difference in the intensity with which c and m use intermediate goods is lower than the difference in the capital-intensity between c and m, so that the effect of more specialization in the intermediate goods sector in reducing the relative cost of producing c is diluted, and so the negative second effect on the wage rate mentioned above is commensurately weak.

This model provides an explanation of why the capital-rich country has a higher wage rate and why the rate of return to capital is depressed in a poor country in spite of capital scarcity. It relies on the effect of endowments and hence of market size on the domestic availability of a wide variety of specialized inputs. The model can be extended to cover the common argument that the rate of return to capital is low in poor countries on account of the absence of a well-developed and well-maintained physical and social infrastructure, particularly in power, transport, communication and job training, and if it is the case that the capital-intensive sector is more dependent on infrastructure (in many empirical studies electricity use, for example, is taken as an index of mechanization, in the absence of data on capital).

But the model in this section is clearly inadequate in fully explaining the observed factor price pattern between a rich and a poor country. For example, in this model the wage–rentals ratio is lower in the rich country, and the rates of return to capital are not (nearly) equal. Of course, one can say, among other things, we often do not have free trade between rich and poor countries. If the poor countries in general tend to protect their capital-intensive import-substitute industries, this may have an effect in raising their rate of return to capital above what is predicted in the model (apart from lowering their wage rate further). It is also unrealistic to assume as we have done in the model of this section, that the rich and the poor countries have similar production functions. Combined with certain types of differences in international production functions as discussed in Sections 2, 3 and 4 above, the model is more likely to yield results on factor prices that are consistent with wage disparity but relative similarity in the rates of return of capital between a rich and a poor country trading with each other but with factors of production immobile between them.

In this paper we have explored alternative explanations of the remarkable asymmetry in the pattern of factor prices between rich and poor countries. We go beyond the usual explanation in terms of greater international mobility of capital relative to labor and concentrate on explanations in terms of particular types of differences in production functions between rich and poor countries, in terms of differential learning effects and differential degrees of specialization in the sector producing intermediate inputs and services. Not all the arguments provide a complete explanation of the observed factor prices (as, for example, is the case with the last explanatory argument noted in the preceding paragraph), but altogether they may contribute to a stronger explanation than the standard one. One interesting avenue, however, needs to be explored further. None of the models in this paper deals with the impact of factor market imperfections[6] (for example, the possible case of labor being paid in the tradeable sectors much more than its opportunity cost in poor countries, or the case of acute information problems leading to capital rationing in poor countries) on the international pattern of factor prices.

Notes

*   I am grateful to two referees for comments on the paper and to Rodrigo Priale for his valuable research assistance on the model in Section 5.
1. Most of the empirical work in connection with the Hirschman hypothesis was, however, in terms of labor productivity, whereas we really need evidence on total factor productivity differentials.
2. This is, unlike in a poor country where the labor-intensive sector often includes a large informal sector with wage rates even lower than in the rest of the economy, which tend to prolong the economic life of capital.
3. Clague (1991) has suggested a fourth reason: densely populated developing countries often specialize in primary products that are *less* labor-intensive than manufacturing products, primarily because the latter require certain capacities of managing large organizations and a network of quality-controlled inputs that these countries are deficient in.
4. While strictly speaking the "hat" calculus here and in later sections is for infinitesimal differences, the qualitative results should be derivable for more general cases.
5. We are, of course, assuming that the rich country has a larger endowment of capital than the poor country. The analysis will be more complicated for comparisons of small rich countries like Belgium with large poor countries like China.
6. We did try to explore the implications of the popular effiency wage theory for the international factor price pattern. If certain jobs require more commitment and responsibility and independent action but are less amenable to regular supervision and monitoring, workers on these jobs are likely to be paid a higher wage (a kind of labor rent) than on jobs with more routine, easily and closely supervised, tasks. It is plausible that the former kind of high-wage jobs are in the more capital-intensive (often also more unionized) sector and that these jobs are more important in rich rather than poor countries. One simple way to capture this intersectoral difference in labor rent may be to assume that in a standard two-sector model the wage paid in the capital-intensive sector is higher by a given absolute margin, say β, and work out how between a rich and a poor country trading with each other the factor prices will change with a larger β for the rich country. But it can be shown in this model that with a larger β while the wage rates are higher in the rich country, the rate of return to capital is even lower than otherwise. So this is not a promising line of explaining similarity in returns to capital between rich and poor countries.

References

Arrow, K., 1962, The economic implications of learning by doing, Review of Economic Studies, June.

Bardhan, P., 1965, International differences in production functions, trade and factor prices, Economic Journal, March.

Bardhan, P., 1966, International trade theory in a vintage capital model, Econometrica, Oct.

Bardhan, P., 1970, Economic growth, development and foreign trade: A study in pure theory (Wiley-Interscience, New York).

Clague, C. K., 1967, An international comparison of industrial efficiency. Peru and the United States, Review of Economics and Statistics, Nov.

Clague, C. K., 1991, Relative efficiency, self-containment and comparative costs of LDC's, Economic Development and Cultural Change 39, April.

Diaz-Alejandro, C., 1965, Industrialization and labor productivity differentials, Review of Economics and Statistics, May.

Ethier, W., 1982, National and international returns to scale in the modern theory of international trade, American Economic Review, June.

Hansen, B., 1991, Factor prices in Egypt and some major developed countries from 1900 to World War II, Research in Economic History 13.

Harberger, A. C., 1978, Perspective on capital and technology in less developed countries, in: M. J. Artis and A. R. Nobay, eds., Contemporary analysis (Croom Helm, London).

Healey, J. M., 1968, Industrialization, capital-intensity and efficiency, Bulletin of Oxford Institute of Statistics, Nov.

Hirschman, A., 1961, The strategy of economic development (Yale University Press, New Haven, CT).

Gouverneur, J., 1970, Hirschman on labor productivity differentials: An empirical analysis, Bulletin of Oxford Institute of Statistics, Aug.

Kravis, I. B., A. W. Heston and R. Summers, 1982, World product and income (Johns Hopkins University Press, Baltimore, MD).

Lucas, R., 1990, Why doesn't capital flow from rich to poor countries?, American Economic Review, May.

Magee, S., 1977, Multinational corporations, the industry technology cycle and development, Journal of World Trade Law, July–August.

Minhas, B. S., 1963, International comparisons of factor costs and factor use (Elsevier, Amsterdam).

Nelson, R. R. and E. S. Phelps, 1966, Investment in humans, technological diffusion and economic growth, American Economic Review, May.

Rodriguez, A., 1996, The division of labor and economic development, Journal of Development Economics, this issue.

Romer, P. M., 1990, Endogenous technological change, Journal of Political Economy, Oct.

Smith, M. A. M., 1976, International trade theory in vintage models, Review of Economic Studies, Feb.

Chapter 6

On Optimum Subsidy to a Learning Industry: An Aspect of the Theory of Infant-Industry Protection[1]

1. Learning Effect in Production

One of the earliest instances of the incorporation of the concept of "learning by doing" in economic theory is the Hamilton-List infant-industry argument. It has been recognized in principle by John Stuart Mill and subsequent writers on international trade. But as any elaboration of this idea involves some explicitly dynamic analysis, it has hardly been integrated into the main corpus of trade theory which is mostly comparative-static in nature; until recently, it has received nothing more than nodding recognition as just one of the few "exceptions" to the doctrine of free trade.

In this paper[2] we take a very simple dynamic model of "learning by doing" in an open economy and work out the optimum *extent* and *time-path* of protection to the learning industry. (In contrast, usual analysis stops at merely pointing out the need for protection in such cases.) In a brief digression in Section 2, we also mention some of the implications for the standard results of "positive" trade theory (regarding patterns of factor prices, output, comparative advantage, etc.) when one introduces the learning effect.

We have two goods, c and m, that use capital, K, and labor, L, in production under constant returns to scale. The learning effect which increases productivity of factors depends on the cumulated volume of *output* in an industry.[3] Since the infant-industry argument is based (at least implicitly) on some kind of differential learning effect, we assume, for simplicity, that learning is operative only in one of the industries, say, in industry m. The production functions are

(1) $Q_c = F_c(K_c, L_c) = L_c \cdot f_c(k_c),$

(2) $Q_m = Q^n \cdot F_m(K_m, L_m) = Q^n \cdot L_m f_m(k_m),$

where Q_i is the current rate of output and k_i the capital-labor ratio employed in i-th industry, $i = m, c$; Q is the cumulated volume of output of m so that $\dot{Q} = (dQ/dt) = Q_m$ (we shall, in Section 3, alter this assumption slightly by introducing a term for depreciation of experience); Q^n incorporates the effect of learning or experience on productivity (we assume $1 > n > 0$);[4] the way we have introduced the learning term also implies our simplifying assumption that the productivity-enhancing effect of learning is neutral with respect to the two factors of production. The stock of experience for the industry is under the control of no single firm; it comes as an irreversible external economy to it.[5]

With full employment of capital and labor,

(3) $K = K_m + K_c,$

(4) $L = L_m + L_c.$

From (3) and (4),

(5) $\dfrac{L_c}{L} = \dfrac{k - k_m}{k_c - k_m},$

(6) $\dfrac{L_m}{L} = \dfrac{k_c - k}{k_c - k_m},$

with $k = K/L$ and $k_c \neq k_m$.

Since we want to concentrate on the operation of the learning effect, we shall assume that the total supply of labor and capital in the economy is given. Without further loss of generality we shall take $L = 1$. (1) and (2) may now be rewritten as

(7) $Q_c = f_c(k_c) \dfrac{[k - k_m]}{[k_c - k_m]},$

(8) $Q_m = Q^n \cdot f_m(k_m) \dfrac{[k_c - k]}{[k_c - k_m]}.$

Before we introduce in this model a planning authority that maximizes a social welfare function over time, let us analyze the behavior of a stylized competitive economy in this model.

With pure competition in both factor and commodity markets and with no individual firm being able to control the amount of experience or learning, the price implications of the model will be like those of a competitive economy with exogenous technical progress. Factors will be paid their marginal products valued at market prices, so that with both goods produced, with c as the numéraire good and the market price of m being P, the wage rate,

$$(9) \quad W = \frac{\partial Q_c}{\partial L_c} = f_c(k_c) - f_c'(k_c)k_c$$

$$= P \cdot \frac{\partial Q_m}{\partial L_m} = P \cdot Q''[f_m(k_m) - f_m'(k_m)k_m]$$

and the rental rate on capital,

$$(10) \quad R = \frac{\partial Q_c}{\partial K_c} = f_c'(k_c)$$

$$= P \cdot \frac{\partial Q_m}{\partial K_m} = P \cdot Q'' \cdot f_m'(k_m).$$

From (9) and (10) the wage-rental ratio,

$$(11) \quad w = \frac{f_i(k_i)}{f_i'(k_i)} - k_i, \ i = c, \ m.$$

With the usual assumptions of $f_i''(k_i) < 0$, etc., we can show k_i and w to be uniquely related from (11). From (10), therefore,

$$(12) \quad P = \frac{f_c'(k_c(w))}{f_m'(k_m(w)) \cdot Q''}$$

which is equal to the ratio of the two marginal products of capital.

2. Learning and Positive Trade Theory

We shall consider the policy question of infant-industry protection in the next section, but let us in this section use equations (11) and (12) for our stylized competitive economy to analyze some of the implications of the phenomenon of learning by doing in a *descriptive* competitive model of international trade. We shall try to be very brief here and only hint at the possibilities of unconventional results.

For illustrative purposes we shall assume in this section that c is the more capital-intensive good, i.e., $k_c > k_m$ (the opposite factor-intensity case may be discussed with the same method of analysis).

From (12),

$$(13) \quad P = \frac{H(w)}{Q''}$$

where

$$H(w) = \frac{f'_c(k_c(w))}{f'_m(k_m(w))}.$$

It can be checked with the help of (11) that $H'(w) > 0$ for $k_c > k_m$. It is self-evident from (13) that unlike in the usual two-sector incomplete specialization model, commodity prices are no longer uniquely determined by (or related to) factor prices *alone*. Thus the usual Stolper-Samuelson results about the relationship between commodity prices and factor prices and the Lerner-Samuelson result of factor-price equalization under free trade may no longer hold true.

Take, for example, the standard Stolper-Samuelson result that a fall in P should lead to a fall in the relative and absolute reward of the factor (labor) used more intensively in producing m. If one takes into account the learning effect, this is no longer guaranteed. With positive current production of m, Q is ever-increasing and the fall in P may be outweighed by the rise in Q^n so that with $H'(w) > 0$, the relative and absolute reward of labor may still go up.[6]

It also follows from (13) that if two trading countries have identical production and learning functions, with the same commodity prices under free trade, the country with larger Q (say, the country with the "earlier start" in producing m) will have the *higher* relative and absolute wage rate.

Can we say anything about the pattern of comparative advantage? For that we shall have to look at the pre-trade relative prices. Once again equation (13) is useful. Suppose again that the two countries have identical production and learning functions. It is possible for the country with more expensive labor (higher w) to have a comparative advantage in the more *labor-intensive* commodity m (i.e., P is lower), if Q is large enough (say, because of earlier start).

It is also not unexpected that the familiar Rybczynski result may no longer hold good. It can easily be checked that an increase in the capital stock with commodity prices constant does not necessarily bring about a drop in the production of the more labor-intensive commodity. Another interesting point to note is that with positive current production of m, i.e., rising Q, constant P means an increasing w; an increase in the wage-rental ratio involves an increase in the sectoral capital-labor ratios and if the total stock of capital and labor is static, full employment necessitates a reallocation of resources in favour of the labor-intensive sector and *against* the capital-intensive sector; so if commodity prices are kept constant all this means declining production in the more capital-intensive sector.

The reader can easily think of other examples[7] of changes in the usual comparative-static results of trade theory when the learning effect is introduced.

3. The Optimality Conditions

In Section 1 we introduced a stylized competitive economy in order to facilitate our analysis of the implications of learning for "positive" trade theory. But let us now introduce a full optimizing model where the planning authority in maximizing social welfare over time takes due account of the productivity-increasing effects of society's experience in producing m.

Suppose the social objective is to maximize

$$(14) \quad \int_0^\infty U(A_c, A_m) \, e^{-\delta t} \, dt$$

with given initial conditions and subject to the following constraints:

$$(15) \quad A_c = Q_c + X_c = f_c(k_c) \frac{[k - k_m]}{[k_c - k_m]} + X_c,$$

$$(16) \quad A_m = Q_m + X_m = Q^n \cdot f_m(k_m) \frac{[k_c - k]}{[k_c - k_m]} + X_m,$$

$$(17) \quad X_c + \bar{P} X_m = 0,$$

$$(18) \quad \dot{Q} = Q_m - \rho Q.$$

A_i is the consumption of the i-th commodity, U is an instantaneous utility function that is concave and has positive marginal utilities, δ is the given positive social rate of discount, X_i is the amount *imported* of the i-th commodity, $\bar{P}$ is the *international* price of m in terms of c and ρ is a constant rate of depreciation of experience.

In (18) we have slightly altered an assumption we made in Sections 1 and 2. Our stock of experience Q in m industry increases by the current rate of production in that industry *net* of a constant rate of depreciation (or "forgetting").[8] (17) gives us the balance of trade equation, i.e., imports are paid by exports. For simplicity, we shall assume that ours is a small country in a large world so that the international price, $\bar{P}$, is given (this helps one to isolate the considerations of infant-industry argument from those of the standard "optimum-tariff" argument). For the time being we are assuming the rest of the world as static. But a more realistic thing would be to have continuous learning going on in the rest of the world as well, possibly changing the international price level. We consider this case in Section 6 of this paper.

For a full solution of the optimizing problem we have to discuss a number of patterns of specialization (specialization in consuming c, in consuming m, in producing c, in producing m, consumption of both m and c, production of both m and c, etc.). But in order to avoid tedium and economize space, we confine ourselves to only the "interior" case – where we produce and consume both the commodities – the case which is usually the most interesting. This means

$$(19) \quad Q_c > 0 \quad \text{and} \quad Q_m > 0$$

and

(20) $A_c > 0$ and $A_m > 0.$

(17) and (20) imply that

(21) $-Q_m < X_m < \dfrac{Q_c}{P}.$

(5), (6), and (10) imply that

(22) $1 > \dfrac{L_c}{L} > 0$ and $1 > \dfrac{L_m}{L} > 0.$[9]

The Hamiltonian H of the present problem is given by

(23) $He^{\delta t} = U(A_c, A_m) + \lambda \left[f_c(k_c) \dfrac{(k - k_m)}{(k_c - k_m)} - \bar{P}X_m - A_c \right]$

$\qquad + \mu \left[f_m(k_m) \cdot \dfrac{(k_c - k)}{(k_c - k_m)} \cdot Q^n + X_m - A_m \right]$

$\qquad + \gamma \left[f_m(k_m) \cdot \dfrac{(k_c - k)}{(k_c - k_m)} \cdot Q^n - \rho Q \right]$

where λ, μ and γ are (positive) imputed prices of the respective constraints.
λ and μ are the demand prices for consumption of c and m respectively and γ is the imputed price of productivity-enhancing experience.
The conditions for maximum are as follows:

(24) $\lambda = \dfrac{\partial U}{\partial A_c},$

(25) $\mu = \dfrac{\partial U}{\partial A_m},$

(26) $\dfrac{\mu}{\lambda} = \bar{P}.$

(26) implies that the ratio of marginal utilities in consumption should be equalized to the given international price ratio. The marginal rate of domestic transformation is given by

(27) $\dfrac{\mu + \gamma}{\lambda} = \dfrac{f_c'(k_c(w))}{f_m'(k_m(w))Q^n}$

where w is given, as before, by (11).

$$(28) \quad \dot{\gamma} = (\rho + \delta)\gamma - (\mu + \gamma)\left[f_m(k_m) \frac{(k_c - k)}{(k_c - k_m)} n \cdot Q^{n-1} \right].$$

(28) gives the optimum rate of change in the shadow price of experience. The transversality condition is given by

$$(29) \quad \lim_{t \to \infty} \gamma Q e^{-\delta t} = 0.$$

In Section 4 we analyze the implications of these conditions.[10] But before that let us introduce another assumption to simplify the problem further. We shall assume that the instantaneous utility function $U(A_c, A_m)$ is homogeneous of degree one (it implies that the income elasticity of demand for either good is unity). This means that in (24) and (25) λ and μ depend only on A_c/A_m, the ratio of consumption of the two goods. But, then, from (26), this ratio is constant so that λ and μ are really constants.

4. Optimum Subsidy

In (27), let us define P^d as

$$(30) \quad \frac{\mu + \gamma}{\gamma} = \frac{f'_c(k_c(w))}{f'_m(k_m(w)) \cdot Q^n} = \frac{H(w)}{Q^n} = P^d$$

where $H(w)$ is defined, as in (13).

P^d is the marginal rate of domestic transformation, while $\bar{P}$ is the marginal rate of transformation through foreign trade as well as the marginal rate of substitution in consumption. Unless the government intervenes, competitive producers of m will produce according to the market price $\bar{P}(= \mu/\lambda)$ and there will be underproduction of m from the social point of view. In order to attain the social optimum, the government should assure the producers a price equal to $P^d(= (\mu + \gamma)/\lambda)$. The optimum rate of subsidy to the learning industry[11] is given by $\bar{P}(1 + \tau) = P^d$, or $\tau = \gamma/\mu$, where τ is the rate of subsidy per unit of output. As long as experience increases productivity its imputed price γ is positive,[12] and so is the rate of subsidy τ. Two points are important to note here. (a) As is by now well recognized (Bhagwati and Ramaswami, 1963; Johnson, 1965), a subsidy is better than tariff in such cases because the latter, in restoring the equality between domestic and foreign marginal rates of transformation, also drives a wedge between the marginal rate of consumer substitution and that of transformation. (b) It should be noted that our good m may be imported or exported, although we have assumed some limits on both sides as implied in (21). So our prescribed subsidization of learning may involve a subsidy to the import-competing industry or to the export industry, as the case may be.[13]

One of our main purposes in this paper is to find out the time-pattern of the optimum subsidy, i.e., the nature of $\dot{\tau}$ over time.

Let us for this purpose take the two differential equations of our model given by (18) and (28).

$$(31) \quad \dot{Q} = Q^n \cdot f_m(k_m(w)) \frac{[k_c(w) - k]}{[k_c(w) - k_m(w)]} - \rho Q,$$

$$(32) \quad \dot{\gamma} = (\rho + \delta)\gamma - (\mu + \gamma)\left[f_m(k_m(w)) \frac{\{k_c(w) - k\}}{\{k_c(w) - k_m(w)\}} nQ^{n-1} \right].$$

Now, from (30), w can be written as a function of P^d and Q. So (31) can be rewritten as

$$(33) \quad \dot{Q} = \phi(Q, P^d).$$

Since μ and λ are constant, from (30) and (32)

$$(34) \quad \dot{P}^d = \frac{\dot{\gamma}}{\lambda} = \frac{\gamma}{\lambda}\left[(\rho + \delta) - \left(1 + \frac{\mu}{\gamma}\right) nQ^{n-1} f_m(k_m(w)) \frac{\{k_c(w) - k\}}{\{k_c(w) - k_m(w)\}} \right].$$

Since from (30), w is a function of P^d and Q, and γ is a function of P^d alone, we can rewrite (34) as

$$(35) \quad \dot{P}^d = \psi(Q, P^d).$$

As explained in detail in the Appendix A, under the sufficient condition of $(\partial Q_m / \partial Q)(Q/Q_m)$ (given P^d) – or what might be called the "learning elasticity of output" of m – being less than unity, the stationary solution (Q_*, P^d_*) to the two differential equations (33) and (35) is unique and is also a saddle point, as is indicated in Fig. 6.1. Under the same sufficient condition, the $\dot{Q} = 0$ curve is uniformly upward-sloping for the ("interior") region we are considering. Under a stronger sufficient condition of the elasticities of factor substitution being small enough,[14] the $\dot{P}^d = 0$ curve is uniformly downward-sloping in the region we are considering.

Given our transversality condition (29), if $Q(0) = Q_*$, the unique optimum path is indicated by the singular solution (Q_*, P^d_*) and the optimum rate of subsidy to the learning industry, $\tau_* = (P^d_* - \bar{P})/\bar{P} = n\rho/(\delta + (1 - n)\rho)$, a constant. If, however, $Q(0) \neq Q_*$, the optimum path of (Q, P^d) lies along the stable branches of the saddle point given the transversality condition. It can be seen from Fig. 6.1 that along the optimum path, *if $Q(0) < Q_*$* (i.e., the initial stock of experience is small enough), *Q steadily increases and P^d steadily decreases to asymptotically approach the stationary solution (Q_*, P^d_*), and therefore, the optimum rate of subsidy, τ, steadily decreases to asymtotically approach the stationary rate τ_*. If, on the other hand,*

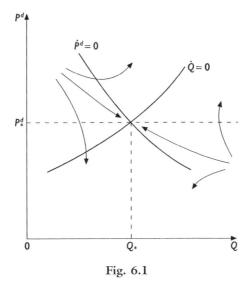

Fig. 6.1

$Q(0) > Q_*$, by similar reasoning the optimum rate of subsidy steadily increases to asymptotically approach the stationary rate τ_*.

5. Temporary Learning

In Section 4 we have characterized the time-path of the optimum rate of subsidy to the learning industry in this model. If the initial stock of experience is small, the optimum rate of subsidy steadily decreases over time to asymptotically approach a stationary rate that is positive. The subsidy always remains positive because with our learning function incorporated in equation (2), experience always enhances productivity and with the spill-over of benefits of the learning process to all firms[15] there tends to be an underproduction of m from the social point of view if the industry is not subsidized. But much of the usual infant-industry argument is concerned with *temporary* protection, where the learning process is more in the nature of overcoming a historical handicap, a matter of catching up with a foreign country's efficiency level than that of a continuous productivity-enhancing phenomenon, and the subsidy is to be removed as soon as the "infant" becomes an adult. The implications of this kind of a learning process can, however, be discussed retaining a large part of the analytic framework in earlier sections of this paper.

Let us rewrite (2) as

(36) $Q_m = G(Q) \cdot F_m(K_m, L_m)$

where G is the learning function, $G(0)$ is a constant, $G'(Q) > 0$, $G''(Q) < 0$ for Q less than a finite positive level of $\bar{Q}$, and for $Q \geq \bar{Q}$, $G(Q) = \bar{G}$, a constant.[16] This means that the stock of experience enhances productivity (at a diminishing rate) up to a point, and then at a certain level of experience, $\bar{Q}$, the country catches up with the foreign efficiency level, $\bar{G}$, and there is no more learning.

How will this affect our analysis of the time-path of the optimum rate of subsidy? As long as $Q < \bar{Q}$, both the $\dot{Q} = 0$ and $\dot{P}^d = 0$ curves will be of the same shape as before, if one makes the same assumptions. The imputed price of experience, γ, will be positive as long as $Q < \bar{Q}$, but for $Q \geq \bar{Q}$, $\gamma = 0$, implying the completion of the learning process. The rate of subsidy, τ, being equal to γ/μ is therefore zero for $Q \geq \bar{Q}$. So if the $\dot{Q} = 0$ and $\dot{P}^d = 0$ curves do not intersect for $Q < \bar{Q}$, then *the optimum rate of subsidy, τ, steadily declines over time until it reaches zero* at $Q = \bar{Q}$. If the $\dot{Q} = 0$ and $\dot{P}^d = 0$ curves intersect before Q reaches $\bar{Q}$, the conclusion of our Section 4 remains valid for the case when the initial stock of experience is small enough.

6. Learning in both Countries

In this section we revert to the case of continuous learning but consider the relaxation of two other assumptions in our model. One of our assumptions has been to take the rest of the world as static. A more interesting model might be one in which learning by doing is continuously going on abroad as well as in our home country. This means that even if ours is a small country in a large world we may no longer take the international price $\bar{P}$ as static: $\bar{P}$ may now change because of learning in the rest of the world. Once we introduce learning abroad, we shall, of course, have to assume something about the transferability of the benefits of that learning. In other words, we have to consider the *international* external economies of the learning process. In this section we shall assume that an increase in the stock of experience in the large world outside will costlessly enhance the productivity[17] in our small country as well. In the process of working out the implications of this factor we shall also do away with another possibly restrictive assumption in our preceding three sections, viz. that of positive depreciation of experience.

In order to simplify our calculations we shall assume that the stock of experience, $\dot{Q}$, in the rest of the world for industry m is growing at a constant rate α and also that the international price of m, $\bar{P}$, is, as a consequence, declining at the rate α. The production function of m in the home country is now given by

(37) $\quad Q_m = G(Q, \dot{Q}) \cdot F_m(K_m, L_m)$

where G is the neutral productivity function, which is increasing (at a diminishing rate) for both Q and $\dot{Q}$. For simplicity we shall assume that the $G(Q, \dot{Q})$ function is homogeneous of degree one so that

(38) $\quad G(Q, \dot{Q}) = \dot{Q} \cdot g(x)$

where

$$x = \frac{Q}{\hat{Q}}.$$

We shall also make a simplifying assumption regarding the utility function $U(A_c, A_m)$. In Section 3 we took U as homogeneous of degree one; for simplification, we shall now take U to be in the more specific Cobb-Douglas form

(39) $U(A_c, A_m) = A_c^{\beta} A_m^{1-\beta}$

where β is a positive constant.

Armed with these simplifying assumptions, we are now ready to tackle our learning model which is much more general than in the preceding sections.

The international price of m, $\bar{P}$, is now declining at a constant rate α, so that in comparison to (26) we now have

(40) $\dfrac{\mu(t)}{\lambda(t)} = \bar{P}(0) e^{-\alpha t}.$

As shown in Appendix B, it is easy to derive from (24), (25), (39), and (40) that

(41) $\lambda(t) = \lambda(0) e^{\alpha(1-\beta)t}$

and

(42) $\mu(t) = \mu(0) e^{-\alpha\beta t}.$

Without loss of generality we shall take $\lambda(0) = \mu(0) = \bar{P}(0) = \hat{Q}(0) = 1$. Comparing with (30) the marginal rate of domestic transformation is now given by

(43) $P^d = \dfrac{\mu(t) + \gamma(t)}{\lambda(t)} = \dfrac{H(w)}{G(Q, \bar{Q})},$

Since $\hat{Q}$ is growing at rate α, we may rewrite (43), with the help of (38) and, (40), as

(44) $\dfrac{H(w)}{g(x)} = 1 + \gamma(t) e^{\alpha\beta t} = 1 + y(t)$

where $y(t) = r(t) e^{\alpha\beta t}$. In Section 4, we have seen that $\tau = \gamma(t)/\mu(t)$. From (42), this means $\tau = y(t)$. We shall be interested in finding out the optimum time-path of $y(t)$.

As explained in Appendix B, under the sufficient condition of $(\partial Q_m / \partial Q)(Q / Q_m)$ – or what might be called the elasticity of output with respect to domestic learning – being less than unity, the stationary solution (x_*, y_*) to the differential equations governing the motion of x and y is unique and is also a saddle point. Under the same sufficient condition, the $\dot{x} = 0$ curve is uniformly upward-sloping, and under a stronger sufficient condition of the price elasticity of supply of m being small enough, the $\dot{y} = 0$ curve is uniformly downward-sloping for the ("interior") region we are considering. The phase diagram looks *exactly* as in Fig. 6.1, when one replaces Q by x and P^d by y.[18]

If $x(0) = x_*$, the unique optimum path is indicated by the singular solution (x_*, y_*) and the optimum rate of subsidy to the learning industry, $\tau_* = y_* = (\alpha g'(x_*)x_*)/(g(x_*)[\delta + \alpha\beta] - \alpha g'(x_*)x_*)$.[19] If, however, $x(0) \neq x_*$, the optimum path of (x, y) lies along the stable branches of the saddle point. *If the home country's initial stock of experience is small enough*, so that $x(0) < x_*$, along the optimum path y, and therefore *the optimum rate of subsidy τ, steadily decreases to asymptotically approach the stationary rate τ_**. If, on the other hand, $x(0) > x_*$, the optimum rate of subsidy steadily increases to asymptotically approach the stationary rate τ_*.

Appendix A

Take our two differential equations (33) and (35). From (31) and (33),

$$(45) \quad \left(\frac{\partial\phi}{\partial Q}\right)_{\phi=0} = Q^n \cdot \frac{dB(w)}{dw} \cdot \frac{\partial w}{\partial Q} - Q^{n-1} \cdot B(w)(1 - n)$$

where $B(w) = f_m(k_m(w))([k_c(w) - k])/([k_c(w) - k_m(w)])$ and $Q^n \cdot B = \rho Q$ when $\phi = 0$. Now the "learning elasticity of output" of m is

$$(46) \quad \frac{\partial Q_m}{\partial Q} \cdot \frac{Q}{Q_m} = n + \frac{Q}{B(w)} \cdot \left[\frac{dB(w)}{dw} \cdot \frac{\partial w}{\partial Q}\right].$$

If this elasticity is less than unity, (45) is obviously negative. Let us find sufficient conditions for this elasticity to be less than unity.

Let e_s be the price elasticity of output of m, so that using the value of $\partial w/\partial P^d$ from (30),

$$(47) \quad e_s = \frac{\partial Q_m}{\partial P^d} \cdot \frac{P^d}{Q_m} = Q^n \cdot B'(w)\frac{\partial w}{\partial P^d}\frac{P^d}{Q_m} = \frac{B'(w)}{B(w)}\frac{H(w)}{H'(w)} > 0$$

where $H(w)$ is defined as in (13).

Now using the value of $\partial w/\partial Q$ from (30), one may rewrite (46) as

$$(48) \quad \frac{\partial Q_m}{\partial Q} \cdot \frac{Q}{Q_m} = n\left[1 + \frac{B'(w)}{B(w)}\frac{H(w)}{H'(w)}\right] = n(1 + e_s).$$

Thus if the "learning elasticity of output" is less than unity it implies that

$$(49) \quad n(1 + e_s) < 1.$$

For example, if the price elasticity of output is m and is less than or equal to unity, a learning coefficient, n, equal to or less than 0.5 is sufficient for (45) to be negative.[20]

If (45) is negative and since with price elasticity of output of m positive, $(\partial\phi/\partial P^d) = (\partial\dot{Q}_m/\partial P^d) > 0$, we can now say that

$$(50) \quad \left(\frac{dP^d}{dQ}\right)_{\phi=0} = -\left[\frac{\partial\phi}{\partial Q}\bigg/\frac{\partial\phi}{\partial P^d}\right]_{\phi=0} > 0.$$

Thus the $\dot{Q} = 0$ curve is upward sloping as in Fig. 6.1. From (30), (34), and (35),

$$(51) \quad \left(\frac{\partial\phi}{\partial Q}\right)_{\psi=0} = -\left[nQ^{n-2}(n-1)B(w) + nQ^{n-1}\frac{dB(w)}{dw}\cdot\frac{\partial w}{\partial Q}\right]P^d.$$

From (46), once again, if the "learning elasticity of output" of m is less than unity, (51) is positive.[21]

From (30), (34), (35), and (47) and since μ and λ are constant,

$$(52) \quad \left(\frac{\partial\psi}{\partial P^d}\right)_{\psi=0} = nQ^{n-1}\left[B\cdot\frac{\mu}{\gamma} - P^d\cdot\frac{dB(w)}{dw}\cdot\frac{\partial w}{\partial P^d}\right] = nQ^{n-1}B\left[\frac{\mu}{\gamma} - e_s\right].$$

Without some extra assumption it does not seem to be possible to be unambiguous about the sign of (52) in general. All we can say is that if the price elasticity of output of m, e_s, is small enough, (52) will be positive.[22] In that case,

$$(53) \quad \left(\frac{dP^d}{dQ}\right)_{\psi=0} = -\left[\frac{\partial\psi}{\partial Q}\bigg/\frac{\partial\psi}{\partial P^d}\right]_{\psi=0} < 0.$$

So under our assumptions the $\dot{P}^d = 0$ curve is downward-sloping as in Fig. 6.1.

Given the shapes of our $\dot{Q} = 0$ and $\dot{P}^d = 0$ curves under our assumptions, the stationary solution is unique. But for proving uniqueness or the saddle-point property of our stationary solution, the last assumption we have just made, viz., the price elasticity of output of m is small enough, is not really necessary. Let us show why.

Although we cannot be unambiguous about the sign of $(\partial\psi/\partial P^d)_{\psi=0}$ in general without this extra assumption, we can show that around the stationary equilibrium point, (Q_*, P_*^d), we know its sign without that assumption. From (31) and (34), when $\dot{Q} = 0$ and $\dot{P}^d = 0$,

$$(54) \quad 1 + \frac{\mu}{\gamma_*} = \frac{\rho+\delta}{B(w)_*\cdot nQ_*^{n-1}} = \frac{\rho+\delta}{n\rho}.[23]$$

Now from (30),

$$(55) \quad \frac{\partial w}{\partial Q} = \frac{nP^d\cdot Q^{n-1}}{H'(w)}$$

Using (49), (54), and (55) in (52)

$$(56) \quad \left(\frac{\partial\psi}{\partial P^d}\right)_{\substack{\psi=0\\\phi=0}} = B(w)_*\cdot Q_*^{n-1}\left[\frac{\delta}{\rho} + 1 - \left\{\left(n + \frac{Q_*}{B(w)_*}\cdot\frac{dB(w)_*}{dw_*}\cdot\frac{\partial w_*}{\partial Q_*}\right)\right\}\right],$$

(56) is positive under our earlier assumption that the "learning elasticity of output" of m is less than unity, as may be checked from (46). So around the stationary equilibrium $\dot{P}^d = 0$ curve must be downward-sloping and the stationary solution is unique, since $\dot{Q} = 0$ is always upward-sloping. Expanding the two differential equations (33) and (35) around the point (Q_*, P_*^d) and using (45), (46), (47), (51), and (56), we can see that under our assumption of the "learning elasticity of output" of m being less than unity, the characteristic roots of the resulting linear system are real and opposite in sign indicating that the stationary solution is a saddle-point.

We need the extra assumption of e_s being small enough to ensure that not merely around the point (Q_*, P_*^d) but $(\partial \psi / \partial P^d)_{\psi=0} > 0$ in general throughout the region we are considering. This ensures the result that for $Q(0) < Q_*$, τ *steadily* decreases.

Appendix B

From (39),

$$\lambda = \beta a^{\beta-1} \text{ and } \mu = (1 - \beta)a^\beta$$

where $a = A_c / A_m$.

Using (57) in (40), $\dot{a}/a = -\alpha$, and that immediately implies (41) and (42).

Let us now analyze the new differential equation of our system. The analysis of the properties of these differential equations is nearly the same as that of our earlier differential equations (33) and (35) analyzed in Appendix A. We shall, therefore, be very brief here.

Since we are no longer assuming depreciation of experience, (31) is to be rewritten, with the use of (37) and (38), as

$$(58) \quad \dot{Q} = Q_m = \dot{Q}g(x) \cdot f_m(k_m(w)) \frac{[k_c(w) - k]}{[k_c(w) - k_m(w)]},$$

since $x = Q/\dot{Q}$, $\dot{x} = \dot{Q}/\dot{Q} - \alpha x$. From (44), w is only a function of x and y. Using $\dot{Q}$ from (58), (59) may now be rewritten as

$$(60) \quad \dot{x} = B(w)g(x) - \alpha x = \phi(x, y)$$

where $B(w)$ is as defined for (45).

As in (45), if the elasticity of output with respect to domestic learning, i.e., $(\partial Q_m / \partial Q)(Q/Q_m) = (g'(x)x)/g(x) + (B'(w)/B(w))(\partial w / \partial x) \cdot x$ is less than unity, then $(\phi_x)_{\dot{x}=0} < 0$. From (13), (44), (47) and (60),

$$(61) \quad \phi_y = g(x)B'(w)\frac{\partial w}{\partial x} = g^2 \frac{B'(w)}{H'(w)} > 0.$$

This means that

$$(62) \quad \left(\frac{dy}{dx}\right)_{\dot{x}=0} = -\frac{\phi_x}{\phi_y} > 0$$

or, the $\dot{x} = 0$ curve is upward-sloping in (x, y) space. With our new production function for m as denoted by (37) and (38), (32) has to be rewritten as

(63) $\dot{\gamma} = \delta\gamma - (\mu + \gamma)g'(x) \cdot f_m(k_m(w)) \dfrac{[k_c(w) - k]}{[k_c(w) - k_m(w)]}$.

From (44),

(64) $\dfrac{\dot{y}}{y} = \alpha\beta + \dfrac{\dot{\gamma}}{\gamma}$.

Since $(\mu + \gamma)/\gamma = 1 + (1/y)$, (64) may be rewritten as

(65) $\dot{y} = y(\delta + \alpha\beta) - (1 + y)g'(x) \cdot B(w) = \psi(x, y)$.

From (65),

(66) $\psi_x = -(1 + y)\left[B(w) \cdot g''(x) + g'(x) \cdot B'(w) \cdot \dfrac{\partial w}{\partial x} \right]$.

As in Appendix A, (66) is positive (since $g'' < 0$) if the price elasticity of output of m is small enough, or alternatively if $g'(x)x/(g(x) - g''(x)x/g'(x)) \geq 1.$[24] From (65),

(67) $(\psi_y)_{\dot{y}=0} = \dfrac{g'(x)}{y}\left[B(w) - y(1 + y)B'(w) \dfrac{\partial w}{\partial y} \right]$.

As in (52) in Appendix A, (67) is positive if the price elasticity of output of m is small enough.
    Thus

(68) $\left(\dfrac{dy}{dx} \right)_{\dot{y}=0} = -\dfrac{\psi_x}{\psi_y} < 0$

or, under our assumptions the $\dot{y} = 0$ curve is downward-sloping in (x, y) space.
    Given the shapes of our $\dot{x} = 0$ and $\dot{y} = 0$ curves the stationary solution is a unique saddle-point. But, as in Appendix A, for proving uniqueness or the saddle-point property of the stationary solution the assumption of price elasticity of output of m being small enough for (67) to be positive is not really necessary. The proof of this statement follows exactly the same kind of proof for a similar statement about the stationary solution in Appendix A and hence is omitted here. We need the assumption about the price elasticity of output of m for (67) to be small in order to ensure that the $\dot{y} = 0$ curve is downward-sloping not merely around the stationary equilibrium point (x_*, y_*) but in general throughout the region we are considering. This ensures the result that for $x(0) < x_*$, y steadily decreases over time.
    The stationary rate of subsidy, τ_*, can easily be calculated by putting (60) and (65) equal to zero. From (60) and (65)

$$\tau_* = y_* = \dfrac{\alpha g'(x_*)x_*}{g(x_*)[\delta + \alpha\beta] - \alpha g'(x_*)x_*}.\text{[25]}$$

Notes

1. I have received useful comments from Tony Atkinson, Harry Johnson, Murray Kemp, Robert Mundell and Takashi Negishi on an earlier draft. Errors are, of course, mine.

2. The essential ideas in this paper may be found in my unpublished Ph.D. dissertation (1965) at Cambridge University, England. Very recently I came across some unpublished work on a broadly similar subject by Harl Ryder and Simone Clemhout and Henry Wan, Jr. Unlike the Ryder paper, I have here abstracted from the added complications of a capital accumulation model in order to bring out the essential learning effect in sharp focus. The Clemhout–Wan paper has a different set of assumptions about learning, production, and objective functions.

3. Arrow in his celebrated model of learning by doing (1962) takes cumulated gross investment as the stock of experience affecting productivity. While this idea is useful in the context of an aggregative growth model like Arrow's, for studying the phenomenon of learning at the industry level it seems more appropriate to take the cumulated volume of industry output as the index of productivity-raising experience. At any rate, most of the empirical evidence of learning in production of airframes, machine tools, etc., relates to the cumulated volume of industry output. See, for example, Hirsch (1956).

4. This is, of course, a very special kind of learning function that is similar to the empirically observed learning function for airframes. Most of our subsequent results, however, carry through (with one exception noted in note 21) if, instead, we take a more general learning function so that

$$Q_m = G(Q) \cdot F_m(K_m, L_m) \text{ with } G'(Q) > 0 \quad \text{and} \quad G''(Q) < 0.$$

The assumption about the derivatives of the $G(Q)$ function means that learning enhances productivity but at a diminishing rate.

   In formalizing the infant-industry concept, however, a more suitable learning function might be one where $G(Q)$ reaches an upper bound $\bar{G}$ for a finite Q, where $\bar{G}$ is a measure of the rest of the world's efficiency level (the thing to be "caught up"). In Section 5 of this paper we explore the implications of such a learning function.

5. That the basic rationale for the infant-industry argument is provided by such irreversible external economies is now well recognized. See Meade [1955, (256)], Haberler [1961, (56)], Kemp [1964, (187)]. For a number of concrete examples of such external economies, see Bardhan [1964].

6. Essentially what is happening is that the system is inherently dynamic so that there is no static equilibrium configuration on which to perform *usual* comparative-static analysis. At some time t_o, *given* the value of Q, the immediate effect of a change in P on w is, of course, as usual.

7. Some more examples (relating to the effect of tariffs) are given in Bardhan [1964]. This is important because the usual results of tariff theory do not carry over to the case of infant-industry tariffs (since they affect production and income in a different way). The impact of an infant-industry tariff has been rather neglected in *descriptive* comparative-static models of protection.

8. Although this is assumed for mathematical convenience, some motivation may be given for this depreciation of experience: for example, in an underdeveloped country an important part of learning is adaptation to industrial employment on the part of the worker from rural areas and this is lost when he leaves the labor force. For those who

find this assumption of depreciation of experience still not very appealing, we have worked out a case without this assumption in Section 6.

9. Both factors are assumed essential for production.

10. Since the Hamiltonian in our problem is concave in control and state variables, any policy satisfying conditions (24)–(28) and the transversality condition (29) is optimal. That H is concave may be more easily checked if we reformulate it in terms of one control variable A_m, and the state variable, Q, as in

$$He^{\delta t} = U(A_c(A_m, Q), A_m) + \gamma[A_m + \bar{X}_m - \rho Q]$$

where $\bar{X}_m$ is the fixed amount of imports of m by the rest of the world, and $A_m = B(w)Q^n - \bar{X}_m$ gives w as a function of A_m and Q, and $A_c = Q_c(w) + \bar{P}\bar{X}_m$ gives A_c as a function of A_m and Q. The Hamiltonian H is concave in A_m and Q, given γ and t.

The essential reason why the Hamiltonian is concave is because we have a strictly concave utility function, a linear Baldwin-envelope curve (since the foreign offer curve is a straight line) and because the second derivative of H with respect to Q is negative for,

$$e^{\delta t}\frac{\partial^2 H}{\partial Q^2} = \frac{\partial^2 U}{\partial A_c^2}\left[\frac{H(w)B(w)n}{Q}\right]^2 - \frac{\partial U}{\partial A_c} \cdot \frac{H(w)B(w)n}{Q^2}\left[1 + n\left(1 + \frac{1}{e_s}\right)\right] < 0.$$

For definitions of $B(w)$, $H(w)$ and e_s, see (45), (13) and (47).

11. It may be a mixture of tax on the non-learning industry and subsidy to the learning industry.

12. This follows from (27), (28) and (29).

13. cf. Haberler [1961, (57)]: "It is, *a priori*, probable that in many cases not a customs duty but an export bounty would be in order in as much as external economies may be realizable in the export rather than in import industries."

14. In the context of developing economies (where the infant-industry argument is supposed to apply with particular relevance) this assumption may not be inappropriate, since such economies are usually characterized by low substitution elasticities in production (low "capacity to transform" in Kindleberger's terms).

15. There are some types of learning processes the benefits of which are specific to the learning firm, and in such cases, obviously, the case for subsidy should not arise.

16. We assume that at the point when $Q = \bar{Q}$, $G'(Q) = 0$ and $G''(Q) = 0$.

17. This is, of course, an extreme assumption of free transferability of knowledge across countries (apart from problems of adaption of foreign technology to the specific pattern of available resources, factor prices, market possibilities, etc., in the home country).

18. We assume that the social rate of discount is high enough so the $\delta > (1 - \beta)\alpha$. This is needed to satisfy the transversality condition (29).

19. That the stationary rate τ_* is positive can be shown as follows. Since under our assumption in n. 18 $\delta > (1 - \beta)\alpha$, the denominator in the expression for y_* is larger than $\alpha[g(x_*) - g'(x_*)x_*]$, which is positive since the bracketed expression is equal to the marginal contribution to domestic output from a rise in the stock of experience abroad.

20. The available empirical estimates of the learning coefficient for airframes as well as different kinds of machine tools, machines and lathes show figures much below 0.5. See, for example, Hirsch [6].

21. If instead of having the special learning function $G(Q) = Q^n$, $1 > n > 0$, we have a more general learning function $G(Q)$ with $G'(Q) > 0$, $G''(Q) < 0$, we have to assume the following for (51) to be positive:

$$\frac{G'(Q)Q}{G(Q)} - \frac{G''(Q)Q}{G'(Q)} \geqq 1.$$

22. An alternative sufficient condition is $1 < \tau e_s$, since $\tau = (\gamma/\mu)$. So if the price elasticity of output of m is less than or equal to the unity and $\tau(0)$ is less than 100%, (52) is positive.
23. This implies that $\tau_* = \gamma_*/\mu = n\rho/\delta + (1 - n)\beta$.
24. If we assume a special form of the $G(Q, \dot{Q})$ function, viz., $G(Q, \dot{Q}) = Q^n \dot{Q}^{1-n}$, $1 > n > 0$, then it is easy to show that $g'(x)x/(g(x) - (g''(x)x)/(g'(x)) = 1$.
25. If we take the special form of the $G(Q, \dot{Q})$ function as in note 24, then

$$\tau_* = \frac{\alpha n}{\delta + \alpha(\beta - n)}.$$

References

Arrow, K. J., "The Economic Implications of Learning by Doing," *Review of Economic Studies*, XXIX (June, 1962), 155–73.

Bardhan, P. K., "External Economies, Economic Development and the Theory of Protection," *Oxford Economic Papers*, XVI (March, 1964).

——, "Economic Growth and the Pattern of International Trade and Investment: A Study in Pure Theory," Ph.D. Dissertation at the University of Cambridge, England, 1966.

Bhagwati, J. and V. K. Ramaswami, "Domestic Distortions, Tariffs and the Theory of Optimum Subsidy," *Journal of Political Economy*, LXXI (February, 1963), 44–50.

Haberler, G., *A Survey of International Trade Theory*, Special Papers in International Economics, No. 1, Princeton University, 1961.

Hirsch, W. Z., "Firm Progress Ratios," *Econometrica*, XXIV (April, 1956), 136–43.

Johnson, H. G., "Optimal Trade Intervention in the Presence of Domestic Distortions," in *Trade, Growth and the Balance of Payments*, Essays in Honor of Gottfried Haberler (Chicago: Rand McNally, 1965).

Kemp, M. C., *The Pure Theory of International Trade* (New Jersey: Prentice Hall, 1964).

Meade, J. E., *Trade and Welfare* (London: Oxford University Press, 1955).

Part II

Vintage Capital Growth Models

Introduction

All the chapters in this Part use a vintage capital growth model, which, among other things, focuses on the endogenously determined life of capital as an important determinant of productivity. If machines unalterably embody the technology of their date of construction, technical progress and the consequent rise in wages reduce the quasi-rents on any given old machine and make some old machines economically obsolete, that is, unprofitable to operate at current wages. Different countries with different wage rates will therefore have different economic lives of machines even if "best-practice" technology (or technology on the newest machine) were the same everywhere, and this is the starting point of Chapter 7. Since average productivity in any industry significantly depends on how modern or outdated its capital stock is, inter-country distribution of comparative advantage depends on inter-country variations in economic lives of capital. To quote from an incisive old empirical study on this question:[1]

> In fact, there is some evidence to suggest that one of the chief reasons for Anglo-American productivity differences lies in standards of obsolescence. It is a common theme in Productivity Mission Reports that the productivity of the best plants in the United Kingdom is comparable with that of the best plants in the United States, and that the difference lies in a much higher proportion of plants employing outmoded methods in the United Kingdom – a much greater "tail" of low-productivity plants. Such a situation is consistent with a higher standard of obsolescence in the United States which follows from a higher level of real wages.

Yet to this day most international trade theorists have largely ignored this source of international productivity difference. Chapters 7 and 8 are an application of a simple vintage capital model to explore this source of productivity difference for a special case where there is no scope for substitution between labor and capital, either *ex ante* (when it is being decided what kind of machine should be built) or *ex post* (when the machine has been built) – what used to be called a "clay-clay" model in the literature. Chapter 7 confirms a Heckscher–Ohlin type result for comparative advantage, although the mechanism involved is quite different from that in usual models. In Chapter 8 we use the same model to look at the effect of protection on productivity (a question of considerable interest to economic historians); we show that the effect is ambiguous and it depends on, among other things, the technological characteristics of the protected industry. We then introduce learning-by-doing in this setup. Even in cases where protection initially lowers productivity by lengthening the economic life of capital, a protection-induced increase in current output at each date in the protected sector results in an increase in the growth rate of productivity on new machines through more rapid learning. A particular case of the model in Chapter 8 then focuses on this dynamic trade-off and a comparison of the time-paths of productivity with and without infant-industry protection.

From this case of learning by doing we go to the models of endogenous growth in recent literature. The idea of a continual introduction of new inputs as an embodiment of technological progress plays an important role in these models, for example in that of P. Romer.[2] But in Romer's model old inputs are never scrapped; new inputs constitute a horizontal expansion of the whole range of inputs. In the Schumpeterian growth models of P. Aghion and P. Howitt[3] and of P. S. Segerstrom et al.,[4] or the related quality ladder models of G. Grossman and E. Helpman,[5] there is economic obsolescence of inputs but it takes place in an extreme fashion: the state-of-the-art product completely and instantaneously displaces all the old varieties. So the richness of the old vintage capital models in this respect, with some old inputs being scrapped while some others coexisting with the latest variety, is missing in the recent literature, and accordingly the differential productivity effects of the different length of the "tail" that Salter talks about are not analyzed. On the other hand, in the old vintage capital models (except those with learning-by-doing) the ultimate source of technical progress embodied in the latest machine was exogenous. In Chapter 9 we therefore set out to combine a Romer-type endogeneity of technical progress (and monopolistic competition and dynamic economies of scale) with an endogenously determined economic life of capital as in the old vintage capital models. In this model policies that affect the economic life of capital (for example, those influencing the gross savings or investment rate, or trade policy in a two-sector open economy) have an effect on the long-run growth rate.

In combining features from these two strands of literature and yet to keep the analysis tractable, we had to adopt quite a few restrictive assumptions in developing our model (including fitting it into the strait-jacket of the steady state). Important beginnings in the area of transitional dynamics for vintage capital growth models have been made by J. Benhabib and A. Rustichini[6] (who have a vintage capital version of an optimal growth model to study the volatile behavior of investment and growth) and by R. Boucekkine, M. Germain, and O. Licandro[7] (who provide a study of replacement dynamics in a model of optimal growth with endogenous scrapping). C.-T. Hsieh[8] has also tried, like us, to combine features of endogenous growth with economic obsolescence of capital, but he takes a simpler "putty-putty" model where there is substitutability between labor and capital and to the same extent both *ex ante* and *ex post*. In such models, unlike in our model, complete obsolescence is only asymptotically reached: a machine will be utilized less intensively as it gets older but will never be completely scrapped. In this simpler case he can discuss interesting new possibilities. For example, he shows that as the rate at which new machines become obsolete depends on expectations of the rate at which new, higher quality machines are expected to be introduced in the future, this creates the possibility of multiple equilibria, one with high growth rates, in which machines quickly become obsolete, and another with low growth rates in which machines are used for a long time.

In Chapters 7, 8, and 9 we have used a "clay-clay" vintage capital model, but a somewhat more realistic model is that of "putty-clay," where there is substitution between capital and labor *ex ante*, i.e., prior to the installation of the machinery, but not *ex post* (this is an approximation to the more general case of lower flexibility of techniques on a machine already installed). This model is more complicated than the "clay-clay" model. Chapters 10, 11, and 12 derive some comparative-dynamic properties of equilibrium in the "putty-clay" model. Chapters 10 and 11 show that these properties are very sensitive to the elasticity of substitution on the *ex ante* production function. One such comparative-dynamic property is explored further in Chapter 12. This relates to the result that for well-defined cases the elasticity of the average productivity of labor with respect to the wage rate is *higher* than the elasticity of substitution along the *ex ante* production function. This is important to note in empirical studies of production functions. Since the original estimation[9] of the constant-elasticity-of-substitution (CES) production function from international cross-section data, it has become a common practice to measure the elasticity of substitution by estimating the coefficient of regression of the logarithm of observed output per unit of labor on that of observed wage rate – following a standard neoclassical production function. But Chapter 12 suggests that this measure will give an overestimate, if the data-generating model is not static, but has the properties of a "putty-clay" vintage capital model.

Notes

1. W. E. G. Salter, *Productivity and Technical Change*, Cambridge University Press, Cambridge, UK, 1960.
2. P. Romer, "Endogenous Technological Change," *Journal of Political Economy*, vol. 98, 1990.
3. P. Aghion and P. Howitt, "A Model of Growth through Creative Destruction," *Econometrica*, vol. 60, 1992.
4. P. S. Segerstrom, T. C. A. Anant, and E. Dinopoulos, "A Schumpeterian Model of the Product Life Cycle," *American Economic Review*, vol. 80, 1990.
5. G. Grossman and E. Helpman, *Innovation and Growth in the Global Economy*, MIT Press, Cambridge, MA, 1991.
6. J. Benhabib and A. Rustichini, "A Vintage Capital Model of Investment and Growth: Theory and Evidence," in R. Becker *et al.* (eds.), *General Equilibrium, Growth, and Trade II*, Academic Press, 1993.
7. R. Boucekkine, M. Germain, and O. Licandro, "Replacement Echoes in the Vintage Capital Growth Model," *Journal of Economic Theory*, vol. 74, 1997.
8. C.-T. Hsieh, "Endogenous Growth and Obsolescence," *Journal of Development Economics*, vol. 66, 2001.
9. K. J. Arrow, H. B. Chenery, B. S. Minhas, and R. M. Solow, "Capital-Labor Substitution and Economic Efficiency," *Review of Economics and Statistics*, vol. 43, 1962.

Chapter 7

International Trade Theory in a Vintage-Capital Model[1]

1

Vintage-capital models are as yet conspicuous by their absence in international trade literature. This paper departs from the perfect-malleability-of-capital assumption of standard international trade theory (as exemplified, *par excellence*, by the Heckscher–Ohlin–Samuelson model) and assumes technical progress to be embodied only in new machines. Substitution between labor and capital is impossible both *ex ante* and *ex post*. Physical depreciation is ignored, and obsolescence takes its toll when rising wages absorb all the revenues from a particular machine.[2] So one of the main points of this paper is to show how changes in capital longevity, like those in capital "depth," affect productivity and therefore comparative advantage.

Owing to mathematical complexities, the literature to date on vintage-capital models hardly ventures into an analysis of the properties of the system when it is off the "golden-age" equilibrium path. Much of it is concerned with the sensitivity of this path with respect to changes in certain parameters; for example, the differences in the operating life of machines or in the sustainable level of consumption between economies on the steady-growth path differing only with respect to saving propensities have been analyzed in [Robinson, 1962; Kurz, 1962, 1963; Phelps, 1963; Matthews, 1964]. This paper takes up this method of comparative dynamics and uses it in the context of the theory of international trade. The theory of comparative advantage is essentially concerned with the factors determining pretrade equilibrium relative commodity prices, and a comparison of two equilibrium positions for the same (closed) economy with some intervening changes in parameters is a useful way of analyzing those factors. For instance, if one takes a closed economy with all the usual Ohlin–Samuelson assumptions in a static equilibrium position, and compares it with the same economy in a different equilibrium position when nothing else has changed except that the capital–labor ratio has increased in between, one finds that in the second equilibrium position the price of the capital-intensive good is lower, indicating the Heckscher–Ohlin proposition regarding the effect of factor endowments on comparative advantage. This paper also resorts to a comparison between two pretrade equilibrium positions for the same economy, but the equilibria referred to are not static but golden-age equilibria.

There are two sectors in the economy, a consumer goods sector (denoted by subscript c) and a capital goods sector (denoted by subscript m). We have fixed-coefficient production functions for machines of each vintage in each sector:

$$(1) \quad F_i(v, t) = \min\{\lambda_i(v)L_i(v, t), a_i(v)I_i(v)\} \quad (i = m, c),$$

where $F_i(v, t)dv$ and $L_i(v, t)dv$ are the rates of output produced and labor employed, respectively, at time t on machines of vintage v in the ith sector; $I_i(v)$ is the number of machines of vintage v in the ith sector; $\lambda_i(v)$ and $a_i(v)$ are the output per man and output per machine, respectively, using machines of vintage v. In the golden-age equilibrium, with no excess capital or labor, (1) can be written as:

$$(1') \quad F_i(v, t) = \lambda_i(v)L_i(v, t) = a_i(v)I_i(v) \quad (i = m, c),$$

The total output in the ith sector is

$$(2) \quad F_i(t) = \int_{t-T_i}^{t} F_i(v, t)dv,$$

where T_i is the (constant) age of the oldest machine in use.

The total labor supply is divided between the two sectors:

$$(3) \quad L(t) = \int_{t-T_m}^{t} L_m(v, t) + \int_{t-T_c}^{t} L_c(v, t)dv.$$

A consumer good at each time t is used as a *numéraire*, and $P(t)$ is the price per unit of new capital goods at time t. Pure competition prevails. From the condition for scrapping of machines,

$$(4) \quad W(t) = \lambda_c(t - T_c) = P(t)\lambda_m(t - T_m),$$

where $W(t)$ is the wage rate at time t in terms of consumer goods. We assume that technical progress is exponential (at rate g), uniform in the two sectors, and Harrod-neutral; entrepreneurs (correctly) expect the wage rate to grow at rate g.

$$(5) \quad \lambda_i(t) = b_i e^{gt},$$

where b_i's are given constants. We also assume that the output–capital ratio is constant, i.e.,

(6) $a_i(t) = a_i.$

As technical progress is Harrod-neutral and uniform in the two sectors, P is constant in the steady state, so that $P(t) = P$. The quasi rent (in terms of the *numéraire*) $R_i(v, t)dv$ in *i*th sector ($i = m, c$) earned at time t per machine of vintage v is:

(7) $R_c(v, t) = a_c \left[1 - \dfrac{W(t)}{\lambda_c(v)} \right],$

$R_m(v, t) = Pa_m \left[1 - \dfrac{W(t)}{P} \dfrac{1}{\lambda_m(v)} \right].$

If the rate of interest r is expected to remain constant over the future, the discounted stream of quasi rents over the lifetime of an investment (with equilibrium in the capital market) is:

$$P = \int_v^{v+T_m} R_m(v, t)\, e^{-r(t-v)}\, dt = a_m P \int_v^{v+T_m} e^{-r(t-v)} [1 - e^{g(t-v-T_m)}]\, dt,$$

or,

(8) $1 = a_m \left[\dfrac{1 - e^{-rT_m}}{r} + \dfrac{e^{-rT_m} - e^{-gT_m}}{r - g} \right] = a_m S(r, T_m).$

Similarly,

(9) $P = a_c \int_v^{v+T_c} e^{-r(t-v)} [1 - e^{g(t-v-T_c)}]\, dt$

$= a_c \left[\dfrac{1 - e^{-rT_c}}{r} + \dfrac{e^{-rT_c} - e^{-gT_c}}{r - g} \right] = a_c S(r, T_c).$

A constant proportion β of total income Y at time t is saved and invested, so that:

(10) $\beta Y(t) = P[I_c(t) + I_m(t)] = PF_m(t).$

Labor supply can be taken as growing at any suitably fixed rate.

2

In Section 1 we have a description of the "golden-age" equilibrium of our closed economy. We take two such equilibria for the same economy, between which only r, the rate of interest, differs, and find out the implications (why we do so will be clear at the end of this section). In particular, we are interested in the sign of dP/dr.

From (4) and (5),

(11) $P = \dfrac{\lambda_c(t - T_c)}{\lambda_m(t - T_m)} = \dfrac{b_c}{b_m} e^{g(T_m - T_c)}$.

From (11),

(12) $\operatorname{sgn}\dfrac{dP}{dr} = \operatorname{sgn}\left[\dfrac{dT_m}{dr} - \dfrac{dT_c}{dr}\right] = \operatorname{sgn}\dfrac{dT_m}{dr}\left[1 - \dfrac{dT_c}{dT_m}\right]$.

From (8),

(13) $\dfrac{dT_m}{dr} = -\dfrac{\dfrac{\partial S(r, T_m)}{\partial r}}{\dfrac{\partial S(r, T_m)}{\partial T_m}}$.

From (8) and (9) it can be shown directly that (putting $v = 0$):

(14) $\dfrac{\partial S(r, T_i)}{\partial r} = \displaystyle\int_0^{T_i} (-t) e^{-rt}[1 - e^{g(t - T_i)}]\, dt < 0 \quad (i = m, c)$.

Equations (8) and (9) can also be rewritten as:

(15) $S(r, T_i) = \dfrac{1}{r}\left[1 + \dfrac{\{ge^{-rT_i} - re^{-gT_i}\}}{r - g}\right] \quad (i = m, c)$.

From (15),

(16) $\dfrac{\partial S(r, T_i)}{\partial T_i} > 0, \quad \text{for } r > g.^3$

Hence, in (13),

(17) $\dfrac{dT_m}{dr} > 0$.

Equation (17) means that the steady-state equilibrium with higher r will have a longer operating life of capital in the capital goods sector. Now, from (9) and (11),

(18) $a_c S(r, T_c) - \dfrac{b_c}{b_m} e^{g(T_m - T_c)} = 0$,

which, when account is taken of the fact that r is an implicit function of T_m in (8), enables us to form a function:

(18') $G(T_m, T_c) = 0.$

From (18'),

(19) $\left[1 - \dfrac{dT_c}{dT_m}\right] = 1 + \dfrac{G_{T_m}}{G_{T_c}}.$

From (18) and (18'),

(20a) $G_{T_m} = a_c \dfrac{\partial S(r, T_c)}{\partial r} \dfrac{dr}{dT_m} - g\dfrac{b_c}{b_m} e^{g(T_m - T_c)},$

(20b) $G_{T_c} = a_c \dfrac{\partial S(r, T_c)}{\partial T_c} + g\dfrac{b_c}{b_m} e^{g(T_m - T_c)}.$

Using (14), (16), and (17) in (20a) and (20b),

(20c) $G_{T_m} < 0,$ and $G_{T_c} > 0.$

From (12), (17), (19), and (20c),

(21) $\operatorname{sgn}\dfrac{dP}{dr} = \operatorname{sgn}[G_{T_c} + G_{T_m}],$

which, using (20a), (20b), and (13), has the same sign as

(21a) $\left[\dfrac{\dfrac{\partial S(r, T_c)}{\partial T_c}}{\left|\dfrac{\partial S(r, T_c)}{\partial r}\right|} - \dfrac{\dfrac{\partial S(r, T_m)}{\partial T_m}}{\left|\dfrac{\partial S(r, T_m)}{\partial r}\right|}\right].$

If we define $x = \dfrac{\partial S(r, T_i)}{\partial T_i}$ and $y = \left|\dfrac{\partial S(r, T_i)}{\partial r}\right|$, $i = m, c$, the sign of the bracketed expression (21a) depends on the sign of $d(x/y)/dT_i$, which is shown to be negative in the Appendix; this means (21a) is positive or negative as $T_m \gtrless T_c$.

Now, which sector has the longer operating life of capital? From (8), (9), and (11), it can be shown that:

(22) $\dfrac{a_m b_c}{a_c b_m} = \dfrac{(r - g)\, e^{gT_c} + g\, e^{-(r-g)T_c} - r}{(r - g)\, e^{gT_m} + g\, e^{-(r-g)T_m} - r} = \dfrac{H(T_c)}{H(T_m)}.$

Since it is an easy matter to show that $H'(T_i) > 0$ for $r > g$, $T_m \gtreqless T_c$ as $a_c b_m \gtreqless a_m b_c$, or as the capital goods sector is more or less capital intensive than the consumer goods sector. The more capital-intensive sector has the higher operating life of capital.[4] This, coupled with our result above, when put in (21a) and (21), gives us $dP/dr \gtreqless 0$, as the capital goods sector is more or less capital intensive than the consumer goods sector.

Thus, between two steady-state equilibria, if the rate of return differs (and therefore the operating life of capital T_i in each sector), the equilibrium with lower r will have a lower price for the output of the sector in which the capital–labor ratio employed is higher. Let us define the country with lower r as the more capital-rich country. Then, analyzing across two countries in a steady-state equilibrium otherwise identical, this means that *the more capital-rich country will have a comparative advantage in the more capital-intensive commodity.*[5]

Suppose capital goods are more capital intensive in production. Then we have shown above that, although the operating life of capital will be smaller in both the sectors of the capital-rich country, compared to those in the capital-poor country, the difference will be larger for the capital goods sector; and since in this model of fixed coefficients of production, both *ex ante* and *ex post*, productivity is inversely related to the length of the operating life of capital, one can see why the more capital-rich country will have a comparative advantage in producing the more capital-intensive capital goods.

3

In the preceding section we have compared two steady-state equilibria with differing r, but with the same rate of technical progress g. But now suppose in the same model that r is the same but g differs between two pretrade equilibria (countries). The country representing the equilibrium with higher g will be taken as the technically more progressive country. It might be interesting to find out the resulting pattern of comparative advantage. In other words, we shall be concerned with the sign of dP/dg.

From (11),

$$(23) \quad \operatorname{sgn}\frac{dP}{dg} = \operatorname{sgn}\left[\left(T_m + \frac{dT_m}{dg}g\right) - \left(T_c + \frac{dT_c}{dg}g\right)\right].$$

Equation (8) can now be defined as:

$$(8') \quad \phi(g, T_m)\, a_m = 1,$$

and (9) as:

$$(9') \quad \phi(g, T_c)\, a_c = P.$$

From (8'),

$$(24) \quad \frac{dT_m}{dg} = -\frac{\frac{\partial \phi(g, T_m)}{\partial g}}{\frac{\partial \phi(g, T_m)}{\partial T_m}}.$$

From (9') and (11),

$$(25) \quad a_c \phi(g, T_c) - \frac{b_c}{b_m} e^{g(T_m - T_c)} = 0,$$

which, when account is taken of the fact that T_m is an implicit function of g^6 in (8'), enables us to form a function

$$(25') \quad E(g, T_c) = 0.$$

From (25'),

$$(26) \quad \frac{dT_c}{dg} = -\frac{E_g}{E_{T_c}}.$$

From (25) and (25'),

$$(27a) \quad E_{T_c} = a_c \frac{\partial \phi(g, T_c)}{\partial T_c} + g \frac{b_c}{b_m} e^{g(T_m - T_c)} = \frac{\partial \phi(g, T_c)}{\partial T_c} a_c + gP,$$

and

$$(27b) \quad E_g = a_c \frac{\partial \phi(g, T_c)}{\partial g} - g \frac{b_c}{b_m} e^{g(T_m - T_c)} \frac{dT_m}{dg} - (T_m - T_c) \frac{b_c}{b_m} e^{g(T_m - T_c)}$$

$$= a_c \frac{\partial \phi(g, T_c)}{\partial g} + PT_c - P\left(T_m + g \frac{dT_m}{dg}\right).$$

From (8), (8'), (9), and (9'),

$$(15a) \quad \phi(g, T_i) = \left[1 + \frac{ge^{-rT_i} - re^{-gT_i}}{r - g}\right] \frac{1}{r} \quad (i = m, c).$$

From (15a),

$$(28a) \quad \frac{\partial \phi(g, T_i)}{\partial g} = \frac{1}{(r - g)^2} [e^{-rT_i} - e^{-gT_i}(1 - (r - g)T_i)] > 0,^7 \quad (i = m, c)$$

(28b) $\dfrac{\partial\phi(g, T_i)}{\partial T_i} = \dfrac{g}{(r - g)}[e^{-gT_i} - e^{-rT_i}] > 0, \quad (i = m, c)$

so that

(29) $g\dfrac{\dfrac{\partial\phi(g, T_i)}{\partial g}}{\dfrac{\partial\phi(g, T_i)}{\partial T_i}} = \dfrac{T_i}{[1 - e^{-(r-g)T_i}]} - \dfrac{1}{r - g}.$

Equation (28b) makes E_{T_c} positive in (27a). Now,

$$\left[T_m + \dfrac{dT_m}{dg}g\right] - \left[T_c + \dfrac{dT_c}{dg}g\right] = \left[T_m + \dfrac{dT_m}{dg}g\right] - \left[T_c - \dfrac{Eg}{E_{T_c}}g\right],$$

which, using (27b) and (27a),

$$= \dfrac{E_{T_c}\left[T_m + \dfrac{dT_m}{dg}g\right] - T_c\dfrac{\partial\phi(g, T_c)}{\partial T_c}a_c - gPT_c + g\left[a_c\dfrac{\partial\phi(g, T_c)}{\partial g} + PT_c - P\left(\dfrac{dT_m}{dg} + T_m\right)\right]}{E_{T_c}},$$

which, using (27a) again,

$$= \dfrac{\left[T_m + \dfrac{dT_m}{dg}g\right]\dfrac{\partial\phi(g, T_c)}{\partial T_c}a_c - T_c\dfrac{\partial\phi(g, T_c)}{\partial T_c}a_c + g\dfrac{\partial\phi(g, T_c)}{\partial g}a_c}{E_{T_c}},$$

which has the same sign, since $E_{T_c} > 0$ and $\dfrac{\partial\phi(g, T_c)}{\partial T_c} > 0$, as

$$\left[T_m + \dfrac{dT_m}{dg}g\right] - \left[T_c - g\dfrac{\dfrac{\partial\phi(g, T_c)}{\partial g}}{\dfrac{\partial\phi(g, T_c)}{\partial T_c}}\right].$$

Putting this in (23), and using (24),

(30) $\operatorname{sgn}\dfrac{dP}{dg} = \operatorname{sgn}\left\{\left[\left[T_m - g\dfrac{\dfrac{\partial\phi(g, T_m)}{\partial g}}{\dfrac{\partial\phi(g, T_m)}{\partial T_m}}\right] - \left[T_c - g\dfrac{\dfrac{\partial\phi(g, T_c)}{\partial g}}{\dfrac{\partial\phi(g, T_c)}{\partial T_c}}\right]\right]\right\}.$

From (29), and after simplification, the expression on the righthand side of (30) can be shown to be equal to:

$$(31) \quad \frac{e^{(r-g)T_m} - [1 + (r - g)T_m]}{(r - g)[e^{(r-g)T_m} - 1]} - \frac{e^{(r-g)T_c} - [1 + (r - g)T_c]}{(r - g)[e^{(r-g)T_c} - 1]} = D(T_m) - D(T_c)$$

where

$$D(T_i) = \frac{e^{(r-g)T_i} - [1 + (r - g)T_i]}{(r - g)[e^{(r-g)T_i} - 1]}.$$

From (31), $D'(T_i)$ has the same sign as

$$(r - g)T_i \, e^{(r-g)T_i} - [e^{(r-g)T_i} - 1],$$

which, as we have seen in note 7, is positive.

Therefore,

$$(32) \quad \frac{dP}{dg} \gtreqless 0, \quad \text{as} \quad T_m \gtreqless T_c, \quad \text{or as} \quad a_c b_m \gtreqless a_m b_c.$$

In other words, analyzing across two countries in steady-state equilibrium, *the technically more progressive country* (where g is higher, or, g being the rate of uniform Harrod-neutral technical progress, where labor is more efficient) *will have a comparative advantage in the more labor-intensive commodity.*

A similar conclusion can be derived from a model somewhat different in kind. So far, we have been assuming that technical knowledge rises simply with the passage of time. It might be interesting to follow Arrow [1962] in postulating that technical progress arises out of experience (learning by doing) and in taking cumulated output of capital goods as the index of experience. In other respects, Arrow's model is broadly similar to that of ours set up in Section 1; in particular, the production process is characterized by fixed coefficients and technical progress is completely embodied in new machines.

We shall keep much of the equational setup and notations of our model in Section 1 and introduce here only the new elements. Let $G(t)$ be the cumulated output of capital goods up to time t. A machine produced when the cumulated output of capital goods has reached $G(v)$ will be said to have serial number $G(v)$ – this is the way we are to redefine our idea of a machine of vintage v used in Section 1. Equation (2) has now to be revised as

$$(2') \quad F_i(t) = \int_{G(t-T_i)}^{G(t)} a_i \, dG \quad (i = m, c),$$

where a_i is, as before, the fixed output-capital ratio. Equation (5) is now revised as

$$(5') \quad \lambda_i[G(v)] = b_i G^n(v), \, 0 < n < 1 \quad (i = m, c),$$

where $\lambda_i[G(v)]$, output per man using the machine with serial number $G(v)$, is a rising function of $G(v)$ (the form of the function is similar to that found in the study of "learning curves" for airframes in United States); we shall call n the learning coefficient (equal for both sectors).

It can be shown (as has been demonstrated by Arrow [1962]) that in the golden age for this sytem, if the exponential rate of growth of labor supply is σ, the rate of increase of G is $\gamma = \sigma/(1 - n)$, and the rate of increase in the wage rate is $g = ny$.

Now, from the scrapping condition similar to (4),

$$(11') \quad P(t) = \frac{b_c}{b_m} \frac{G^n(t - T_c)}{G^n(t - T_m)}.$$

The quasi rents at time t from a machine with serial number $G(t)$ are:

$$R_c[G(t), t] = a_c\left[1 - \frac{W(t)}{\lambda_c(G(t))}\right] = a_c\left[1 - \frac{G^n(t - T_c)}{G^n(t)}\right],$$

and

$$R_m[G(t), t] = a_mP\left[1 - \frac{W(t)}{P} \frac{1}{\lambda_m(G(t))}\right] = a_mP\left[1 - \frac{G^n(t - T_m)}{G^n(t)}\right].$$

But W rises at a constant rate g. Therefore, $R_c[G(t), t]$ is also equal to $a_c[1 - e^{-gT_c}]$ and $R_m[G(t), t]$ equal to $a_mP[1 - e^{-gT_m}]$.

This means, from $(7')$,

$$(7a) \quad G^n(t) = G^n(t - T_i)e^{gT_i}, \quad (i = m, c).$$

Thus, our crucial earlier equations (8), (9), and (11) remain valid, even in terms of the present model.

Now suppose between two countries in steady-state equilibrium everything else is the same, except that n, the learning coefficient, varies, i.e., one country has a higher propensity to learn by doing than the other. Let us find out the sign of dP/dn. From (8), (9), and (11), it follows, as we have shown in the earlier part of this section, that $dP/dg \geq 0$ as $a_cb_m \geq a_mb_c$. Now, since $g = n\sigma/(1 - n)$, $dg/dn > 0$, it follows that $dP/dn \geq 0$, as $a_cb_m \geq a_mb_c$.

In other words, all other things being the same, *the country* (in golden-age equilibrium) *with a higher propensity to learn by doing will have a comparative advantage in the more labor-intensive commodity.* If instead of n, we vary σ between the two equilibria, it is easy to show from above (since $dg/d\sigma > 0$) that *the country with a higher rate of growth in the labor force will have a comparative advantage in the more labor-intensive commodity.*

Before we close, two comments might be made about the models used in this paper. The first is regarding the impossibility of factor substitution both *ex ante* and *ex post*. As has been shown in [Matthews, 1964], in a vintage-capital model the values of the elasticity of factor substitution, both *ex ante* and *ex post*, are very important determinants of the average age of capital and hence of productivity. If, for example, the elasticity of factor substitution, both *ex ante* and *ex post*, is equal to unity, the average age of capital is invariant with respect to a change in the rate of return r. It can, however, be shown, in terms of a model akin to that in [Kurz, 1962], that in this case also the country with lower r (in golden-age equilibrium) will have a comparative advantage in the more capital-intensive commodity. An interesting extension of our model will be to consider the case when the *ex ante* production function is a Cobb–Douglas one, but there is no *ex post* factor substitutability; we are sure that this will be very much more complicated than our simple model.

Our second comment concerns the method of comparative dynamics employed in this paper. There is no doubt that our analysis is on an extremely high level of abstraction, since we only compare two golden-age equilibria, while so many things remain conveniently constant. But at the same time it is worth mentioning that this level of abstraction may not be higher than that involved in comparing two static equilibria, which is the staple of much of current international trade theory. In particular, the analysis of how comparative advantage may be affected by intercountry variations in capital longevity, even though couched in terms of the very special case of golden-age equilibrium, might be a useful addition to the literature.

Appendix

In this Appendix we will show that y/x is an increasing function of T_i, where $x = \dfrac{\partial S(r, T_i)}{\partial T_i}$, and $y = \left| \dfrac{\partial S(r, T_i)}{\partial r} \right|$, with $S(r, T_i)$ being given by (15). From (15),

$$(33) \quad x = \frac{g}{(r - g)} [e^{-gT_i} - e^{-rT_i}],$$

and

$$(34) \quad y = \frac{1}{r^2(r - g)^2}[(r - g)^2 + g(r - g) e^{-rT_i}(1 + rT_i) + r(g\, e^{-rT_i} - r\, e^{-gT_i})].$$

From (33) and (34),

$$(35) \quad \frac{y}{x} = \frac{1}{gr^2(r - g)} \cdot \left[\frac{(r - g)^2 + g(r - g) e^{-rT_i}(1 + rT_i) + r(g\, e^{-rT_i} - r\, e^{-gT_i})}{[e^{-gT_i} - e^{-rT_i}]} \right]$$

$$= \frac{1}{gr^2(r - g)} \left[-r^2 + (r - g)g \frac{\{(\alpha - 1) e^{\alpha z} + 1 + \alpha z - \alpha\}}{e^{(\alpha-1)z} - 1} \right],$$

where $\alpha = r/g > 1$, and $z = gT_i > 0$. Let us write:

$$(36) \quad J(z) = \frac{(\alpha - 1)e^{\alpha z} + 1 + \alpha z - \alpha}{e^{(\alpha-1)z} - 1}.$$

From (36),

$$(37) \quad \frac{J'(z)}{J(z)} = \frac{\alpha(\alpha - 1)e^{\alpha z} + \alpha}{(\alpha - 1)(e^{\alpha z} - 1) + \alpha z} - \frac{(\alpha - 1)e^{(\alpha-1)z}}{e^{(\alpha-1)z} - 1}.$$

The two denominators on the righthand side of (37) are positive, since $\alpha > 1$. Hence, $J'(z) > 0$, if, by crossmultiplying on the righthand side of (37) and dividing through by $e^{(\alpha-1)z}$,

$$(38) \quad V(z) = \alpha(\alpha - 1) e^{\alpha z} + \alpha - \alpha(\alpha - 1) e^{z} - \alpha e^{-(\alpha-1)z} - (\alpha - 1)^2 e^{\alpha z} - \alpha(\alpha - 1)z$$
$$+ (\alpha - 1)^2.$$

$$V(0) = \alpha(\alpha - 1) + \alpha - \alpha(\alpha - 1) - \alpha - (\alpha - 1)^2 + (\alpha - 1)^2 = 0, \text{ and}$$

$$V'(z) = \alpha^2(\alpha - 1) e^{\alpha z} - \alpha(\alpha - 1) e^{z} + \alpha(\alpha - 1) e^{-(\alpha-1)z}$$
$$- \alpha(\alpha - 1)^2 e^{\alpha z} - \alpha(\alpha - 1)$$

$$= \alpha(\alpha - 1)[e^{\alpha z} - e^{z} + e^{-(\alpha-1)z} - 1]$$

$$= \alpha(\alpha - 1)(e^{\alpha z} - 1)[1 - e^{-(\alpha-1)z}] > 0, \text{ since } \alpha > 1.$$

Therefore, $V(z) > 0$ for $z > 0$, and

$$(39) \quad J'(z) > 0 \text{ for } z > 0.$$

Putting this in (35), and remembering the definition of $J(z)$ given by (36) and that $z = gT_i$, we can say that y/x is an increasing function of T_i.

Notes

1. I am indebted to Dr. J. A. Mirrlees and Professor R. M. Solow for very helpful comments on an earlier draft. All errors are, of course, mine.
2. Our model is akin to the so-called "clay-clay" model in a one-sector closed economy analyzed in detail by Solow, Tobin, von Weizsäcker, and Yaari [1965]. The stimulus to think along these lines was provided to me by Solow's Marshall Lecture in Cambridge, England, in October, 1963.
3. As is usual in the literature on vintage-capital models, we shall henceforth always assume that $r > g$, i.e., the rate of return is higher than the rate of technical progress, which is not very implausible.
4. This is true not merely in "clay-clay" models, but also in all "putty-clay" models.
5. The conclusion may be familiar enough but, considering the nature of the model, it is not at all self-evident (as may be seen from the next paragraph in the text). The whole thing is determined by the *relative* difference in the operating lives of capital in the two sectors in the two countries. It may also be noted, in contrast to the standard Heckscher–Ohlin model, that although production functions *ex ante* are internationally identical the extent of *utilization* of new technical knowledge in the industry as a whole is not the same between countries because of differences in the scrapping ages of machines.

6. From (28a), (28b), and (24) $dT_m/dg < 0$, i.e., the steady-state equilibrium with higher g will have a shorter operating life of capital in the capital goods sector.

7. Multiplying both sides by e^{rT_i}, $\partial\phi(g, T_i)/\partial g$ has the same sign as

$$M(T_i) = (r - g)T_i\, e^{(r-g)T_i} - [e^{(r-g)T_i} - 1].$$

$M(0) = 0$, and $M'(T_i) = (r - g)^2\, T_i\, e^{(r-g)T_i} > 0$. Hence $M(T_i) > 0$ for $T_i > 0$.

References

Arrow, K. J.: "The Economic Implications of Learning by Doing," *Review of Economic Studies*, June, 1962.

Kurz, M.: "Patterns of Growth and Valuation in a Two-sector Model," *Yale Economic Essays*, Fall, 1962.

——: "Substitution versus Fixed Production Coefficient: A Comment," *Econometrica*, January–April, 1963.

Matthews, R. C. O.: "The New View of Investment: Comment," *Quarterly Journal of Economics*, February, 1964.

Phelps, E. S.: "Substitution, Fixed Proportions, Growth and Distribution," *International Economic Review*, September, 1963.

Robinson, Joan: "A Neo-Classical Theorem," *Review of Economic Studies*, June, 1962.

Solow, R., J. Tobin, C. von Weizsäcker and M. Yaari: "A Model of Fixed Capital without Substitution," Cowles Foundation Discussion Paper, no. 188, August 6, 1965.

Chapter 8

Dynamic Effects of Protection on Productivity*

1. Introduction

In the literature on import substitution and economic growth it is often argued that protection, by sheltering markets and enhancing the profitability of current methods of production, delays modernization of the capital stock and thus dampens the growth of labor productivity. In the economic history literature, however, one occasionally notices a contrary presumption: for example, Williamson (1971) has emphasized the importance of highly protective tariffs in early nineteenth-century United States in encouraging a faster scrapping of capital in favor of technologically superior equipment in the textile industry and thus fostering rapid productivity growth in that industry. Temin (1966), in interpreting the relative decline of the British steel industry in the period from the 1880s to World War I, has referred to the tariff-induced adoption of superior capital equipment in the United States and Germany. We shall not here go into the large differences in the social, political and economic pre-conditions of growth prevailing in the protectionist regimes in the nineteenth century as opposed to those in today's poor countries to which the trade and development literature usually refers. Nor shall we deal with the question that even when protection helps modernization of capital, it is not usually the most efficient method of achieving that result. Our more limited aim in this paper is to formulate a simple theoretical model of an open economy with embodied technical progress and heterogeneous capital and to show how the effect of protection on economic obsolescence of machines and hence average labor productivity is not unambiguous and that it depends on, among other things, the technological characteristics of the protected industry.

We assume that all technical progress is embodied in new machines, machines embody the technology of their date of construction, that there is no substitutability between capital and labor either ex ante or ex post (what is usually called the "clay–clay" assumption)[1] and that there are constant returns to scale in production. In our model of sections 2 and 3 two sectors produce tradable outputs using labor and a vintage stock of capital; one sector produces machines and the other produces a consumption good. Harrod-neutral technical progress occurs exogenously at the same rate in both sectors. Comparing across long-run growth equilibria, tariff protection of the relatively capital-intensive sector *lengthens* the economic life of capital in *both* the tradable producing sectors; protection of a labor-intensive sector, on the other hand, *shortens* the economic life of capital.

In section 4 we introduce learning by doing. Even when protection initially lowers productivity by lengthening the economic life of capital, the tariff-induced increase in current output at each date in the protected sector results in an increase in the growth rate of productivity on new machines through more rapid learning. The model in section 4 focuses on this dynamic trade-off. Since we are now essentially concerned with adjustment toward the long-run equilibrium path, our model, like most vintage capital models off the steady state, tends to get unmanageably complicated. In order to focus on the qualitative properties of the dynamic trade-off we adopt a simplifying partial equilibrium model with the (growing) wage rate and price of the capital good as exogenous and with learning as linear (or log-linear) in cumulated output. Comparing the time-paths of productivity, as given in fig. 8.1 in section 4, we show how protection in our model induces a higher level of average productivity in the protected sector, *after* some date. The length of the period for which productivity is depressed depends upon relative prices, rate of learning and the rate of saving. The concluding section (section 5) suggests some extensions of the models in this paper.

2. A Two-Sector Vintage-Capital Model

There are two sectors in the economy, the first producing machines used in both sectors and the other producing a consumable. In each sector we have fixed-coefficient production functions for machines of each vintage:

$$F_i(v, t) = \min\{a_i(v)I_i(v), b_i(v)L_i(v, t)\}, \quad i = 1, 2, \tag{1}$$

where $F_i(v, t)\,dv$ and $L_i(v, t)\,dv$ are the rates of output produced and labor employed, respectively, at time t on machines of vintage v ($v \leq t$) in the ith sector. In long-run equilibrium, without unemployed labor or capital, this is:

$$F_i(v, t) = a_i(v)I_i(v) = b_i(v)L_i(v, t), \quad i = 1, 2. \tag{2}$$

Total output of the ith sector is:

$$F_i(t) = \int_{t-T_i}^{t} F_i(v, t)\,dv, \quad i = 1, 2, \tag{3}$$

where $(t - T_i)$ is the vintage of the oldest machine in use. In the steady state, T_i is independent of t.

The capital good produced in sector 1 is the numéraire and $P(t)$ is the relative price of the consumer good output of sector 2. Perfect competition is assumed. If old machines cannot be traded, then a machine is scrapped when the wage bill for operating it exhausts the value of its output. Thus:

$$W(t) = b_1(t - T_1) = P(t)b_2(t - T_2), \tag{4}$$

where $W(t)$ is the wage rate at time t in terms of the numéraire

Technical progress consists of an improvement in the input–output coefficients. We assume that technical progress is Harrod-neutral (purely labor-augmenting) at a constant rate, g, in each sector, so that:

$$b_i(t) = b_i e^{gt}, \quad i = 1, 2, \tag{5}$$

$$a_i(t) = a_i, \quad i = 1, 2, \tag{6}$$

where the a_i and b_i are given constants. Entrepreneurs correctly expect the wage rate to grow at rate g. We assume that $P(t)$, the relative price of consumption, is a given constant world price.

For equilibrium in the capital market, the discounted stream of quasi-rents earned on a machine during its life must equal its cost of production. Thus, since r, the interest rate, is constant for steady-state growth in the clay–clay model:

$$
\begin{aligned}
1 &= \int_v^{v+T_1} a_1 \left(1 - \frac{W(t)}{b_1 e^{gv}} \right) e^{-r(t-v)} \, dt \\
&= \int_v^{v+T_1} a_1 \left(1 - e^{g(t-v-T_1)} \right) e^{-r(t-v)} \, dt \\
&= a_1 \left[\frac{(r-g) + g e^{-rT_1} - r e^{-gT_1}}{r(r-g)} \right],
\end{aligned} \tag{7}
$$

and

$$
\begin{aligned}
1 &= \int_v^{v+T_2} Pa_2 \left(1 - \frac{W(t)}{Pb_2 e^{gv}} \right) e^{-r(t-v)} \, dt \\
&= Pa_2 \left[\frac{(r-g) + g e^{-rT_2} - r e^{-gT_2}}{r(r-g)} \right].
\end{aligned} \tag{8}
$$

The steady-state values of T_1, T_2, and r are determined by eqs. (4), (7), and (8). Rewriting (4) as

$$P = \frac{b_1}{b_2} e^{g(T_2 - T_1)}, \tag{9}$$

we see that (7), (8), and (11) determine T_1, T_2, and r simultaneously. Bardhan (1970) shows that $T_1 > T_2$ as sector 1 is more capital-intensive than sector 2, and conversely [eqs. (7), (8), and (9) together show $a_1 b_2 / b_1 a_2 \lessgtr 1$ as $T_1 \gtrless T_2$].

For completeness, the steady-state distribution of the labor force across the sectors is given by the equilibrium savings equal investment (with s as the proportional savings rate) and full-employment conditions:

$$\int_{t-T_1}^{t} b_1 \, e^{gv} L_1(v, t) \, dv = s \int_{t-T_1}^{t} b_1 \, e^{gv} L_1(v, t) \, dv + s \int_{t-T_2}^{t} P b_2 \, e^{gv} L_2(v, t) \, dv, \tag{10}$$

and

$$L(t) = \int_{t-T_1}^{t} L_1(v, t) \, dv + \int_{t-T_2}^{t} L_2(v, t) \, dv. \tag{11}$$

Our assumption of an exogenous rate of saving makes it difficult to carry out full rigorous welfare comparisons of alternative policies. A comparison of optimal time-paths for a vintage-capital model with optimal saving would be the natural approach to addressing the welfare consequences of protection in a complete model. However, with optimal saving, complete specialization occurs in the steady state except for a particular choice of the social rate of discount in the small-country model. In a two-country model with the terms of trade endogenous, each country will completely specialize unless the social rates of discount are equal. An optimal saving model can be written out for the two-sector economy with vintage capital. While a solution for the optimal path is difficult to derive, an inspection of the conditions indicates that starting with any initial capital stock distributed across vintages and sectors, new machines will be added only to the sector in which the country completely specializes in the steady state, so that the labor force is shifted entirely toward that sector in a short time – as soon as the most modern machine initially in the other sector is economically unviable. Therefore, such a model does not allow a meaningful analysis of protection; a "putty–clay" model with optimal saving would, but the difficulties encountered with such a model are well known.

3. Effects of a Tariff Rate Increase

The effects of a tariff rate increase (or equivalent quota) on the long-run equilibrium values of T_1 and T_2 determine its effect on the average productivity of labor within each sector. Lengthening the steady-state economic life of capital adds machines of lower than average output–labor ratios to the stock of capital in use. In the steady state, the proportion of the labor force employed in each sector is constant and the distribution of labor over capital of different vintages within each sector depends only upon the growth rate of the labor force, so that average productivity declines with an increase in the economic life of capital in a sector.

We proceed by differentiating the system of eqs. (7)–(9) with respect to or after replacing P by $P(1 + \tau)$, for an ad valorem tariff. The resulting system of equations is:

$$0 = a_1 \frac{\partial \phi_1}{\partial T_1} \frac{dT_1}{d\tau} + a_1 \frac{\partial \phi_1}{\partial r} \frac{dr}{d\tau}, \tag{12}$$

$$0 = \left(a_2 \frac{\partial \phi_2}{\partial T_2} + g \frac{1}{p(1 + \tau)} \right) \frac{dT_2}{d\tau} + a_2 \frac{\partial \phi_1}{\partial r} \frac{dr}{d\tau}, \tag{13}$$

$$\frac{1}{g(1 + \tau)} = \frac{dT_2}{d\tau} - \frac{dT_1}{d\tau}, \tag{14}$$

where

$$\phi_i = \frac{(r - g) + g e^{-rT_i} - r e^{-gT_i}}{r(r - g)}, \quad i = 1, 2, \tag{15}$$

and

$$\frac{\partial \phi_i}{\partial T_i} = \left(\frac{g}{r - g} \right) (e^{-gT_i} - e^{-rT_i}) > 0, \quad \text{for} \quad T_i > 0, \tag{16}$$

$$\frac{\partial \phi_i}{\partial r} = \frac{-1}{r^2} \left(1 + \frac{g}{r - g} (1 + rT_i) e^{-rT_i} \right) + \frac{r e^{-gT_i} - g e^{-rT_i}}{r(r - g)^2} < 0, \quad \text{for} \quad r > g. \tag{17}$$

As a standard in such models we assume $r > g$ since the economy's savings rate is not yet high enough to take it beyond the "golden-rule" growth path.

Elimination of $dT_2/d\tau$ leaves the system:

$$\begin{bmatrix} a_1 \dfrac{\partial \phi_1}{\partial T_1} & a_1 \dfrac{\partial \phi_1}{\partial r} \\[2ex] a_2 \dfrac{\partial \phi_2}{\partial T_2} & a_2 \dfrac{\partial \phi_2}{\partial r} \end{bmatrix} \begin{bmatrix} dT_1/d\tau \\ dr/d\tau \end{bmatrix} = - \begin{bmatrix} 0 \\ \left[a_2 \dfrac{\partial \phi_2}{\partial T_2} + gP \right] \Big/ g(1 + \tau) \end{bmatrix}, \tag{18}$$

which is solved as:

$$\frac{dT_1}{d\tau} = \frac{1}{D} \left[\frac{a_2 \dfrac{\partial \phi_2}{\partial T_2} + \dfrac{g}{P}}{g(1 + \tau)} \right] \cdot a_1 \frac{\partial \phi_1}{\partial r}, \tag{19}$$

$$\frac{dr}{d\tau} = \frac{-1}{D} \left[\frac{a_2 \dfrac{\partial \phi_2}{\partial T_2} + \dfrac{g}{P}}{g(1+\tau)} \right] \cdot \left[a_1 \frac{\partial \phi_1}{\partial T_1} \right], \tag{20}$$

where

$$D = a_1 a_2 \left(\frac{\partial \phi_1}{\partial T_1} \frac{\partial \phi_2}{\partial r} - \frac{\partial \phi_1}{\partial r} \frac{\partial \phi_2}{\partial T_2} \right)$$

is the determinant of the matrix defined in (18). In the appendix this determinant is shown to be positive if sector 1 is more capital-intensive and negative if sector 2 is capital-intensive.

The change in the economic life of capital in the second sector is given by:

$$\frac{dT_2}{d\tau} = \frac{1}{D} \left[\frac{a_1 a_2 \dfrac{\partial \phi_1}{\partial T_1} \dfrac{\partial \phi_2}{\partial r} + a_1 \dfrac{1}{P} \dfrac{\partial \phi_1}{\partial r}}{g(1\tau)} \right]. \tag{21}$$

Therefore, each of these derivatives is negative if sector 1 is capital-intensive and positive if it is labor-intensive, so that protection of the capital-intensive sector causes a fall in average productivity within both sectors, a rise in the interest rate, and a fall in the wage rate relative to all other prices. Opposite conclusions follow for protection of the labor-intensive sector. Thus, Stolper–Samuelson-like conclusions are obtained, but the mechanism involved is different from the standard model where changes in the *intensive* margin take place through changes in the capital–labor ratio, whereas in our vintage model changes in the *extensive* margin through changes in economic life of machines bring about the result.

4. Infant-Industry Protection in the Vintage-Capital Model

The simple two-sector vintage-capital trade model can be modified to incorporate Harrod-neutral learning-by-doing by replacing the exogenously growing output–labor coefficients by increasing functions of cumulative sectoral output or investment. When only one sector is modified, a pattern of specialization will arise which depends upon the rate at which learning occurs and initial levels of productivity across sectors. Both this model and one in which learning takes place in all sectors are very difficult to analyze and involve too many variables to provide for a simple two-dimensional phase diagram.

Since our main purpose is to focus on the qualitative properties of a dynamic trade-off between the productivity-dampening effect of any lengthening of the economic life of capital and the effects of tariff-induced learning, we adopt a simplifying partial equilibrium model of learning-by-doing with a vintage stock of capital under the assumptions that the growing wage rate and price of capital are exogenous and learning is a linear, or log-linear, function of cumulative output. As before, technical progress will be Harrod-neutral.

The production function is given by:

$$q(v, t) = \min\{I(v), bQ(v)L(v, t)\}, \tag{22}$$

where $Q(v) = \int_0^v q(t)dt$ is cumulative output in the industry. Machines are retired when the wage bill for operating them exhausts the value of their output, or:

$$w\,e^{gt} = PbQ(t - T), \tag{23}$$

where $w(t) = w\,e^{gt}$ is the wage rate, P is the price of output, and T is the economic life of capital.

Output and labor use at time t are, respectively:

$$q(t) = \int_{t-T}^{t} bQ(v)L(v, t)\,dv \tag{24}$$

and

$$L(t) = \int_{t-T}^{t} L(v, t)\,dv. \tag{25}$$

Fixed proportions without excess capacity or unemployment imply:

$$I(v) = bQ(v)L(v, t), \tag{26}$$

and the investment equation assumed is:

$$sPq(t) = P_m(t)I(t). \tag{27}$$

Both of these are used to solve for $L(t)$:

$$L(t) = \left(s\frac{P}{bP_m}\right)[\log Q(t) - \log Q(t - T)]$$

$$= \left(s\frac{P}{bP_m}\right)\left[\log Q(t) - \log \frac{w\,e^{gt}}{Pb}\right],$$

letting $P_m(t) = P_m$ be constant.

To find the equation of motion for $q(t)$, we differentiate (23) and (24) with respect to time:

$$Pbq(t - T)\left(1 - \frac{dT}{dt}\right) = g(w\,e^{gt}) \tag{28}$$

$$\dot{q}(t) = b\left[Q(t)L(t,\,t) - Q(t-T)L(t-T,\,t)\left(1 - \frac{dT}{dt}\right)\right], \tag{29}$$

noting that fixed proportions imply that $dL(v,\,t)\,dt = 0$, unless a machine is retired. The investment equation (27) implies

$$bQ(t)L(t,\,t) = sPq(t)/P_m$$

and

$$bQ(t-T)L(t-T,\,t) = sPq(t-T)/P_m.$$

These equations and (28) can be substituted into (29) to obtain:

$$\dot{q}(t) = \frac{sP}{P_m}\left[q(t) - \frac{wg}{bP}e^{gt}\right], \tag{30}$$

which can be solved as:

$$q(t) = A\,e^{gt} + (q_0 - A)\exp\left(\frac{sP}{P_m}t\right), \tag{31}$$

where $q_0 \equiv q(0)$ and

$$A \equiv \frac{g(w/b)}{P - gP_m/s}.$$

The present value of quasi-rents earned on a machine cannot be less than its purchase price if investment is to take place at all in the industry. Thus,

$$P_m \leqq P\left[\frac{(r-g) + g\,e^{-rt} - r\,e^{-gt}}{r(r-g)}\right].$$

$$\leqq P/r$$

$$< P/g, \quad \text{for} \quad g \leqq r.$$

However, we will further assume that $P_m < s(P/g)$, so that $A > 0$ and that $q_0 > A$ [otherwise $q(t)$ would vanish in finite time].

The purpose of this exercise is to evaluate the effect on $q(t)/L(t)$ of an increase in P relative to w and P_m, i.e. evaluate:

$$\frac{d}{dP}\left[\frac{q(t)}{L(t)}\right].$$

We have:

$$\frac{dq(t)}{dP} = \left[\frac{A}{P - gP_m/s}\right] \cdot [e^{at} - e^{gt}] + (q_0 - A)\frac{a}{P}te^{at},$$

$$\frac{dL(t)}{dP} = \frac{s}{bP_m}\left[\log Q(t) - \log\frac{we^{gt}}{Pb}\right]$$

$$+ \frac{a}{b}\left[\frac{1}{P} + \frac{1}{Q(t)}\left\{\left(\frac{A}{P - gP_m/s}\right)\left(\frac{e^{at} - 1}{a} - \frac{e^{gt} - 1}{g}\right)\right.\right.$$

$$\left.\left. + \left(\frac{q_0 - A}{P}\right)te^{at} + \left(\frac{q_0 - A}{P}\right)\left(\frac{1 - e^{at}}{a}\right)\right\}\right],$$

where $a \equiv sP/P_m$. This leads to:

$$\left[L(t)\frac{dq(t)}{dP} - q(t)\frac{dL(t)}{dP}\right] = \left[\frac{s}{P_m}\frac{q_0 - A}{P}\right]\left[L(t) - \frac{q(t)}{bQ(t)}\right]te^{at}$$

$$+ \frac{q(t)}{bQ(t)}\left[\frac{q_0 - A}{P}\right][e^{at} - 1] + \left[\frac{A}{P - gP_m/s}\right](e^{at} - e^{gt})L(t) - \frac{s}{bP}[L(t)q(t) + q(t)]$$

$$- \frac{s}{b}\left[\frac{q(t)}{Q(t)}\right]\left[\left(\frac{A}{P - gP_m/s}\right)\left(\frac{e^{at}}{a} - \frac{e^{gt}}{g}\right) + \frac{A}{gP}\right]. \tag{32}$$

Evaluated at $t = 0$,

$$L(0)\frac{dq(0)}{dP} - q(0)\frac{dL(0)}{dP} = -\frac{sq_0}{bP_m}\left[L(0) + 1 + \frac{w/b}{AQ_0}\right] < 0.$$

However, there exists some $\hat{t}$ such that for all $t \geq \hat{t}$, $d(q/L)/dP > 0$, since the positive part of (32) increases as te^{at} and the negative part as e^{at} [note that if there are any old machines in use,

$$L(t) > q(t)/bQ(t)].$$

Average productivity can be written:

$$\frac{q(t)}{L(t)} = \frac{d/dt(Q(t))}{\frac{a}{b}\left[\log Q(t) - \log\left(\frac{we^{gt}}{bP}\right)\right]},$$

which increases asymptotically as $(1/t)\,e^{at}$, given our assumption that $a > g$.

These results are described graphically in Fig. 8.1, where the solid path is drawn for a lower relative price of output than the dotted path.

This exercise can be repeated with log-linear learning, resulting in more complex computations.

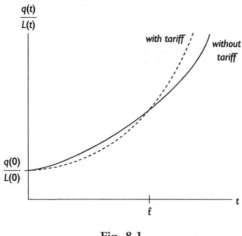

Fig. 8.1

The above demonstration shows that on account of the particular form learning takes, there are always eventual gains to improving the relative price of output of the learning industry in this model, even when protection initially lowers productivity by lengthening the economic life of capital. Whether or not protection is desirable thus depends crucially upon the length of time until productivity is improved (and, of course, upon the discount rate), which will vary depending upon the rate of growth of productivity in the rest of the economy, the rate at which learning occurs, and the savings rate.

5. Conclusion

Using a simple vintage-capital trade model, this paper shows that the effects of protection on average labor productivity vary with the relative capital-intensity of the protected sector. The direction of tariff-induced changes in the economic lives of machines and, consequently, the extent of adoption of new technical knowledge within industries depends upon whether or not the tariff raises the wage rate relative to the prices of outputs. Protection of the more capital-intensive sector causes a fall in labor productivity in both sectors, while imposition of a tariff on the output of the more labor-intensive sector increases productivity in each sector. These results may help to partially clarify why protection has appeared to encourage modernization of capital stocks within industries in some instances, while discouraging it in others.

The partial equilibrium analysis of learning-by-doing in a vintage-capital growth model demonstrates the possibility that even if protection increases the economic life of capital, average productivity gains may result eventually. In this case, a tariff initially reduces productivity, but greater volumes of output and investment create more rapid learning, ultimately leading to a higher growth path of productivity. These results are only suggestive, and the actual effect of infant protection of a capital-intensive industry will depend upon the functional form and rapidity of learning-by-doing in the industry.

We have extended our analysis of protection in this paper to a three-sector model, in which machines are sector-specific and non-traded. Suppose the two types of machines are produced jointly by labor alone under constant returns to scale, and all other assumptions of our model in section 2 are retained. The results differ in one respect from those of section 3: if the two sectors have fairly similar capital intensities and the responsiveness of output of different machine types to changes in their relative prices is small, then the protected sector experiences a fall in average productivity and the unprotected sector a rise in average productivity. That is, the pattern of relative capital intensities does not matter. If the capital intensities of the sectors are not too similar, or the responsiveness of machine outputs is large, the effects of protection are the same as for our model in section 3.

Another extension we have tried is to introduce in our vintage-capital model the taxation of quasi-rents with a depreciation allowance at a constant proportional rate. A natural alternative to tariff or quota protection in such models is the acceleration of the rate at which the capital stock is depreciated. The uniform acceleration of the depreciation allowance across both sectors increases average labor productivity within each sector and the wage rate. Acceleration of the depreciation allowance in the labor-intensive sector improves average productivity in the economy, while the same policy applied to the capital-intensive sector lowers average productivity in both sectors along with the wage rate.

Appendix

The determinant of the matrix defined in eq. (18) is:

$$D = a_2 \frac{\partial \phi_2}{\partial r} a_1 \frac{\partial \phi_1}{\partial T_1} - a_1 \frac{\partial \phi_1}{\partial r} a_2 \frac{\partial \phi_2}{\partial T_2}$$

$$= a_1 a_2 \frac{\partial \phi_2}{\partial r} \frac{\partial \phi_1}{\partial T_1} - a_1 a_2 \frac{\partial \phi_1}{\partial r} \frac{\partial \phi_2}{\partial T_2}.$$

To determine the sign of D, we note $\partial \phi_i / \partial T_i > 0$ and $\partial \phi_i / \partial r < 0$ for $T_i > 0$, and differentiate

$$\left(\frac{\partial \phi_i}{\partial r} \right) \Big/ \left(\frac{\partial \phi_i}{\partial T_i} \right)$$

with respect to T. The sign of this derivative is given by the sign of:

$$-\frac{\delta^2 \phi}{\partial r \partial T} \left(\frac{\partial \phi}{\partial T} \right) + \frac{\partial \phi}{\partial r} \left(\frac{\partial^2 \phi}{\partial T^2} \right).$$

$$\frac{\partial^2 \phi}{\partial T \partial r} = \frac{g e^{-gT}}{(r-g)^2} [(1 + (r-g)T) e^{-(r-g)T} - 1] < 0,$$

$$\frac{\partial^2 \phi}{\partial T^2} = \left(\frac{g}{r-g} \right) (r e^{-rT} - g e^{-gT}) < 0.$$

Since $\partial\phi/\partial r < 0$ and $\partial\phi/\partial T > 0$, we have that $-(\partial\phi/\partial r)/(\partial\phi/\partial T)$ is increasing in T. Therefore, $D \gtreqless 0$ as $T_1 \gtreqless T_2$.

Notes

*   Comments on an earlier draft by a referee and partial research support by the National Science Foundation under Grant no. SES-7804022 are gratefully acknowledged.
1.   The properties of a "clay–clay" growth model have been analyzed by Solow, Tobin, von Weizsäcker and Yaari (1966).

References

Bardhan, P., 1970, Economic growth, development and foreign trade: A study in pure theory (John Wiley, Inc., New York).

Solow, R., J. Tobin, C. von Weizsäcker and M. Yaari, 1966, Neoclassical growth with fixed factor proportions, Review of Economic Studies 33, 79–115.

Temin, P., 1966, The relative decline of the British steel industry, 1880–1913, in: H. Rosovsky, ed., The industrialization of two systems (Harvard University Press, Cambridge, Mass.).

Williamson, J., 1971, Optimal replacement of capital goods: The early New England and British textile firm, Journal of Political Economy 79, 1320–1324.

Chapter 9

Endogenous Growth Theory in a Vintage Capital Model[1]

I. Introduction

In the development of the endogenous growth models over the last decade, the idea of a continual introduction of new inputs as an embodiment of technological progress has played a central role. In particular, the original formulations by Ethier (1982) and Romer (1990) in terms of an expanding variety of intermediate goods contributing to final good productivity have been very popular. In the "old" growth theory literature, the vintage capital models also carried the idea of a continual introduction of new inputs, with the latest technology embodied in the newest machine that comes into operation. Some of the early formulations of this type of models are associated with Johansen (1959), Solow (1962), Phelps (1963) and Solow, Tobin, von Weizsäcker, and Yaari (1966).[2] However, in all these vintage models, the ultimate source of technical progress embodied in the latest machine was exogenous; in particular, the steady-state growth rate was not amenable to policy influence. In contrast, in the more recent models, growth is driven by endogenous processes of research and development (R & D) or learning, and these processes can be influenced by policy. Furthermore, most of the earlier models assumed competitive markets, whereas growth theory in the 1990's has formalized endogenous technical progress in terms of a tractable imperfect-competition framework, in which temporary monopoly power sometimes acts as a motivating force for private innovators and there are scale economies.

On the other hand, in many of the recent models – for example, in that of Romer (1990) – technical progress works through a horizontal expansion of the range of inputs, and the wider the range the better for productivity. In these models, the old abacus goes on being utilized for calculation jobs side by side with the latest desktop computer. In most of the vintage models, as new inputs arrive, some of the old varieties are no longer profitable to use, and a central focus of these models was the endogenous obsolescence of machines.

In this case the economic life of machines becomes an important determinant of productivity. Different countries with different wage rates (that are paid to operators of machines) will thus have a different economic life of machines, even if "best-practice" technology (or technology on the newest machine) is the same every-where.[3] One of the earliest economists to have a serious empirical treatment of this issue was Salter (1960). To quote him for an example:

> In fact there is some evidence to suggest that one of the chief reasons for Anglo-American productivity differences lies in standards of obsolescence. It is a common theme in Productivity Mission Reports that the productivity of the best plants in the United Kingdom is comparable with that of the best plants in the United States, and that the difference lies in a much higher proportion of plants employing outmoded methods in the United Kingdom – a much greater "tail" of low-productivity plants. Such a situation is consistent with a higher standard of obsolescence in the United States which follows from a higher level of real wages. (pp. 72–73)

Clearly, productivity differences on such grounds will be much sharper between rich and poor countries.

Of course, obsolescence of inputs is captured in part of the recent growth litera-ture, most notably in the Schumpeterian models of Aghion and Howitt (1998, chapter 2, for their latest version) and Segerstrom *et al.* (1990), or the related quality ladder models of Grossman and Helpman (1991). But in those models obsolescence of inputs takes place in an extreme fashion: the state-of-the-art pro-duct completely and instantaneously displaces all the old varieties.[4] So the richness of the vintage models in this respect, with some old inputs being scrapped while some others coexisting with the latest variety, is missing in the recent literature, and accordingly the differential productivity effects of the different length of the "tail" that Salter talks about is not analyzed.

In this paper we combine this aspect of richness of the old vintage models with endogeneity of technical progress and monopolistic competition and dynamic eco-nomies of scale (aspects in which the recent models are richer). In particular, we show how the endogenously determined economic life of a machine, denoted by T in our model, affects not just the level of productivity, as in the old vintage models, but also the steady-state growth rate. Policies can affect the equilibrium value of T (for example, those influencing the gross savings rate in the economy, accelerated depreciation allowance in tax laws, etc.), and that will have an effect on the long-run growth rate. We also present a two-sector extension of the basic model where we show that trade policy, by influencing the relative price of goods, can affect T and thus the long-run growth rate of a trading economy.[5]

While our model is abstract, oversimplified and extremely limited in applicability, it may not be entirely out of place to link the results with some of the issues that have come up in the empirical and policy literature on comparative economic growth and economic history. For example, in comparisons of fast economic growth in East

Asia with relative stagnation in Latin America in recent history, it is commonplace to point to the significant differences in the rates of saving in the two areas. Our model may suggest an additional dimension of the effects of higher saving and investment on the growth rate in terms of modernization of the capital stock. Our result is also consistent with the significant correlation observed by de Long and Summers (1991) between equipment investment and growth. We may also venture to suggest that embodied technical progress in new machines may have some implications for the widely noted and remarkable empirical work of Young (1995) which shows that factor accumulation largely explains the high growth in East Asia. If a high rate of capital accumulation also leads to a modernization of the capital stock and if embodiment matters, it may be statistically difficult to disentangle the effects of factor accumulation from those of technical progress. For a group of seven OECD countries over the last century Wolff (1991) shows that catch-up in total factor productivity is positively associated with capital accumulation and he considers the embodiment effect as one of the important elements in this association. Consistent with our model, Wolff shows that the average age of capital stock in these seven countries for the hundred years since 1880 moves inversely with changes in the rate of growth of the capital stock.

In the economic history literature, the relationship between trade policy and modernization of capital stock has sometimes been commented upon. For example, Williamson (1971) has emphasized the importance of highly protective tariffs in early nineteenth-century United States in encouraging a faster scrapping of capital in favor of technologically superior equipment in the textile industry and thus fostering rapid productivity growth in that industry. Temin (1966), in interpreting the relative decline of the British steel industry in the period from the 1880's to World War I, has referred to the tariff-induced adoption of superior capital equipment in the United States and Germany. For all its limitations, our two-sector model may provide a simple framework for analyzing such questions of the impact of trade policy on the economic life of capital and thus on the rate of growth, even though our particular results about the effects of protection may be model-specific.

The plan of the rest of the paper is as follows. In section II we enumerate the basic vintage capital model with endogenous technical progress and economies of scale, both external and internal, in the production of capital goods. In section III we derive some of the comparative-dynamic results. In section IV we present a two-sector extension of the basic model to focus on the effect of trade policy and relative price changes. Section V provides some conclusions.

II. The Basic Model

Let us consider an economy in which a single final good is produced, with a fixed-coefficient production function, using labor and capital goods of different vintages.[6] If factors of production are fully employed, the final good is produced with the following production function:

$$\Upsilon(v,\, t) = a(v)\, K(v) = b(v)\, L_\Upsilon(v,\, t) \tag{1}$$

where $\Upsilon(v,\, t)$ is output of the final good produced at time t using capital goods of vintage v, $L_\Upsilon(v,\, t)$ is labor used to produce that output, and $K(v)$ is the composite of capital goods of vintage v.

Since the final good can be produced using capital goods of different vintages, total production in the final good sector at time t, $\Upsilon(t)$, is given by

$$\Upsilon(t) = \int_{t-T}^{t} \Upsilon(v,\, t)\, dv \tag{2}$$

where $t - T$ is the vintage of the oldest machines in use, and T is the economic life of the machines.

In this economy, at any time t, $n(v)$ differentiated capital goods are produced by $n(v)$ monopolistic competitive firms, each of them producing $I_i(v)$ units of capital good i of vintage v. The composite of those capital goods of vintage v, $K(v)$, is

$$K(v) = \left[\int_{0}^{n(v)} I_i(v)^\alpha \, di \right]^{\frac{1}{\alpha}} \quad 0 < \alpha < 1 \tag{3}$$

where $I_i(v)$ stands for units of capital good i of vintage v, and $n(v)$ is the number of differentiated capital goods of vintage v.

In the production of these capital goods we assume increasing returns to scale, both external and internal; this has family resemblance to the internal and external scale economies assumed in the production, through the R & D process, of differentiated capital goods in recent growth models, like that of Romer (1990). To produce each capital good of vintage v, $F/K_H(v)$ units of labor has to be invested first, where $K_H(v)$ is the stock of general knowledge capital available at the moment of producing the new machines of vintage v. Once the fixed cost in terms of labor is invested, it is possible to produce $\beta(S(v))$ units of $I_i(v)$ with one unit of labor, where $S(v)$ is the quality index of machines of vintage v. This implies that

$$I_i(v) = \beta(S(v))\, L_i(v) \tag{4}$$

That quality index increases as new machines are produced, according to the following equation

$$\dot{S}(v) = n(v)\, I(v) \tag{5}$$

where, as we shall see later, $I(v) = I_i(v)$ for all i. Thus, we have internal scale economies through the fixed cost and external scale economies through learning effects. The learning effect operates both on reducing the fixed cost as general knowledge capital improves and on the variable cost through the cumulated quality index, $S(v)$. This index has a learning effect akin to that of the "serial number of machines" used in Arrow's (1962) original learning by doing model.

With these assumptions, the variable cost of producing capital goods of vintage v is $w(t) L_i(v)$, where $w(t)$ is the wage rate at time t. Using (4), we can write the marginal cost of producing capital good i of vintage v at time t, for all i, as

$$MC(v, t) = \frac{w(t)}{\beta(S(v))} \tag{6}$$

Because of the symmetric way in which each capital good i of a given vintage v enters in the sub-production function (equation (3)) and also because the cost of producing each capital good of a given vintage is the same, equal quantity of the capital goods of the same vintage are produced, that is, $I_i(v) = I(v)$ for all i. Then, from (3) it is easy to obtain that

$$K(v) = I(v) n(v)^{\frac{1}{\alpha}} \tag{7}$$

Let $X(v) = \int_0^{n(v)} I_i(v)\, di$ be the aggregate demand for capital goods of vintage v. Since $I_i(v) = I(v)$ for all i, then

$$X(v) = n(v) I(v) \tag{8}$$

Using equation (8), equation (7) can be rewritten as follows:

$$K(v) = N(V)^{(1-\alpha)/\alpha} X(V) \tag{9}$$

Let us assume that in the final good sector technological progress is purely labor-augmenting. Additionally, to simplify the model's solution, we are going to assume that labor productivity in the production of final goods is also a function of past experience and depends on the quality index, that is,

$$b(v) = b(S(v)) \tag{10}$$

and

$$a(v) = a \tag{11}$$

Firms in the final good sector are competitive and maximize profits. They maximize $\Pi_f(t) = P_Y(t) \int_{t-T}^{t} Y(v, t)\, dv - \int_{t-T}^{t} w(t) L_Y(v, t)\, dv - \int_{t-T}^{t} [\int_0^{n(v)} R_i(v, t) I_i(v)\, di]\, dv$, where $P_Y(t)$ is the price of the final good, and $R_i(v, t)$ is the price of the capital good i of vintage v, at time t. Taking the price of the final good as the numéraire, so that this price is unity, the first order conditions of profit maximization are:

$$b(S(v)) = w(t) \tag{12}$$

$$I_i(v) = \left[\frac{aK(v)^{1-\alpha}}{R_i(v, t)} \right]^{\frac{1}{1-\alpha}} \tag{13}$$

In the capital good sectors, to maximize profits, each monopolistic competitive firm equates marginal revenue to marginal cost. Marginal revenue is equal to $MR_i(v, t) = (1 - 1/\eta)R_i(v, t)$, where η is the price elasticity of the demand for $I_i(v)$. From equation (13) we have that $\eta = 1/(1 - \alpha)$. Therefore, $MR_i(v, t) = \alpha R_i(v, t)$, whereas the marginal cost is given by equation (6). Thus, each firm in the capital good sector maximizes profits setting $\alpha R_i(v, t) = w(t)/\beta(S(v))$, which implies that[7]

$$R_i(v, t) = \frac{w(t)}{\alpha\beta(S(v))} \tag{14}$$

In the final good sector, a machine is scrapped when the wage bill paid to operate it exhausts the value of total output.[8] Then, from equation (1) the following scrapping condition is obtained

$$b(t - T) = b(S(t - T)) = w(t) \tag{15}$$

Let $P_k(v, t)$ be the price of the composite of capital goods $K(v)$. Then the following relationship must hold: $P_k(v, t)K(v) = \int_0^{n(v)} R_i(v, t) I_i(v)\, di$. But since $I_i(v) = I(v)$ and $R_i(v, t) = R(v, t)$ for all i, from this last relationship we obtain

$$P_k(v, t)K(v) = n(v)R(v, t)I(v) \tag{16}$$

Combining equations (7) and (16), the price of the composite of capital goods is determined by

$$P_k(v, t) = R(v, t)\,n(v)^{\frac{\alpha-1}{\alpha}} \tag{17}$$

In the final good sector, wages plus quasi-rents must exhaust the value of output, that is,

$$Y(v, t) = L_Y(v, t)w(t) + K(v)\rho_k(v, t) \tag{18}$$

where $\rho_k(v, t)$ is the quasi-rents of the composite of capital goods of vintage v at time t. Using equations (1), (10), (11) and (15), from equation (18) we find that the quasirents are given by

$$\rho_k(v, t) = a\left[1 - \frac{b(S(t - T))}{b(S(v))}\right] \tag{19}$$

In equilibrium, the price at time t of the composite of capital goods $K(v)$ must be equal to the present value of the expected quasi-rents, discounted at the market rate of interest, $r(t)$. Since $P_k(v, t)$ is the price of $K(v)$ at time t, then

$$P_k(v, t) = \int_t^T \rho_K(v, u)\, e^{-\int_t^u r(z)dz}\, du \tag{20}$$

As $v = t$, equation (20) gives $P_k(t, t)$, which is the market price of the composite of capital goods at the moment of their construction. Since in steady-state the interest rate, r, is constant, setting $v = t$ equation (20) becomes

$$P_k(t, t) = \int_t^{t+T} \rho_k(t, u)\, e^{-r(u-t)}\, du \tag{21}$$

Labor market equilibrium requires that the supply of labor at time t be equal to the sum of labor used to produce final goods and capital goods. Assuming that labor supply is constant and equals L, this implies that

$$L = L_\Upsilon(t) + \int_{t-T}^t n(v)L_i(v)\, dv + F \tag{22}$$

where $L_\Upsilon(t)$ is labor used to produce final goods, and $\int_{t-T}^t n(v)L_i(v)\, dv$ is labor used to produce capital goods. Since $F/K_H(v)$ units of labor are required to develop capital goods, and since to obtain a simpler solution we are assuming that the fixed costs are paid each period, at time t, $\int_{t-T}^t n(v)F/K_H(v)\, dv$ is the amount of labor devoted to research and development. Let us now suppose that the stock of capital knowledge is proportional to the economy's cumulative experience in research and development. With that assumption and by an appropriate choice of units, the factor of proportionality may be set to one, so that $K_H(v) = n(v)T$.[9] Therefore, at time t, labor employed in the development of new capital goods is given by $\int_{t-T}^t n(v)F/K_H(v)dv = F$, which is the third term of the right-hand side of equation (22).

Labor employed in the production of final goods is equal to $L_\Upsilon(t) = \int_{t-T}^t L_\Upsilon(v, t)\, dv$. But from equation (1) we have that $L_\Upsilon(v, t) = a(v)K(v)/b(v)$, and since from (7), (8), and (11) we know that $K(v) = I(v)n^{1/\alpha}$, $X(v) = n(v)I(v)$, and $a(v) = a$, then $L_\Upsilon(t) = \int_{t-T}^t n^{(1-\alpha)/\alpha}X(v)/b(v)\, dv$. Therefore, using this last expression together with equations (4) and (8), the labor market equilibrium condition becomes

$$L = a\int_{t-T}^t n(v)^{\frac{1-\alpha}{\alpha}}\frac{X(v)}{b(S(v))}\, dv + \int_{t-T}^t \frac{X(v)}{B(S(v))}\, dv + F \tag{23}$$

The operative profits at time t of a typical firm that produces capital good i of vintage v are equal to $\Pi(v, t) = R(v, t)I(v) - w(t)L_i(v)$. But since from (4) we know that $L_i(v) = I(v)/\beta(S(v))$, then $\Pi(v, t) = [R(v, t) - w(t)/\beta(S(v))]I(v)$. Using equation (14), this last expression can be rewritten as $\Pi(v, t) = (1 - \alpha)R(v, t)I(v)$.

There is free entry in the capital good sectors. Therefore, firms in these sectors are going to enter until the operative profits are equal to the entry costs, that is, until $\Pi(v, t) = (1 - \alpha)R(v, t)I(v) = w(t)F/n(v)T$.[10] Recalling that $I(v) = X(v)/n(v)$, and using (14), the following zero-profit condition is obtained

$$X(v) = \frac{\alpha}{(1 - \alpha)}\beta(S(v))\frac{F}{T} \tag{24}$$

To close the model it remains to specify the equilibrium in the final good sector. To this end, let us assume that consumers save a constant fraction, s, of their income,[11] so that total investment at time t, $I_T(t)$, is given by

$$I_T(t) = sQ_T(t) \tag{25}$$

where $Q_T(t)$ is the economy's income (or total output).

III. Comparative Dynamics

Having specified the basic equations of the model, in this section we are going to show how the economic life of the machines, denoted by T, and the growth rate of the economy are jointly determined.

To simplify the model's solution, let us now assume that $\beta(S(v)) = \beta S(v)$, and $b(S(v)) = bS(v)$, where β and b are positive constants. Since from (8) we know that $X(v) = n(v)I(v)$, equation (5) implies that the quality index, S, accumulates according to $dS(v)/dt = n(v)I(v) = X(v)$, which in turn implies that

$$\frac{\dot{S}(v)}{S(v)} = \frac{I(v)n(v)}{S(v)} = \frac{X(v)}{S(v)} \tag{26}$$

Substituting equation (24) in (26), and then integrating both sides of the resulting equation, it is obtained that $\beta(S(v)) = \beta e^{\lambda v}$ and $b(S(v)) = be^{\lambda v}$, where $\lambda = \beta \alpha F (1 - \alpha)T$. With these results, equation (19) becomes

$$\rho_k(v, t) = a[1 - e^{\lambda(t-T-v)}] \tag{27}$$

Substituting equation (27) in (21) and then integrating, after some algebraic manipulations, we get that the price of the composite of capital goods at the moment of their construction is equal to

$$P_K(t, t) = a\left[\frac{(r - \lambda) - r\,e^{-\lambda T} + \lambda\,e^{-rT}}{r(r - \lambda)}\right] \tag{28}$$

From equation (17) we have that as $v = t$, $n(v = t)^{(1-\alpha)/\alpha} = R(t, t)/P_k(t, t)$ and from (14) we know that $R(t, t) = w(t)/\alpha\beta(S(t))$. Therefore, $n(v = t)^{(1-\alpha)/\alpha} = w(t)/[\alpha\beta(S(t))P_k(t, t)]$. Since $\beta(S(v)) = \beta e^{\lambda v}$, substituting equation (28) in this last expression, for the case in which $v = t$, and using the scrapping condition, equation (15), it is obtained that the number of differentiated capital goods of vintage v, when they are first produced, that is, as $v = t$, is given by

$$n(v)^{\frac{1-\alpha}{\alpha}} = \frac{b\,e^{-\left[\beta\frac{\alpha}{1-\alpha}F\right]}}{\beta a\alpha} \frac{r(r - \lambda)}{[(r - \lambda) - r\,e^{-\lambda T} + \lambda\,e^{-rT}]} \tag{29}$$

Equation (29) implies that if the rate of interest and the economic life of the machines are constants, the number of differentiated capital goods is the same for all vintages.[12] Replacing equation (24) in the resource constraint equation (23), after integrating we get

$$L = \frac{F}{(1-\alpha)} \left[\frac{\beta \alpha a n^{\frac{1-\alpha}{\alpha}}}{b} + 1 \right] \tag{30}$$

To be able to solve the model, it remains to determine the economy's income. To do so, let us define the value of the economy's stock of capital, $K_T(t)$, as follows:

$$K_T(t) = \int_{t-T}^{t} n(v) R(v, t) I(v) \, dv = \int_{t-T}^{t} P_k(v, t) K(v) \, dv \tag{31}$$

Differentiating this last equation with respect to time we obtain that

$$K_T(t) = K(t) P_k(t, t) + \int_{t-T}^{t} \dot{K}(v) P_k(v, t) \, dv + \int_{t-T}^{t} K(v) \dot{P}_k(v, t) \, dv \tag{32}$$

But $K(t) P_k(v, t) = n(v = t) R(t, t) I(t)$ is the economy's gross investment at time t, $I_T(t)$, and since $dK(v)/dt = 0$, equation (32) becomes

$$\dot{K}_T(t) = I_T(t) + \int_{t-T}^{t} K(v) \dot{P}_k(v, t) \, dv \tag{33}$$

In turn, if we differentiate equation (20) with respect to time we find that

$$\frac{\rho_K(v, t)}{P_K(v, t)} + \frac{\dot{P}_K(v, t)}{P_K(v, t)} = r \tag{34}$$

which implies that $dP_k(v, t)/dt = rP_k(v, t) - \rho_k(v, t)$. Substituting this expression in equation (33) we have that

$$\dot{K}_T(t) = I_T(t) + rK_T(t) - \int_{t-T}^{t} K(v) \rho_k(v, t) \, dv \tag{35}$$

Equation (35) can be rewritten as follows

$$I_T(t) - \dot{K}_T(t) = \int_{t-T}^{t} K(v) \rho_k(v, t) \, dv - rK_T(t) \tag{36}$$

This last equation states that gross investment, $I_T(t)$, minus net investment, $dK_T(t)$ dt, is equal to gross quasi-rents, $\int_{t-T}^{t} K(v) \rho_k(v, t) dv$, minus net profits, $rK_T(t)$. Both terms of equation (36) can be identified as "true depreciation." Since we are ignoring physical depreciation, as in Solow, Tobin, von Weizsäcker and Yaari (1966), only "obsolescence" of the machines accounts for "true depreciation." Knowing that, the economy's GDP, from the income side, must be equal to wages plus capitalists' gross income, which in turn must be equal to net profits plus "true depreciation," that is, capitalists' income is equal to $rK_T(t) + I_T(t) - dK_T(t)/dt$. This implies, using equation (36), that GDP from the income side, $Q_T(t)$, is given by

$$Q_T(t) = w(t)L + \int_{t-T}^{t} K(v)\rho_k(v,\, t)\, dv \tag{37}$$

where, as was mentioned before, L is the amount of labor available in the economy. Then, substituting equations (9) and (27) in (37), and then using (24), after integrating, the following equation is obtained

$$Q_T(t) = w(t)L + a n^{\frac{1-\alpha}{\alpha}} e^{\lambda t} [1 - e^{-\lambda T}] - a \frac{\alpha}{1-\alpha} \beta F n^{\frac{1-\alpha}{\alpha}} e^{\lambda(t-T)} \tag{38}$$

In turn, total investment at time t, $I_T(t) = n(v = t)R(t,\, t)I(t)$. But $n(v = t)I(t) = X(t)$, and from equations (14) and (24) we know that $R(t,\, t) = w(t)/\alpha\beta(S(t))$ and $X(t) = \alpha\beta(S(t))F/(1 - \alpha)T$, which implies that $I_T = w(t)F/(1 - \alpha)T$. Replacing equation (15) in this last expression, we obtain that

$$I_T(t) = \frac{1}{(1-\alpha)} \frac{bFe^{\lambda(t-T)}}{T} \tag{39}$$

And, finally, replacing equations (38) and (39) in equation (25), after some algebraic manipulations, we get that

$$\frac{1}{(1-\alpha)} b \frac{F}{T} = s\left[bL + a n^{\frac{1-\alpha}{\alpha}} [e^{\lambda T} - 1] - a \frac{\alpha}{1-\alpha} \beta F n^{\frac{1-\alpha}{\alpha}} \right] \tag{40}$$

The economy can be described by a system of three equations ((29), (30) and (40)) with three unknowns: the number of differentiated capital goods of a given vintage, n, the rate of interest, r, and the economic life of the machines, T. Combining those three equations, the following expression can be obtained, through which the economic life of the machines, T, is determined

$$\left[(1-\alpha)\frac{L}{F} - 1 \right] = \frac{\alpha\beta\left[\dfrac{1}{1-\alpha}\dfrac{F}{T} - sL \right]}{s\left[e^{\beta\frac{\alpha}{1-\alpha}F} - 1 - \dfrac{\alpha}{1-\alpha}\beta F \right]} \tag{41}$$

Equation (41) can be solved graphically in a plane in which the left- and right-hand side of that equation are measured along the vertical axis, and T is measured

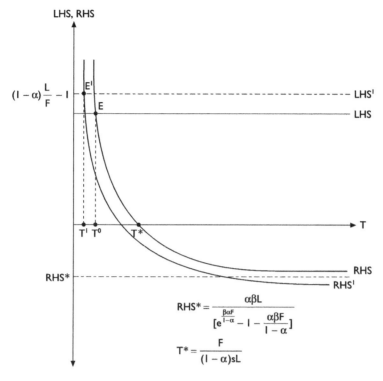

$$RHS^* = \frac{\alpha\beta L}{[e^{\frac{\beta\alpha F}{1-\alpha}} - 1 - \frac{\alpha\beta F}{1-\alpha}]}$$

$$T^* = \frac{F}{(1-\alpha)sL}$$

Fig. 9.1

along the horizontal axis. As shown in figure 9.1, in that plane the LHS schedule is represented by an horizontal line. In turn, the RHS schedule tends to infinity as T approaches zero, and tends to $- \alpha\beta L/[e^{\beta\alpha F/(1-\alpha)} - 1 - \alpha\beta F/(1-\alpha)]$ as T tends to infinity. Therefore, in figure 9.1, the RHS can be represented by a downward-sloping curve, which intersects the horizontal axis as $T = F/[(1-\alpha)sL]$. The economic life of the machines, T, is determined at the intersection point of both schedules, point E. As the labor force, L, increases, the LHS curve would shift upwards, to LHS', whereas the RHS curve would shift downwards, to RHS'. Therefore, in the new equilibrium point, point E', the economic life of the machines, T, is smaller.

Recalling that $w(t) = be^{\lambda(t-T)}$, from equation (38) it is easy to see that the growth rate of income, $Q_T(t)$ is equal to $\lambda = \beta\alpha F/(1-\alpha)T$. Therefore, this vintage capital model predicts that as the labor force, L, increases, the economic life of the machines, T, decreases and the rate of growth of the economy rises. This growth effect of a larger labor force is similar to the size or scale effect noted in the new growth literature.

Figure 9.2 illustrates the impact of an increase of the saving rate on T. In that figure, as the saving rate, s, increases, the LHS curve would remain unchanged, but the RHS schedule would shift downwards, to RHS'. Thus, in this case, also in the new intersection point, E', the economic life of the machines is smaller and consequently the growth rate of income increases. Again, this growth-promoting effect of higher saving rates is similar to that obtained in the new growth models.

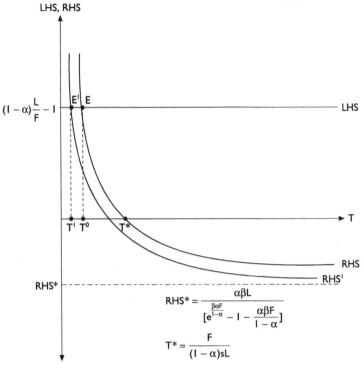

Fig. 9.2

While both of these results are comparable to those obtained in other growth models, in this vintage capital model both the size effect of a larger labor force and higher savings rates reduce the time of profitable operability of machines, and thus modernize the economy's stock of capital sooner, whereby the productivity of the economy grows faster.

IV. The Two-Sector Extension

In this section we are going to analyze how trade policies, by influencing the relative price of goods, can affect the economic life of the machines and thus the long-run rate of growth of the economy.

To this end, let us now consider an economy in which two final goods are produced: good Y and good Z. For simplification, good Z is produced using only labor, whereas good Y is produced using labor and capital goods of different vintages. The production function used to produce good Y is the same as in section II, and is given by equation (1). Thus, equations (1) to (21) of the previous section remain unaltered and describe the production side of the capital intensive sector. In this two-sector economy, the price of good Y is taken as the numéraire. On the other hand, output in sector Z, the labor intensive one, is produced using labor as the only variable factor of production, which is given by

$$Z(t) = A(t)L_Z(t)^{\Upsilon}N^{1-\Upsilon} \qquad \Upsilon < 1 \tag{42}$$

where $Z(t)$ is output of good Z, $L_Z(t)$ is labor employed in the production of good Z, $A(t)$ is a productivity parameter, and N is the fixed amount of land available in the economy.

With this production function, profit maximization in sector Z implies that

$$\Upsilon P_Z(t)\frac{Z(t)}{L_Z(t)} = w(t) \tag{43}$$

where $P_Z(t)$ is the relative price of good Z at time t. Since it is assumed that labor market is competitive, equations (15) and (43) imply that

$$b(t - T) = bS(t - T) = \Upsilon P_Z(t)\frac{Z(t)}{L_Z(t)} = w(t) \tag{44}$$

In turn, labor market equilibrium requires that the supply of labor, L, be equal to the sum of labor used to produce both final goods and capital goods, that is,

$$L = L_{\Upsilon}(t) + \int_{t-T}^{t} n(v)L_i(v)\,dv + F + L_Z(t) \tag{45}$$

where $L_{\Upsilon}(t)$ and $L_Z(t)$ stand for labor employed in the production of final goods Y and Z, respectively, and as was explained in section II, $\int_{t-T}^{t} n(v)L_i(v)\,dv$ is labor used to produce capital goods, and F is labor devoted to R & D.

Following the same procedure as in the previous section (see equation (23), (24) and from (26) to (29)), equation (45) becomes

$$L = \frac{F}{(1-\alpha)}\left[\frac{\beta\alpha an^{\frac{1-\alpha}{\alpha}}}{b} + 1 + \frac{(1-\alpha)}{F}L_Z(t)\right] \tag{46}$$

Then, let us assume that it is the case of a two-sector small open economy in which both final goods can be traded internationally. In the absence of barriers to trade, and under the assumption that the economy is small, the "law of one price" applies, and consequently the relative price of the labor intensive good (Z) is determined in the world economy and is taken as given by the small open economy. From equation (44), this implies that $P_z(t)$ is given by

$$P_Z = P_Z^* = \frac{bS(t-T)L_Z(t)}{\Upsilon Z(t)} \tag{47}$$

To close the model we need to specify the equilibrium in the final good sectors. Let us assume that consumers spend a constant fraction of their income on the consumption of the two final goods, that is,

$$C_Y(t) = c_1 Q_T(t) \tag{48}$$

$$P_Z(t)C_Z(t) = c_2 Q_T(t) \tag{49}$$

where c_1 and c_2 are the fractions of income that are spent on the consumption of good Y and good Z, respectively, and as before $Q_T(t)$ is the economy's income (or total output). In this case also the economy's income, $Q_T(t)$, is obtained adding labor income and capitalists' income, as was done in section II, and is given by equation (38).

Also in this small open economy, at any time t, each household devotes its income to consume the homogeneous final goods or to save. Therefore, the equilibrium in the product markets requires that total income be equal to total expenditure, that is,

$$C_Y(t) + P_Z(t)C_Z(t) + I_T(t) = Q_T(t) \tag{50}$$

where, $I_T(t)$ is total investment at time t. Implicitly, in equation (50) it is assumed that trade is balanced, so that $NX_T(t) = 0$, where NX_T stand, for net exports. This implies that

$$NX_T(t) = NX_Y(t) + P_Z(t) NX_Z(t) = 0 \tag{51}$$

where $NX_Y(t)$ and $NX_Z(t)$ stand for net exports of good Y and good Z, at time t, respectively.

Substituting equations (48) and (49) in (50) we have that

$$I_T(t) = (1 - c_1 - c_2) Q_T(t) = s Q_T(t) \tag{52}$$

where s is the saving rate, and $I_T(t) = n(v = t)R(t, t)I(t)$ is gross total investment at time t, which is given by equation (39). Replacing equations (38) and (39) in equation (52), after some algebraic manipulations, we get that

$$\frac{b}{(1-\alpha)} \frac{F}{T} = s \left[bL + an^{\frac{1-\alpha}{\alpha}} [e^{\lambda T} - 1] - a \frac{\alpha}{1-\alpha} \beta F n^{\frac{1-\alpha}{\alpha}} \right] \tag{53}$$

Since it is the case of a small open economy, in sector Z total consumption of good Z plus net exports of that good must equal total output, that is, $C_Z(t) + NX_Z(t) = Z(t) = A(t)L_Z(t)^Y N^{1-Y}$. From equation (49) we know that $P_Z(t)C_Z(t) = c_2 Q_T(t)$, which implies that $c_2 Q_T(t) + P_Z(t) NX_Z(t) = P_Z(t)Z(t) = P_Z(t)A(t)L_Z(t)^Y N^{1-Y}$. But from equation (44) we know that $w(t) = Y P_Z(t) Z(t)/L_Z(t)$. Using these expressions, we obtain that

$$L_Z(t) = \frac{Y[c_2 Q_T(t) + P_Z(t)NX_Z(t)]}{w(t)} \tag{54}$$

Using equation (38), and since $w(t) = b e^{\lambda(t-T)}$, where $\lambda = \beta \alpha F/(1 - \alpha)T$, labor employed in the production of final good Z can be rewritten as follows

$$L_Z(t) = \Upsilon c_2 \left[L + \frac{an^{\frac{1-\alpha}{\alpha}}}{b}[e^{\lambda T} - 1] - a\frac{\alpha}{1-\alpha}\frac{\beta F}{b}n^{\frac{1-\alpha}{\alpha}} \right] + \frac{\Upsilon P_Z(t)NX_Z(t)}{be^{\lambda(t-T)}} \tag{55}$$

If in steady-state technical progress in sector Z grows at the same rate as that of in sector Y, that is, if $A(t) = A_0 e^{\lambda t}$, where A_0 is a constant, from equations (29), (46), (47), (53) and (55), the following relationship can be obtained, through which the economic life of capital is determined

$$(1-\alpha)\frac{L}{F} - 1 - \frac{(1-\alpha)N}{F}\left[\Upsilon P_Z A_0 e^{\beta\frac{\alpha}{1-\alpha}F\frac{1}{1-\Upsilon}}\frac{1}{b}\right] = \frac{\alpha\beta\left[\frac{1}{1-\alpha}\frac{F}{T} - sL\right]}{s\left[e^{\beta\frac{\alpha}{1-\alpha}F} - 1 - \frac{\alpha}{1-\alpha}\beta F\right]} \tag{56}$$

As shown in figure 9.3, equation (56) can be solved graphically, in a plane in which the left and right hand side of that equation are measured along the vertical axis, and the economic life of the machines, T, is measured along the horizontal axis. In that plane, the LHS schedule can be represented by an horizontal line. In

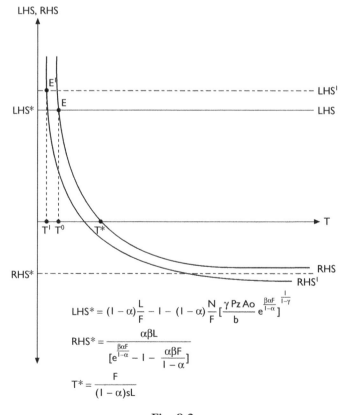

$$\text{LHS}^* = (1-\alpha)\frac{L}{F} - 1 - (1-\alpha)\frac{N}{F}[\frac{\gamma P_Z A_0}{b}e^{\frac{\beta\alpha F}{1-\alpha}}]^{\frac{1}{1-\gamma}}$$

$$\text{RHS}^* = \frac{\alpha\beta L}{[e^{\frac{\beta\alpha F}{1-\alpha}} - 1 - \frac{\alpha\beta F}{1-\alpha}]}$$

$$T^* = \frac{F}{(1-\alpha)sL}$$

Fig. 9.3

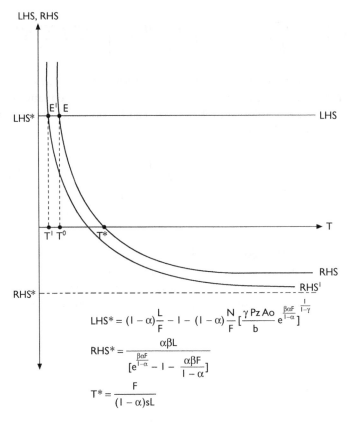

Fig. 9.4

turn, the RHS schedule tends to infinity as T approaches zero, and tends to $-\alpha\beta L/[e^{\beta\alpha F/(1-\alpha)} - 1 - \alpha\beta F/(1 - \alpha)]$ as T tends to infinity. Therefore, in figure 9.3, the RHS can be represented by a downward sloping curve, which intersects the horizontal axis as $T = F/[(1 - \alpha)sL]$. The economic life of the machines, T, is determined at the intersection point of both schedules. As the labor force, L, increases, the LHS curve shifts upwards, whereas the RHS curve shifts downwards. Therefore, in the new equilibrium point, E^1, the economic life of the machines is smaller. In this case, as in the one-sector model, the economy's income is given by equation (38), whereby the growth rate of income (and income per-capita) is equal to $\lambda = \beta\alpha F/(1 - \alpha)T$. Thus, this two-sector extension of the model predicts also that as the size of the labor force increases, T falls, and income grows faster.

Figure 9.4 depicts the case of an increase of the saving rate. As in the previous section, in this case if the saving rate, s, increases, the LHS curve would remain the same, but the RHS schedule would shift downwards. Thus, at the new intersection point, E^1, the economic life of the machines would be smaller and consequently the growth rate of income would increase.

Finally, in this open economy, if the relative price of good Z, P_Z, decreases, perhaps due to the adoption of trade policy aimed at protecting the more capital

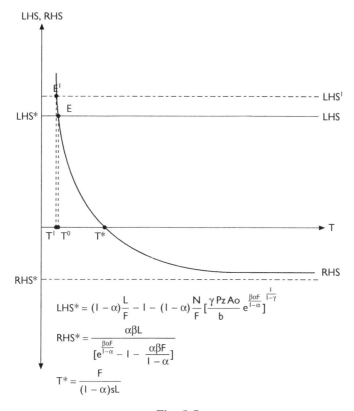

$$\text{LHS*} = (1 - \alpha)\frac{L}{F} - 1 - (1 - \alpha)\frac{N}{F}[\frac{\gamma\,Pz\,Ao}{b}\,e^{\frac{\beta\alpha F}{1-\alpha}}]^{\frac{1}{1-\gamma}}$$

$$\text{RHS*} = \frac{\alpha\beta L}{[e^{\frac{\beta\alpha F}{1-\alpha}} - 1 - \frac{\alpha\beta F}{1-\alpha}]}$$

$$T* = \frac{F}{(1-\alpha)sL}$$

Fig. 9.5

intensive industry (sector Y), the LHS curve shifts upwards, whereas the RHS curve remains unaltered. In that case, as shown in Fig. 9.5, in the new equilibrium point, E^1, the economic life of the machines, T, decreases and consequently the growth rate of the economy $\lambda = \beta\alpha F/(1 - \alpha)T$ increases.

V. Conclusions

In this paper we have tried to add an extra dimension to the standard endogenous growth story. This is provided by the endogenously determined economic life of capital, T, when machines embodying the different technology of their different dates of construction coexist as is usual in the old vintage capital models. But unlike in the latter models, T will now have an effect on the long-run growth rate of the economy. Policies that affect T will thus change this growth rate. For example, we show in section III that an increase in the savings rate will lower T and raise the growth rate. Similarly, in the two-sector version of the basic model presented in section IV, we show that if the two final goods are tradeable, protection of the capital-intensive good may increase the growth rate by reducing T.

We should add that the purpose of this paper is to illustrate a richer variety of questions that may open up in the endogenous growth theory literature if we borrow some aspects of the vintage capital models, but our answers to them should not be interpreted as conclusive. This is particularly because some of those answers may be model-specific, as is not uncommon in much of the endogenous growth literature. For example, there is a whole slew of assumptions to fit the model into the strait-jacket of the steady state. Those who have dabbled in the old vintage models are aware that these models can become very cumbersome once we are off the steady state. Yet this area of transitional dynamics is an obvious area that needs to be explored; important beginnings have been made by Benhabib and Rustichini (1993) and Boucekkine, Germain and Licandro (1997). The former paper has a vintage-capital version of an optimal growth model to study the volatile behavior of investment and growth. The latter paper provides a study of replacement dynamics in a model of optimal growth with endogenous scrapping. Our full-employment model also ignores the importance of vintage capital for issues like the link between growth and unemployment, as discussed in Aghion and Howitt (1998, chapter 4). We have also ignored structural problems arising from vintage human capital, as analyzed, for example, in Chari and Hopenhayn (1991).

We have also made a number of other assumptions to keep our analysis tractable, for example about the fixed-coefficients production function with each vintage of machines, no machines used in producing one of the final goods in the two-sector version, similarity of rates of technical progress in final goods and in capital goods production, about the particular approximate measure of the stock of knowledge capital, and so on. The fixed-coefficients production function assumption makes our model akin to what used to be known as a "clay-clay" model in the vintage capital literature, the best example of which is that of Solow, Tobin, von Weizsäcker, and Yaari (1966). It is well-known in the vintage literature – see, for example, Bardhan (1969) – how introducing some elasticity of substitution between capital and labor ex ante (i.e., prior to the installation of the machinery), but not ex post (or what used to be called a "putty-clay" model), can have a significant effect on the comparative-dynamic results with respect to T, the economic life of capital.

Another assumption that needs to be relaxed is that of tradeability only of final goods, but not of the capital goods, in our two-sector version where we discuss the impact of trade policy on the growth rate. This may have a particular bearing on the discussion relating to East Asian growth where trade allowing for imports of machines from abroad embodying the latest technology is supposed to have played a very important role.

Notes

1. We are grateful to Gene Grossman and Paul Romer for valuable comments on an earlier draft. Of course, all errors remain ours alone.
2. For extensions of these models, see Bliss (1968) and Bardhan (1969).

3. For an early model of international trade patterns based on differences in comparative advantage following from differences in the economic life of machines, see Bardhan (1966).

4. One exception is the paper by Redding (1996) where an innovation renders obsolete only a fraction of the machines in use, but this paper addresses a different set of issues, those relating to the disadvantage of an early starter.

5. In Bardhan and Kletzer (1984) there is an analysis of the dynamic effect of protection on the time path of productivity in a partial equilibrium model of learning. Grossman and Helpman (1991a) give several examples of how trade policies, by altering relative prices, can affect the growth rate.

6. In this respect, our vintage model is akin to that of Solow, Tobin, von Weizsäcker, and Yaari (1966).

7. Equation (14) states that profit maximization in the capital good sectors implies that $R_i(v, t) = R(v, t)$, for all i, which according to equation (13) allows us to conclude that $I_i(v) = I(v) = [aK(v)^{(1-\alpha)}/R(v, t)]^{1/(1-\alpha)}$, for all i.

8. Machines of vintage v are scrapped when $w(t)L_\Upsilon(v, t) = \Upsilon(v, t)$, that is, when $w(t) = \Upsilon(v, t)/L_\Upsilon(v, t)$.

9. While one may postulate that R&D experience is proportional to $K_H(t) = \int_{t-T}^{t} n(v)\, dv$, in this model we are assuming that this experience "depreciates" over time, so that only the experience with the recent capital goods is predominant in the determination of the stock of knowledge capital. Therefore, an "approximation" for the stock of knowledge capital is given by $K_H(t) = \int_{t-T}^{t} n(v)\, dv$. We will see later that due to the assumption that technical progress in both the final good sector and the capital good sectors depend on the quality index, and as a result both grow at the same rate, it is obtained that $n(v) = n$ for all v. This implies that $K_H(t) = n(t)T$.

10. Here we are assuming that the fixed costs are paid each period by the monopolistic competitive firms. However, this is a simplifying assumption which allows us to obtain a cleaner solution. The model has been solved for the general case in which in equilibrium, at time t, the entry costs $w(t)F/n(v)T$ (paid once) are equal to the present value of the stream of profits, that is, $w(t)\, F/n(v)T = \int_{t}^{t+T} \Pi(v, u)e^{-\int r(z)\, dz}du$. Under certain conditions on the parameters, the results obtainid for that general case are similar to the ones obtained here. The proof is available on request from the authors.

11. We have worked out a more general non-constant savings rate case (with a constant-elasticity intertemporal utility function) for the one-sector model, but we omit it here.

12. This result is mainly obtained due to the assumption that technical progress in both the final good sector and the capital good sectors is a function of the quality index $S(v)$. Without this assumption, $n(v)$ would not be the same across vintages and it would be much more complicated to derive an analytical solution for the model.

References

P. Aghion and P. Howitt, *Endogenous Growth Theory*, MIT Press, Cambridge, MA 1998.

K. J. Arrow, "The Economic Implications of Learning by Doing," *Review of Economic Studies*, 1962.

P. Bardhan, "International Trade Theory in a Vintage Capital Model," *Econometrica*, 1966.

P. Bardhan, "Equilibrium Growth in a Model with Economic Obsolescence of Machines," *Quarterly Journal of Economics*, 1969.

P. Bardhan and K. Kletzer, "Dynamic Effects of Protection on Productivity," *Journal of International Economics*, 1984.

J. Benhabib and A. Rustichini, "A Vintage Capital Model of Investment and Growth: Theory and Evidence," in R. Becker *et al.* (eds.), *General Equilibrium, Growth, and Trade II*, Academic Press, 1993.

C. J. Bliss, "On Putty-Clay," *Review of Economic Studies*, 1968.

R. Boucekkine, M. Germain, and O. Licandro, "Replacement Echoes in the Vintage Capital Growth Model," *Journal of Economic Theory*, 1997.

V. V. Chari and H. Hopenhayn, "Vintage Human Capital, Growth, and the Diffusion of New Technology," *Journal of Political Economy*, 1991.

B. de Long and L. Summers, "Equipment Investment and Economic Growth," *Quarterly Journal of Economics*, 1991.

W. J. Ethier, "National and International Returns to Scale in the Modern Theory of International Trade," *American Economic Review*, 1982.

G. M. Grossman and E. Helpman, "Quality Ladders in the Theory of Growth," *Review of Economic Studies*, 1991.

G. M. Grossman and E. Helpman, *Innovation and Growth in the Global Economy*, MIT Press, Cambridge, MA, 1991a.

L. Johansen, "Substitution vs. Fixed Proportions in the Theory of Economic Growth: A Synthesis," *Econometrica*, 1959.

E. S. Phelps, "Substitution, Fixed Proportions, Growth and Distribution," *International Economic Review*, 1963.

S. Redding, "Is There a Penalty to being a Pioneer," Nuffield College, Oxford University, Working Paper no. 109, 1996.

P. M. Romer, "Endogenous Technological Change," *Journal of Political Economy*, 1990.

W. E. G. Salter, *Productivity and Technical Change*, Cambridge University Press, Cambridge, 1960.

P. S. Segerstrom, T. C. A. Anant, and E. Dinopoulos, "A Schumpeterian Model of the Product Life Cycle," *American Economic Review*, 1990.

R. M. Solow, "Substitution and Fixed Proportions in the Theory of Capital," *Review of Economic Studies*, 1962.

R. M. Solow, J. Tobin, C. von Weizsäcker, and M. Yaari, "Neoclassical Growth with Fixed Factor Proportions," *Review of Economic Studies*, 1966.

P. Temin, "The Relative Decline of the British Steel Industry, 1880–1913," in H. Rosovsky (ed.), *The Industrialization of Two Systems*, Harvard University Press, Cambridge, Mass., 1966.

J. Williamson, "Optimal Replacement of Capital Goods: The Early New England and British Textile Firm," *Journal of Political Economy*, 1971.

E. N. Wolff, "Capital Formation and Productivity Convergence over the Long Term," *American Economic Review*, June 1991.

A. Young, "The Tyranny of Numbers: Confronting the Statistical Realities of the East Asian Growth Experience," *Quarterly Journal of Economics*, 1995.

Chapter 10

Equilibrium Growth in a Model with Economic Obsolescence of Machines*

I. Introduction

Leif Johansen formalized the idea of *ex post* rigidity of factor proportions in a "vintage-capital" growth model with technical progress embodied only in new equipment.[1] Edmund Phelps,[2] and very recently, Murray Kemp and Pham Chí Thánh[3] have investigated the properties of steady-state growth equilibrium in such a model for the special case of *ex ante* Cobb-Douglas production functions.[4] In view of the extremely complicated relationships in this model *even in the steady state*, the simplification of the Cobb-Douglas assumption is very helpful. But, as is shown in this paper, the Cobb-Douglas assumption obscures many of the important properties of this model. For example, the relationship between the economic life of capital and the rate of interest, the uniqueness of growth equilibrium,[5] the needed concavity of the present-value function of profits, etc., are all very sensitive to the assumption about the *ex ante* elasticity of substitution of factors, and by assuming the latter to be unity one tends to overlook a rich variety of issues and problems. The present paper is an attempt at a fuller generalization of this model.[6]

We have a model in which machines embody the technology of their date of construction, and once a machine is built there is no scope for altering its labor requirement. Technical progress is completely embodied and Harrod-neutral at a constant rate g. Physical depreciation is ignored (it should be the easiest thing to introduce a fixed rate of depreciation in this model) and obsolescence takes its toll when rising wages absorb all the revenues from a particular machine. The total labor force grows at constant rate μ and gross investment is taken to be a fixed proportion s of gross output. As for our expectations assumption, we assume that the entrepreneurs (correctly) expect the wage rate, W, to grow at rate g – the case of "perfect foresight." Kemp and Thánh also consider the other extreme case of "zero foresight" where entrepreneurs *persist* in their erroneous expectation of a constant wage, an assumption which we find rather unattractive.

One easy criticism of this paper – as of the papers by Phelps and Kemp and Thánh – is that throughout we confine ourselves to the long-run equilibrium growth path. This is certainly a matter of mathematical convenience. But there is probably much more justification for analyzing the steady-state properties for this model than for the usual neoclassical growth model, because due to the complex structure of this model some of these properties are not even now well known or well understood in the literature and, as the elaborate calculations needed for the proofs of this paper would testify, the answers to some very simple but important questions asked in terms of this model are quite complicated indeed, even when we are in the relatively comfortable world of the steady state.

II. The Model and Uniqueness of Equilibrium

For each vintage of equipment there is a production relationship of the form

(1) $F_v(t) = F_v[I_v, e^{gv} \cdot L_v]$

where $F_v(t)\, dv$ stands for the rate of output at time t produced on machines of vintage v (i.e., capital installed during a period $(v, v+dv)$ with $t \geq v$), $I_v\, dv$ the number of machines installed in the period $(v, v+dv)$, and $L_v\, dv$ the labor employed on capital of vintage v. Since this is a one sector model, we measure capital goods in units identical with the unit of output. Total output at time t accrues at a rate

(2) $F(t) = \displaystyle\int_{t-T}^{t} F_v(t)\, dv$

where T is the *economic* life of the oldest machine in use. In the steady state T is constant.

Since the production function in (1) is assumed to be homogeneous of degree one, labor productivity on capital of vintage v is

(3) $\dfrac{F_v}{L_v} = e^{gv} f_v[k_v e^{-gv}]$

where $k_v = I_v/L_v$. (For our purpose of investigating the properties of long-run equilibrium, it is enough to study the equilibrium at time zero. At $t = 0$, labor productivity on current machines is $F_0/L_0 = f_0(k_0)$. Just for convenience, from now on we shall drop the subscript 0; a variable without the vintage label will denote the value of the variable at $t = 0$.) In competitive equilibrium the present value of net profit is zero (i.e., the present value of current investment $= I_t$).

If r is the constant rate of interest at which future quasi-rents are discounted and if the wage rate, W, is expected to grow at rate g,[7] the present value of profits from investment designed to employ one man is[8]

$$(4) \quad V = f(k)\frac{[1 - e^{-rT}]}{r} - W\frac{[1 - e^{-(r-g)T}]}{(r - g)} - k = 0.$$

Now, maximizing v with respect to k and T,

$$(5) \quad f'(k) = \frac{r}{1 - e^{-rT}}$$

and

$$(6) \quad f(k) = W\,e^{gT}.$$

Equation (6) is, of course, the well-known scrapping condition, viz., that capital of a particular vintage is scrapped when its output is absorbed in labor costs. As Bliss,[9] has pointed out, the second order conditions for maximizing V depend on the value of the elasticity of factor substitution, σ, along the *ex ante* production function, and if σ is very large we may not have a maximum. But we have checked[10] that in this case the second order conditions for a maximum are satisfied under the sufficient condition of $\sigma \leqq 1$.

Why some kind of a restriction like this is needed may be explained in the following intuitive way. An important feature of a vintage-capital model like ours is that capital in such a model has two dimensions, one *intensive*, represented by k, the technique on current machines, and the other *extensive*, represented by T, the economic lifetime of machines. "Capital deepening" through concavity of the *ex ante* production function, tends to make the present value function for net profits concave, but, at the same time, it leads to "capital lengthening" (since for a given W, the more capital-intensive machines are scrapped later) which, in its turn, tends to detract from concavity of the present-value function. For ensuring that the present-value function is concave, we have to assume that the forces of diminishing returns generated by capital deepening are strong enough (one way of securing that is not to have too high σ) to outweigh the lengthening effect.

Now equations (5) and (8) give us two relationships among r, T and k. Totally differentiating both the equations with respect to r one can work out the value of dk/dr and dT/dr.

As proved in Appendix E of my paper and also in Bliss, $dk/dr < 0$, i.e., the (long-run) equilibrium with the higher rate of interest is characterized by a more labor-intensive technique for current equipment. More complicated is the relationship between T and r. But as indicated by Matthews[11] and proved in Appendix D of my paper as well as in Bliss, the (long-run) equilibrium with *higher* rate of interest will have *longer* economic life of equipment (i.e., $dT/dr > 0$) if the elasticity of substitution σ, along the *ex ante* production function is near zero, and a *shorter* life of equipment (i.e., $dT/dr < 0$) if σ is near or equal to unity. When σ is significantly below unity but above zero, one is not sure of the sign of dT/dr.

Since the long-run equilibrium total output is growing at an exponential rate of $\lambda (= \mu + g)$, output from new equipment at time t is related to total output as follows:

$$(9) \quad F(t) = \frac{F_t[1 - e^{-\lambda T}]}{\lambda}.$$

If s is the constant fraction of total gross output saved and currently invested,

$$(10) \quad sF(t) = I_t.$$

Using equations (3) and (9), (10) may be rewritten as

$$(11) \quad s = \frac{k}{f(k)} \cdot \frac{\lambda}{[1 - e^{-\lambda T}]}.$$

This is the same equation as equation (63) in Bliss. One may ask whether the growth equilibrium as characterized by equation (11) is unique for a given gross saving ratio s. This is important since most of the comparative-dynamic propositions which have been derived in terms of such vintage-capital models in the literature are of limited usefulness unless, among other things, uniqueness of growth equilibrium is proved.[12]

The R.H.S. of (11) may be written as $A(k)/B(T)$ where $A(k) = k/f(k)$ and $B(T) = (1 - e^{-\lambda T})/\lambda$. Since $dk/dr < 0$, $A(k)$ is a declining function of r. $B(T)$ is an increasing function of T, and if $dT/dr \geq 0$, we immediately see that the R.H.S. of (11) is a declining function of r and therefore the growth equilibrium is unique. Bliss[13] also gets this result.

More difficult is the case when $dT/dr < 0$, since *both* A and B are declining functions of r. But I have proved[14] in Appendix F of my paper that $(dA/dr)(1/A) < (dB/dr)(1/B)$ under the sufficient condition of $\sigma \leq 1$. So under this condition the R.H.S. of equation (11) is a decreasing function of r and the resulting uniqueness of growth equilibrium is shown in Figure 10.1.

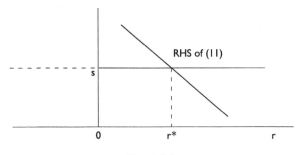

Fig. 10.1

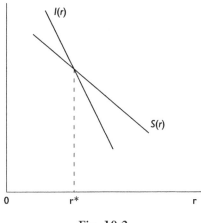

Fig. 10.2

A rough intuitive explanation of why some condition of this type is needed may be given. Let us go back to equations (10) and (11). A fall in the interest r increases k, i.e., current gross investment per man; in other words, the investment function is a negatively sloped curve corresponding to changes in r. Now let us look at the savings function. With a constant fraction of gross output being saved, it depends on how output itself behaves corresponding to changes in r. A fall in r through capital deepening means a larger output on the current machine, but depending on the sign of dT/dr, it also affects the economic lifetime of capital. If $dT/dr < 0$, a fall in r implies capital lengthening, and that tends to increase total output, so that on both counts savings tend to be a declining function of r as well. With both the saving and investment functions negatively sloped, the problem of multiple equilibria arises. What in effect we have shown above is that if σ is not very large, at the intersection of the two curves the absolute value of the slope of the investment function exceeds that of the savings function and the equilibrium is unique. (See Figure 10.2). There are two factors that bring this about: (a) because of the concavity of the *ex ante* production function, the effect of capital deepening on output of current machines in the savings function is swamped by capital deepening itself in the investment function, and (b) as long as σ is not very large, the impact of a change in r on output, and therefore savings, through capital lengthening is relatively small, since the *absolute* value of the elasticity of T with respect to r is an increasing function of σ for given r and T. If $dT/dr > 0$ (which we know is the case at least for very small σ), then, of course, the capital shortening effect of a fall in r on output reinforces the cause of uniqueness of growth equilibrium.[15]

III. Comparative Dynamics

Having proved the uniqueness result, one might also use this model to derive some comparative-dynamic propositions. For example, as the R.H.S. of equation (11) is a decreasing function of r for $\sigma \leq 1$, it is immediately seen that $dr/ds < 0$, i.e., comparing between two steady-state equilibria, the equilibrium with the *higher* gross saving ratio should have the *lower* rate of interest under our elasticity of substitution condition.[16]

How about distributive shares? With exponential growth of the labor force at rate μ, labor assigned to new machines is related to the total labor force $L(t)$ in the following way:

$$(17) \quad L_t = \frac{L(t) \cdot \mu}{[1 - e^{-\mu T}]}.$$

Using equations (6), (9), and (17), the total wage share in the economy is

$$(18) \quad Q(t) = \frac{W(t) \cdot L(t)}{F(t)} = \frac{[e^{\mu T} - 1]\lambda}{[e^{\lambda T} - 1]\mu}.$$

It is easy to check that the extreme R.H.S. of equation (18) is a decreasing function of T. We have already seen that when σ is very near or equal to unity, $dT/dr < 0$; in this case, therefore, we may say $dQ/ds < 0$, i.e., between two steady-state equilibria the one with the *higher* gross saving ratio has a *lower* wage share. We get the opposite result when σ is very near zero and $dT/dr > 0$.

In Appendix C of my paper, as in Bliss, it is shown that $dW/dr < 0$, i.e., the wage rate and the rate of interest are always inversely related in this model. It can also be shown that the absolute value of the elasticity of what might be called the "factor-price frontier" in this model, $(dW/dr)(r/W)$, is *less* than (whereas in usual neoclassical models it is equal to) the ratio of investment elasticity of output to the labor elasticity of output along the *ex ante* production function.

Another interesting comparative-dynamic result, as shown in Appendix G of my paper, is that in this model the elasticity of the average productivity of labor with respect to the wage rate (i.e., $\{d[F(t)/L(t)]/dW(t)\} \cdot \{W(t)/[F(t)/L(t)]\}$) is *higher* than the elasticity of substitution (for $\sigma \leq 1$ and $r \geq \lambda$) along the *ex ante* production function, whereas in usual neoclassical models the former is always *equal* to the latter. This implies that the well-known method of estimating elasticity of factor substitution à la Arrow, Chenery, Minhas and Solow[17] – i.e., by estimating the coefficient of regression of the logarithm of observed output per unit of labor on that of observed wage rate – may give an overestimate, if the data-generating model is not static, but has the properties of a vintage-capital model of the type analyzed here.[18]

A corollary of the above result is that the average productivity of labor is always an increasing function of the wage rate. This implies that comparing countries in steady states, the country with the higher wage rate will have a higher productivity of labor.[19] Labor productivity in this model depends not merely on the capital-intensity of the machines in use but also on the economic life of the machines, and both are affected by the wage rate.

Finally, given the gross saving ratio, does a higher rate of (Harrod-neutral) technical progress imply a higher or a lower rate of interest? It is proved in Appendix I of my paper[20] that given the gross saving ratio and the rate of growth of population, $dr/dg > 0$ for $r \geq \lambda$[21] and $\sigma \leqq 1$.

Reviewing the whole of our analysis in this paper it seems imperative to underline the important role of σ, the elasticity of factor substitution, in shaping the different types of interrelationships in the model and that role this tends to be obscured by the usual Cobb-Douglas assumption. We have seen how very large σ might cause problems in maximizing the present-value function of net profits as given by our equation (4). We have also found some restriction like $\sigma \leqq 1$ as a (sufficient) condition for uniqueness of growth equilibrium. Then again we have noticed how the value of σ is important in finding out the type of relationship that holds in equilibrium between T, the economic lifetime of capital, and r, the rate of interest. As it turns out, the sign of dT/dr is one of the most important items of information one needs for deriving all sorts of comparative-dynamic propositions in such vintage-capital models. The latter, therefore, are very sensitive to the particular value of σ.

Before ending we may also note that *all* the results of this paper carry over to a generalized model of Arrow-type "learning by doing"[22] with *ex ante* factor substitutability and *ex post* rigidity. (This is largely because despite differences in the origin of technical progress, the structures of the two types of models are very similar particularly in their steady-state solutions.) Levhari in his extension[23] of Arrow's model has been able to avoid some of the problems mentioned in this paper by assuming the far easier case of *ex post* factor substitutability.

Notes

*   This paper was first written in Oct. 1966, and presented at the Dec. 1967 meeting of the Econometric Society in Washington. A slightly revised version came out as M.I.T. Department of Economics Working Paper, No. 17, in March 1968, under the title, "Equilibrium Growth in a Model with Economic Obsolescence of Machines." The present version omits the long Appendix of that paper where some of the results mentioned here without proof are proved. These proofs involve cumbersome calculations which, on editorial advice, I have decided not to inflict on the general reader. Those who want to check the results may write to me and I shall be glad to supply copies of that article.

1.   Johansen, "Substitution vs. Fixed Proportions in the Theory of Economic Growth: A Synthesis," *Econometrica*, XXVII (April 1959).

2.   E. S. Phelps, "Substitution, Fixed Proportions, Growth and Distribution," *International Economic Review*, IV (Sept. 1963).

3.   M. C. Kemp and P. C. Thánh, "On a Class of Growth Models," *Econometrica*, XXXIV (April 1966).

4.   R. M. Solow, J. Tobin, C. C. von Weizsäcker and M. Yaari, "Neo-Classical Growth with Fixed Factor Proportions," *Review of Economic Studies* XXXIII (April 1966), extensively discuss the properties of a vintage-capital model where there is no choice of substitution either *ex ante* or *ex post*. The popular nickname for their model is "clay-clay," whereas our is a "putty-clay" model.

5.   As mentioned in n. 3, this has not been proved by Phelps, *op. cit.*, or Kemp and Thánh, *op. cit.*, *even* for the Cobb-Douglas Case.

6. Recently C. J. Bliss, "On Putty-Clay," *Review of Economic Studies*, XXXV (April 1968), has attempted a similar generalization. To the extent that our results coincide with his we have only summarized them and referred the reader to his article. But in some important respects our paper goes beyond what is available there. For example, we have proved that we may dispense with the "admittedly unsatisfactory form" of Bliss's crucial uniqueness assumption – his condition (46) with the inequality reversed – if we have *ex ante* production functions with elasticity of substitution less than or equal to unity. Similarly, the latter assumption is sufficient for the uniqueness of growth equilibrium for a given gross saving ratio and also for the inverse comparative-dynamic relationship between the rate of interest and the gross saving ratio. Neither of these results are found in Bliss. In Section III of our paper we also provide some additional comparative-dynamic propositions.

7. In this paper it will be assumed that $r \neq 0$ and $r \neq g$. In Appendix (J) of my paper, *op. cit.*, I refer to the cases of $r = 0$ and $r = g$.

8. For a derivation of this equation, see Bliss, *op. cit.*

9. *Op. cit.*, p. 114.

10. Totally differentiating V and using equations (5) and (6), $d^2V/dk^2 < 0$, if

$$(7) \quad \frac{[e^{rT} - 1]g}{r} \cdot \frac{[f(k) - f'(k)k]}{f'(k)k} > \sigma$$

where

$$\sigma = -\frac{f'(k)[f(k) - f'(k)k]}{f''(k)f(k)k}.$$

Readers will recognize equation (7) as equation (46) in Bliss, *op. cit.*, p. 115, with the inequality sign reversed.

We shall prove that when V vanishes, as it does in competitive equilibrium, equation (7) is satisfied for $\sigma \leq 1$. Multiplying both sides of equation (5) by $-k$ and using equations (4) and (6) we get

$$(8) \quad \frac{f(k)}{f(k) - f'(k)k} = \frac{[e^{rT} - 1](r - g)}{[e^{(r-g)T} - 1]r}.$$

This is equation (60) in Bliss *op. cit.*, p. 119.

From equation (8), the L.H.S. of (7) may be rewritten as

$$\frac{[e^{rT} - 1][e^{(r-g)T} - 1]g}{(r - g)[e^{rT} - 1] - r[e^{(r-g)T} - 1]},$$

which is greater than unity if

$$\frac{re^{rT}}{[e^{rT} - 1]} > \frac{(r - g)e^{(r-g)T}}{[e^{(r-g)T} - 1]}.$$

This is so since if $y(x) = x e^x/(e^x - 1)$, $y'(x) > 0$. Thus $d^2V/dk^2 < 0$, for $\sigma \leq 1$. It is also indicated in Appendix (B) of my paper, *op. cit.*, that this sufficient condition on σ can be significantly weakened if r is positive: in that case $d^2V/dk^2 < 0$ for $\sigma \leq 2$. This is useful to know since R. Britto, "Some Micro-economic Properties of Vintage-Type Capital Models" (unpublished), has shown that at least for C.E.S. *ex ante* production functions, equilibrium r must have a lower positive bound for the case of $\sigma > 1$.

11. R. C. O. Matthews. "The New View of Investment: A Comment," this *Journal*, LXXVII (Feb. 1964).

12. Phelps observes, "We are able to find a golden-age solution to the equations. The difficulty lies in showing that it is the *only* asymptotic solution possible" (italics mine), *op. cit.*, p. 276. He then goes on to assume the problem away. Kemp and Thánh, *op. cit.*, p. 269, seem to assert uniqueness, but their Figure 2, to which they refer, has two downward sloping curves for their equations (4.8) and (4.9), and there is nothing on the face of it which precludes multiple intersection. The limit of those two curves seem to ensure existence but not uniqueness of equilibrium. Murray Kemp has confirmed this in correspondence.

The crucial problem of asymptotic stability of growth equilibrium in such models (with "perfect foresight") has so far defied our attempt to prove. The major difficulty is the very complicated nature of non-steady-state behavior in such models.

Solow, Tobin, von Weizsäcker, and Yaari, *op. cit.*, have proved asymptotic stability for $\sigma = 0$ case. Following on their work, E. Sheshinksi, "Balanced Growth and Stability in the Johansen Vintage Model," *Review of Economic Studies*, XXXIV (April 1967), has proved asymptotic stability for the case of $0 < \sigma \leq 1$, but under the naive assumption of "zero foresight" on the part of the entrepreneurs.

13. *Op. cit.*, p. 121.

14. Hints of the proof:

Totally differentiating equation (5), we get the value of dk/dr. Using it and equation (5) in equation (11),

$$\frac{dA}{dr}\frac{1}{A} - \frac{dB}{dr}\frac{1}{B} < 0$$

if

$$(12) \quad \frac{\sigma}{r}[z(m) - 1] > \frac{dT}{dr}\frac{1}{T}\left[\sigma - \frac{z(m)}{z(q)}\right]$$

where $z(x) = (e^x - 1)/x$, $m = rT$ and $q = \lambda T$.

Since the L.H.S. of (12) is positive and $dT/dr < 0$, (12) is immediately proved if $\sigma \geq z(m)/z(q)$. Let us, therefore, assume $\sigma < z(m)/z(q)$. If $r > 0$, all we have to prove is that

$$(13) \quad \frac{\sigma[z(m) - 1]z(q)}{[z(m) - \sigma z(q)]} > -\frac{dT}{dr}\frac{r}{T}.$$

Totally differentiating in (8) and using the value of dk/dr,

$$\frac{dT}{dr}\frac{r}{T} = \frac{[z(m) - 1][\sigma z(n) + (1 - \sigma)z(m)] - z(m)[z(n) - 1]\frac{m}{n}}{z(m)z(n)(m - n) - \sigma[z(m) - z(n)]}$$

when $n = (r - g)T$. Using this in (13) and deducting 1 from both sides, we have to prove that

(14) $$\frac{\dfrac{(m-n)}{n}[1 + (n-1)z(n)] + (1 - \sigma)[z(m) - z(n)]}{z(m)z(n)(m-n) - \sigma[z(m) - z(n)]} > \frac{1 - \sigma z(q)}{[z(m) - 1] + [1 - \sigma z(q)]}.$$

Since the L.H.S. is positive, the inequality (14) is immediately proved if $\sigma z(q) \geq 1$. So let us assume $1 > \sigma z(q)$.

Define

$$a = (m-n)z(m)z(n) > 0$$
$$b = z(m) - z(n) > 0$$
$$c = \frac{(m-n)}{n}[1 + (n-1)z(n)] > 0.$$

The denominators on both sides of equation (14) are positive. On cross multiplication and simplification it is enough for us to show that

(15) $(1 - \sigma)(a - b - c) < [z(m) - 1][b(1 - \sigma) + c].$

But since $a - b - c = [z(m) - 1][b + c + z(m)(m/n)] - b(m/n)z(m)$, all we have to prove is that

(16) $[z(m) - 1]\sigma c > \dfrac{(1 - \sigma)}{n}z(m)[(m-n)\{z(m) - 1\} - bm].$

The L.H.S. of (16) is positive. On the R.H.S., the bracketed expression is negative, using the value of b and since $[z(m) - 1]/m > [z(n) - 1]/n$ with $m > n$. Therefore the R.H.S. is nonpositive if $\sigma \leq 1$, and that proves inequality (16). The proof for $r < 0$ follows essentially the same line.

15. Figure 10.2 seems also to suggest *local* stability of equilibrium under $\sigma \leq 1$, if the dynamic behavior equation relates dr/dt positively with $(I - S)$.
16. The contrary assertion by Bliss, *op. cit.*, p. 119, fn. 1, seems to be wrong.
17. K. J. Arrow, H. B. Chenery, B. S. Minhas and R. M. Solow, "Capital-Labor Substitution and Economic Efficiency," *Review of Economics and Statistics,* XLIII (Aug. 1962).
18. In "On Estimation of Production Functions from International Cross-Section Data," *Economic Journal,* LXXVII (June 1967), I pointed to this over-estimation bias in the Arrow-Chenery-Minhas-Solow procedure for the cases of *ex ante* production functions of Cobb-Douglas and fixed-coefficients types. In this paper I generalized the result for all $\sigma \leq 1$.
19. In P. K. Bardhan, "International Trade Theory in A Vintage-Type Capital Model," *Econometrica,* XXXIV (Oct. 1966), we have a model which explains intercountry productivity differentials, and therefore trade, in terms of differences in the economic life of equipment as determined by factor prices. Even when the stream of new technical knowledge (embodied in new machines) is the same for all countries, their rate of utilization of this knowledge, as reflected in the economic life of machines, is different, since different wage rates lead them to scrap machines at different dates.

20. "Equilibrium Growth in a Model with Economic Obsolescence of Machines," *op. cit.*

21. A faster rate of technical progress may imply a *lower* rate of return when $\lambda > r$. This is in contrast to the case of *ex ante* fixed-coefficients production functions discussed in Solow, Tobin, von Weizäcker and Yaari, *op. cit.*

22. K. J. Arrow, "The Economic Implications of Learning by Doing," *Review of Economic Studies*, XXIX (June 1962).

23. D. Levhari, "Extensions of Arrow's 'Learning by Doing'," *Review of Economic Studies*, XXXIII (April 1966).

Chapter 11

More on Putty-Clay

The seeming intractability of many of the relationships in the putty-clay model (where machines embody the technology of their date of construction, there is a choice of techniques at the moment of new investment, but once a machine is built there is no scope for altering its labor requirement) has come in the way of any extensive analysis of this model which is otherwise very rich in implications that most of the usual growth models lack. In an excellent paper Bliss (1968) despaired of deriving meaningful comparative-dynamic propositions in this model because he was unable to prove (a) the uniqueness of a net present-value maximizing competitive equilibrium and (b) the uniqueness of growth equilibrium for a given gross saving ratio. Bardhan (1969) and Britto (1969) have, however, proved (a) under the none-too-restrictive sufficient condition that the *ex ante* production function has an elasticity of substitution, σ, that does not exceed unity. Under the same sufficient condition, Bardhan (1969) has proved[1] (b) and, as a direct corollary, the inverse comparative-dynamic relationship between the rate of interest, r, and the gross saving ratio, s.

All this has now made it somewhat easier to derive interesting comparative-dynamic propositions (under the above-mentioned sufficient condition) in the model, some of which we report in this paper: (i) It is now well-known[2] that the equilibrium with a higher rate of interest, r, will have a *longer* economic life of capital, T, (i.e., $dT/dr > 0$) if σ is near zero, and a *shorter* life of capital (i.e., $dT/dr < 0$) if σ is near or equal to unity; but the sign of dT/dr is generally regarded as indeterminate when σ is significantly different[3] from both zero and unity. It is proved in this paper that dT/dr is always positive as long as σ is not above $2/3$. This reduces our zone of ignorance, although does not quite eliminate it. This also implies that when σ does not exceed $2/3$, the equilibrium with a higher group saving ratio, s, has also a *larger* wage share in gross output. (ii) For a given rate of interest, a higher rate of embodied Harrod-neutral technical progress, g, implies a *shorter* economic life of capital (i.e., $\partial T/\partial g < 0$). The same is true even if the rate of interest is not given, but what is given is only the gross-saving ratio (which is assumed not to exceed its "golden rule" value) and that the *ex ante* production function is Cobb-Douglas. This result in the Cobb-Douglas putty-clay case is in contrast with the "clay-clay" case of Solow, Tobin, von Weizsäcker and Yaari (1966) where a faster rate of technical progress always implies a *longer* life of capital. (iii) The factor-price frontier in this model is downward-sloping as in usual models, but at any point on this frontier the elasticity (positively defined) is *less* than the ratio of investment elasticity of output to the labor elasticity of output along the *ex ante* production function. So, empirically, if one tries to get an estimate of this ratio from the elasticity of an observed factor-price frontier, because of the specification error one will always get an *underestimate*, if the data-generating model is putty-clay. (iv) We confirm for the putty-clay model a result obtained by Levhari and Sheshinski (1970) for the "putty-putty" vintage model that the factor-price frontier shrinks towards the origin (i.e., the wage rate is *lower* at a given rate of interest) the higher is g, the rate of embodied technical progress.[4] (v) The relationship between the rate of interest, r, and the rate of embodied technical progress, g, for a given gross saving ratio and rate of growth of the labor force, is monotonically positive as long as the rate of savings is not above its "golden rule" value. This result is in some contrast with that of Levhari and Sheshinski (1969) for the "putty-putty" vintage model. (vi) Finally, for a given gross saving ratio, with an *ex ante* Cobb-Douglas production function a higher rate of embodied technical progress implies a *lower* (the same) wage-share in gross output if the rate of saving is less than (equal to) its "golden rule" value.

These six sets of results are shown in the following six sections.

1

In order to save space, we shall assume that the paper by Bliss (1968) or that of Bardhan (1969) is familiar to the reader, and go directly to the fundamental equations relevant for our purpose.[5] If r is the constant rate of interest at which future quasi-rents are discounted and if the wage rate, W, is correctly expected to grow at rate g, the rate of embodied Harrod-neutral technical progress, the present value of profits, V, from investment designed to employ one man is given by the following equation and should in competitive equilibrium be equal to zero, so that[6]

$$(1) \quad V = f(k)\frac{[1 - e^{-rT}]}{r} - \frac{W[1 - e^{-(r-g)T}]}{(r - g)} - k = 0,$$

where k is investment per man, f is the labor productivity on the new investment and T is the economic life of the oldest machine in use. Maximizing V with respect to k and T,

$$(2) \quad f'(k) = \frac{r}{1 - e^{-rT}},$$

and the well-known scrapping condition for economically obsolete machines:

(3) $f(k) = W e^{gT}$.

Multiplying both sides of equation (2) by $(-k)$ and using equations (1) and (3) we get

(4) $\dfrac{f(k)}{f(k) - f'(k)k} = \dfrac{z(m)}{z(n)}$

where

$z(x) = \dfrac{e^x - 1}{x}, \quad x = m, n$

and

$m = rT \quad \text{and} \quad n = (r - g)T.$

Now totally differentiating in (4), using the value of dk/dr obtained from total differentiation in (2), applying the value of σ, the elasticity of substitution, which is equal to

$\dfrac{-f'(k)[f(k) - f'(k)k]}{f''(k)f(k)k},$

and after considerable simplifications with the use of (2) and (4),

(5) $\dfrac{dT}{dr} \dfrac{r}{T} = \dfrac{[z(m) - 1][\sigma z(n) + (1 - \sigma)z(m)] - z(m)[z(n) - 1](m/n)}{z(m)z(n)(m - n) - \sigma[z(m) - z(n)]}.$

In Appendix (B), it is shown that the denominator on the R.H.S. of (5) is positive when σ does not exceed unity, which we assume anyway in this paper to ensure uniqueness of competitive equilibrium. It is also proved there that the numerator is positive for σ not exceeding 2/3. So for the value of elasticity of substitution not exceeding 2/3, a higher rate of interest implies a *longer* economic life of capital.

This result has also its implications for distributive shares. The wage share, w, in this model is given[7] by

(6) $w = \dfrac{z(p)}{z(q)}$

where $p = \mu T$, μ being the constant rate of growth of labor and $q = \lambda T$, $\lambda (= \mu + g)$ being the rate of growth of output. Now it is easy to check that the R.H.S. of (6) is a decreasing function of T. Since in Bardhan (1969) we have proved that $dr/ds < 0$ and since we have proved above that $dT/dr > 0$ for σ not exceeding 2/3, we can now say that under this sufficient condition a higher gross-saving ratio implies a *larger* wage share. This is in contrast to the case when the *ex ante* production function is Cobb-Douglas, as in Phelps (1963) and Kemp and Thánh (1966).

2

Given the rate of interest, equation (2) gives us a relationship between T and k, and using this in equation (4) we get a relationship between k and g. From (2), for a given r,

$$(7) \quad \frac{dT}{dk} = \frac{[e^{rT} - 1]}{r} \frac{[f(k) - f'(k)k]}{\sigma f(k)k} > 0.$$

From (4), with the use of (19) in Appendix (A) and the definition of σ, we can work out

$$(8) \quad \frac{dk}{dg} = \frac{-z(m)[1 + (n - 1)z(n)] \dfrac{T}{n}}{\dfrac{(1 - \sigma)}{\sigma k}[z(m) - z(n)]z(n) + \dfrac{dT}{dk} \dfrac{1}{T}[(m - n)z(m)z(n) - z(m) + z(n)]}.$$

From (19) in Appendix (A) it is easy to see that the numerator on the R.H.S. of (8) is negative, while from (20) in Appendix (B), from (7) and our general assumption that $\sigma \leq 1$, the denominator is positive. This means dk/dg is negative.

Hence, for given r,

$$(9) \quad \frac{dT}{dg} = \frac{dT}{dk} \cdot \frac{dk}{dg} < 0,$$

or, *for a given rate of interest* a faster rate of embodied technical progress implies a shorter economic life of machines.

Of course, *for a given gross saving ratio*, a faster rate of technical progress does not leave the rate of interest unchanged. As will be shown in Section 5, for a given gross saving ratio (that does not exceed its "golden rule" value), $dr/dg > 0$.

This means, at least for the case of *ex ante* Cobb-Douglas production functions (9) implies that T is negatively associated with g, *even* taking into account the accompanying change in r, since in this case dT/dr is negative. Thus in this case the total impact of a faster rate of embodied technical progress is to *reduce* the economic life of capital.

3

Since in this model the concept of an aggregate capital stock is meaningless, the properties of the factor-price frontier relating W and r, are useful to know both for analytical and empirical purposes. Bliss (1968) has already shown that in the putty-clay model the frontier is downward-sloping as in usual models. But if we want to compute the elasticity of this frontier, we totally differentiate (1) and use (2) and (3) to get

$$(10) \quad -\frac{dW}{dr}\frac{r}{W} = \frac{[z(m) - 1] - \dfrac{m}{n}[z(n) - 1]}{z(n)}.$$

It is easy to show that this elasticity is *less* than the ratio of investment elasticity of output to the labor elasticity of output along the *ex ante* production function. The latter may be expressed as $kf'(k)/(f - f'(k)k)$, which, from (4), is equal to $[z(m) - z(n)]/z(n)$. This, as easily checked, is larger than (10), since $m > n$. This result is in contrast with the implication of a usual neo-classical model.[8]

Of course, in the putty-clay model the ratio of the two output elasticities does *not* in general correspond to the ratio of factor shares. How does the elasticity of the factor-price frontier, as given by (10), compare with the ratio of profit to wage share in gross output? From (6) and (10), it is easy to see that the former is *smaller* in value than the latter in the case corresponding to the so-called "golden rule" i.e. when r, the interest rate, is equal to λ, the growth rate of output. This only confirms the result in the preceding paragraph, because in the "golden rule" case the ratio of the two output elasticities is exactly equal to the ratio of factor shares. But when r is larger than λ, we cannot be definite. For high enough r compared to λ, it is possible for the elasticity of the factor price frontier to be equal to or to exceed the ratio of profit to wage share.

4

Now we want to find out the relationship between W and g for a given rate of interest, r.

From (3),

$$(11) \quad \frac{dW}{dg} = e^{-gT}\left[f'(k)\frac{dk}{dg} - f(k)\left(T + g\frac{dT}{dk}\frac{dk}{dg}\right)\right].$$

In Appendix (C) it is shown that (11) is negative. This means that for a given rate of interest the higher is the rate of embodied technical progress the lower is the wage rate; in other words, the factor-price frontier shrinks towards the origin with faster technical progress.[9] Essentially what is happening is as follows: the capital scrapping condition given by our equation (3) implies that today's new machine will be scrapped T years from now when the wage rate will rise to be equal to the average productivity of today's new machine. Now, the higher is the rate at which the wage rate increases due to technical progress, the smaller can today's wage rate be to catch up with this average productivity over the same period. Of course, this period does not remain the same with a higher rate of technical progress (it is shorter, as we have seen in Section 2) but, on the other hand, the average productivity of today's machine – the thing to be caught up with – is also smaller (since with a higher rate of technical progress the amount of investment per man on new machines is also smaller, as we have seen in Section 2). So the first-mentioned effect dominates to keep the level of the wage rate smaller for a given rate of interest.

Of course, with a higher rate of technical progress the rate of interest will not remain the same. In the next section we show that for a given gross saving ratio, as long as this saving ratio does not exceed its "golden rule" value, a higher rate of technical progress is associated with a higher rate of interest. The effect of this on the level of the wage rate reinforces that described in the preceding paragraph, because along the factor-price frontier a higher rate of interest also implies a lower wage rate. So for a given gross saving ratio, the total effect of a higher rate of embodied technical progress is to lower the wage rate. This is a paradoxical result: between two otherwise identical economies in long-run equilibrium with the same gross saving ratio, the technically more progressive economy will have the *lower* wage rate.

5

If in this economy s is the constant fraction of total gross output saved and currently invested, the savings-investment equation may be written[10] as

$$(12) \quad s = \frac{k}{f(k)} \frac{\lambda}{1 - e^{-\lambda T}}$$

where, as before, $\lambda \ (= \mu + g)$ is the growth rate. For the given gross-saving ratio, s, and the rate of growth of labor force, μ, we can denote the R.H.S. of (12) as M and get

$$(13) \quad \frac{dr}{dg} = -\frac{\dfrac{\partial N}{\partial g}}{\dfrac{\partial N}{\partial r}}.$$

Since in Bardhan (1969) we have proved that dr/ds is negative under our general assumption that $\sigma \leq 1$, this implies that $\partial N/\partial r$ is negative. So (13) will have the same sign as that of $\partial N/\partial g$.

From (12), and after substituting the value of dT/dk from (7),

$$(14) \quad \frac{\partial N}{\partial g} \frac{1}{N} = \frac{[f(k) - f'(k)k]}{f(k)k} \left[1 - \frac{(e^{rT} - 1)\lambda}{r(e^{\lambda T} - 1)\sigma} \right] \frac{dk}{dg} + \frac{(e^{\lambda T} - 1 - \lambda T)}{\lambda(e^{\lambda T} - 1)}.$$

Since from (8) dk/dg is negative, and since

$$\frac{e^{rT}-1}{r} \geqq \frac{e^{\lambda T}-1}{\lambda} \quad \text{for} \quad r \geqq \lambda,$$

(14) is positive under our assumption that $\sigma \leqq 1$.

Thus, given the gross-saving ratio, a higher rate of embodied technical progress is associated with a higher rate of interest under our general assumption that $\sigma \leqq 1$, as long as the rate of interest is not below the growth rate (i.e. the rate of savings is not above its "golden rule" value). This result is in some contrast with that in the "putty-putty" vintage model of Levhari and Sheshinski (1969) who stated that "it can be shown that a negative relation between the rate of return and the rate of embodied technical progress can occur even when the rate of savings is below its Golden Rule value." Part of the difference may lie in our general assumption in this paper that $\sigma \leqq 1$, which ensures the uniqueness of equilibrium in the putty-clay model.

6

Classical as well as modern economists have been deeply interested in finding out the impact of technical progress on factor shares. It is thus worth noting the impact of embodied Harrod-neutral technical progress on the factor shares in the putty-clay model, particularly because this model has some extra dimensions (like the economic obsolescence of machines) which were lacking in earlier models.

The equation for w, the wage-share in gross output is given by equation (6) in Section 1. Given μ, the rate of growth of the labor force, w depends on g and T. Given T, w is a declining function of g; but T also depends on g, directly as well as indirectly through the associated change in r (for a given gross-saving ratio). So

$$(15) \quad \frac{dw}{dg} = \frac{\partial w}{\partial g} + \frac{\partial w}{\partial T}\left[\frac{\partial T}{\partial r}\frac{dr}{dg} + \frac{\partial T}{\partial g}\right]$$

From our analysis in the preceding Sections we know that on the R.H.S. of (15), $(\partial w/\partial g) < 0$, $(\partial w/\partial T) < 0$, $(dr/dg) > 0$ (when the rate of saving does not exceed its "golden rule" value, as we assume), $\partial T/\partial r$ is positive for $\sigma \leqq \frac{2}{3}$ and is negative when $\sigma = 1$, and $(\partial T/\partial g) < 0$. This implies that to work out the sign of (15) is quite a complicated affair. We have been able to get clear-cut results only for the case of *ex ante* Cobb-Douglas production functions.

Working out the values of $\partial w/\partial g$ and $\partial w/\partial T$ from (6), that of $\partial T/\partial r$ from (5) for the Cobb-Douglas case where $\sigma = 1$, that of dr/dg from (12), (13) and (14) and that of $\partial T/\partial g$ from (7), (8) and (9), and substituting them in (15) and after simplification,

$$(16) \quad \frac{dw}{dg}\frac{1}{wT} = \frac{-z'(q)}{z(q)} + \left[\frac{z'(q)}{z(q)}q - \frac{z'(p)}{z(p)}p\right]\frac{z(m)A}{B}$$

where

$$A = \frac{[z(q) - 1]}{qz(q)} + \frac{[z(m) - 1]z'(n)}{z(m)\dfrac{m}{n}[z(n) - 1] - z(n)[z(m) - 1]}$$

and

$$B = 1 - \frac{z(m)}{z(q)} + \frac{[z(m) - 1][(m - n)z(m)z(n) - \{z(m) - z(n)\}]}{z(m)\dfrac{m}{n}[z(n) - 1] - z(n)[z(m) - 1]}$$

and where $z(x)$, as before, is $(e^x - 1)/x$ and $q = \lambda T$, $p = \mu T$, $m = rT$ and $n = (r - g)T$. From (19) in Appendix (A) and (22) in Appendix (B) it is easy to check that both A and B are positive.

In Appendix (D) we show that

$$(17) \quad \left[\frac{z'(q)}{z(q)}q - \frac{z'(p)p}{z(p)}\right] \lesseqgtr \frac{[(m - n)z(m)z(n) - \{z(m) - z(n)\}]}{z(m)z(n)} \quad \text{for} \quad q \lesseqgtr m$$

$m \geq q$ or $r \geq \lambda$, of course, implies that the rate of saving does not exceed its "golden rule" value, which we have assumed anyway. Using (17) and applying (19) of Appendix (A) and after simplification we can show that the R.H.S. of (16) is less than or equal to the following expression

$$(18) \quad \frac{-[z(n) - 1]}{nABz(n)}\left\{\frac{mz(m)[z(q) - 1]}{qz(q)} - [z(m) - 1]\right\}$$

$$- \frac{[1 + (q - 1)z(q)][z(m) - z(q)]}{qz^2(q)B[(m - n)z(m)z(n) - \{z(m) - z(n)\}]}.$$

From (20) (22) in Appendix (B) it is easy to check that (18) is non-positive. This implies that (16) is also non-positive. (16) is exactly equal to zero in the "golden rule" case ($m = q$) and negative in the case when $m > q$ (the rate of saving is less than its "golden rule" value). So in the "golden rule" case with an *ex ante* Cobb-Douglas production function a faster rate of embodied technical progress leaves the wage share unchanged; in the case when the rate of saving is less than its "golden rule" value, the equilibrium with a faster rate of technical progress has a *lower* wage-share.[11]

Appendix

(A) We define

$$z(x) = \frac{e^x - 1}{x} > 0 \quad \text{for} \quad x \lessgtr 0.$$

x will be alternatively used as

$$m = rT$$
$$n = (r - g)T$$
$$g = \lambda T$$
$$p = \mu T$$

so that $(e^{rT} - 1)/rT = z(m)$ and so on. One should also note that $m - n = q - p = gT > 0$.
It is easy to check that

(19) $z'(x) = \dfrac{1 + (x - 1)z(x)}{x} > 0$ for $x \gtrless 0.$

(B) In equation (5) we first prove that the denominator on the R.H.S. is positive for σ not exceeding unity. All we have to prove is that

(20) $z(m)z(n)(m - n) > z(m) - z(n).$

Define $y(x) = x + (1/z(x))$, then with the help of (19) $y'(x)$ has same sign as $([z(x) - 1][1 + xz(x)]/x) > 0$. This implies that $m + (1/z(m)) > n + (1/z(n))$, which in turn implies (20).
   Now let us take the numerator on the R.H.S. of (5). It is obvious that the smaller is the value of σ, the larger is the value of the numerator. If we can show that the numerator is positive for $\sigma = \frac{2}{3}$, then it is positive for all positive σ below $\frac{2}{3}$ as well.
   It is easy to see that the numerator is equal to zero if $g = 0$, i.e. $m = n$. But since $g > 0$, all we have to show is that the derivative of the numerator with respect to g is positive. Differentiating with respect to g and using (19), we find that we have to prove

(21) $\dfrac{mz(m)}{z(m) - 1} > \dfrac{\sigma n[1 + (n - 1)z(n)]}{[nz(n) - 2\{z(n) - 1\}]}$

We prove this in two steps. First we show that

(22) $\dfrac{mz(m)}{z(m) - 1} > \dfrac{nz(n)}{z(n) - 1},$

since $m > n$; and then we show that under the condition that $\sigma = \frac{2}{3}$, the R.H.S. of inequality (22) is larger than the R.H.S. of inequality (21). Define

$$p(x) = \dfrac{z(x)x}{z(x) - 1}.$$

Using (19), the sign of $p'(x)$ is the same as that of $[z^2(x) - 1 - xz(x)]$ which is positive, since by expansion in Taylor series it can be shown that $((e^x - 1)/x) > e^{x/2}$. This proves inequality (22).
   The R.H.S. of inequality (22) is larger than the R.H.S. of (21) if, as can be shown after cross-multiplication, use of $\frac{2}{3}$ as the value of σ and simplification,

(23) $[z(n) + 2]n^2 z(n) - 2[z(n) - 1][1 + 2z(n)]n > 0$

The L.H.S. of (23) is obviously positive when n is negative, but when n is positive, dividing through by n, the L.H.S. of (23) may be rewritten, after simplification, as

$$F(n) = (n - 4)(e^n - 1)^2 + 2n(e^n - 1)(1 + n) + 2n^2.$$

Since $F(0) = 0$ and $F'(n) > 0$, (5) is valid.

(C) For (11) to be negative all we have to prove is

$$(24) \quad \frac{f(k)}{f'(k)} T > \frac{dk}{dg}\left[1 - \frac{f(k)}{f'(k)} g \frac{dT}{dk}\right].$$

Putting the value of dk/dg from (8) this may be rewritten as

$$(25) \quad \frac{f(k)}{f'(k)} \frac{(1 - \sigma)}{\sigma}[z(m) - z(n)]z(n) + \frac{z(m)}{n}[1 + (n - 1)z(n)]$$

$$> \frac{f(k)}{f'(k)} \frac{dT}{dk} \frac{1}{T}\left[z(n)[z(m) - 1] - z(m)[z(n) - 1]\frac{m}{n}\right].$$

The L.H.S. of (25) is positive and on the R.H.S. dT/dk is positive from (7) and the whole bracketed expression is negative which follows from (22). So inequalities (24) and (25) are valid.

(D) Using (19), the L.H.S. of (17) is

$$(26) \quad q\frac{z'(q)}{z(q)} - p\frac{z'(p)}{z(p)} = (q - p) - \frac{[z(q) - z(p)]}{z(q)z(p)}$$

The R.H.S. of (17) is equal to $(m - n) - ([z(m) - z(n)]/z(m)z(n))$. Since $(m - n) = gT = q - p$, all we have to prove for showing the validity of (17) is that

$$(27) \quad \frac{z(q) - z(p)}{z(q)z(p)} \geqq \frac{z(m) - z(n)}{z(m)z(n)}, \quad \text{for} \quad m \geqq q.$$

Define $\alpha = r/g$, $\beta = \lambda/g$, and $\theta = gT$. Since we take $r \geqq \lambda$ and $\lambda = \mu + g$, $\alpha \geqq \beta > 1$. Then,

$$(28) \quad \frac{z(m) - z(n)}{z(m)z(n)} = \frac{z[\alpha\theta] - z[(\alpha - 1)\theta]}{z[\alpha\theta]z[(\alpha - 1)\theta]}$$

and

$$(29) \quad \frac{z(q) - z(p)}{z(q)z(p)} = \frac{z[\beta\theta] - z[(\beta - 1)\theta]}{z[\beta\theta] \cdot z[(\beta - 1)\theta]}.$$

If $r = \lambda$, then, of course, $\alpha = \beta$, and (28) = (29). Let us assume $r > \lambda$, or $\alpha > \beta$. Define

$$(30) \quad J(y) = \frac{z[y\theta] - z[(y - 1)\theta]}{z[y\theta] \cdot z[(y - 1)\theta]}, \quad y = \alpha, \beta.$$

We have to prove that $J'(y) < 0$, since that will imply (28) smaller than (29).

Working out the value of $J'(y)/J(y)$ from (30), and after cross multiplication and simplification what remains for us to prove is that

(31) $\dfrac{z'[y\theta]}{z^2[y\theta]} < \dfrac{z'[(y-1)\theta]}{z^2[(y-1)\theta]}$

Noting the value of $z'(x)$ from (19), all we have to prove is that

$p'(x) < 0,$

where

(32) $p(x) = \dfrac{1 + [x-1]z(x)}{x \cdot z^2(x)}, \quad x = y\theta, (y-1)\theta.$

Using (19) again, and upon simplification $p'(x)$ has the same sign as that of

(33) $2[z(x)-1] - xz(x)[3 + \{x-2\}z(x)].$

We have to show that this is negative. First we show

(34) $xz(x) - 2[z(x)-1] > 0.$

Using the definition of $z(x)$, (34) is equal to

$\dfrac{1}{x}[x\,e^x - 2\,e^x + x + 2].$

Define

$P(x) = x\,e^x - 2\,e^x + x + 2.$

This is positive since $P(0) = 0$ and $P'(x) > 0$. It immediately follows from (34) that

(35) $3 + [x-2]z(x) > 1.$

Using (34) and (35), it is easy to see that (33) is negative.

Notes

1. The method of proof also suggests local stability of growth equilibrium. See Bardhan (1969, footnote 6).
2. See Matthews (1964), Bliss (1968) and Bardhan (1969).
3. According to Arrow, Chenery, Minhas and Solow (1961) this is commonly the case. However, as shown in Bardhan (1967), if the data-generating model is putty-clay, the elasticity of average labor productivity with respect to the wage rate – which is taken as the elasticity of substitution in Arrow et al. (1961) – may be significantly different from zero and yet σ in the *ex ante* production function may be zero.

4. The same result is valid for the "clay-clay" case of Solow, Tobin, von Weizsäcker and Yaari (1966).
5. Our subsequent equations (1), (2), (3), and (4) correspond to equations (35), (49), (51) and (60) respectively in Bliss (1968). For our purpose of investigating the properties of balanced-growth equilibrium, it is enough to study the equilibrium at time zero. All our subsequent variables without any vintage label refer to time zero; this convenient procedure was also adopted in Bliss (1968) and Bardhan (1969).
6. In the subsequent analysis we assume $r \neq 0$ and $r \neq g$. If $r = 0$, (1) changes to

$$V = f(k)T - \frac{W[e^{gT} - 1]}{g} - k = 0;$$

and (2) to $f'(k) = 1/T$. If $r = g$, (1) changes to

$$V = f(k)\frac{[1 - e^{-rT}]}{r} - WT - k = 0.$$

In either of these two cases the model is much more simplified, and the analysis is left to the reader.

7. For a derivation of this equation see that for equation (66) in Bliss (1968).
8. Levhari and Sheshinski (1970) also find that in their "putty-putty" vintage model the elasticity of the factor-price frontier is not equal to the ratio of the two output elasticities.
9. For a similar result in the "putty-putty" vintage model see Levhari and Sheshinski (1970).
10. For a derivation of this equation see equation (63) in Bliss (1968).
11. It is interesting to note, as Phelps (1963) and Kemp and Thánh (1966) have shown, that in the *ex ante* Cobb-Douglas case, for the same rate of technical progress, the equilibrium with the higher gross saving ratio also has a *lower* wage share.

References

Arrow, K. J. H. B. Chenery, B. S. Minhas and R. M. Solow, "Capital-Labour Substitution and Economic Efficiency," *Review of Economics and Statistics* XLIII (August, 1961), 225–250.

Bardhan, P. K., "On Estimation of Production Functions from International Cross-Section Data," *Economic Journal*, LXXVII (June, 1967), 328–335.

Bardhan, P. K., "Equilibrium Growth in a Model with Economic Obsolescence of Machines," *Quarterly Journal of Economics*, LXXXIII (May, 1969), 312–323.

Bliss, C. J., "On Putty-Clay," *Review of Economic Studies*, XXXV (April, 1968), 105–132.

Britto, R., "On Putty-Clay: A Comment," *Review of Economic Studies*, XXXVI (July, 1969), 395–398.

Kemp, M. C. and P. C. Thánh, "On a Class of Growth Models," *Econometrica*, XXXIV (April, 1966), 257–282.

Levhari D. and E. Sheshinski, "The Relation between the Rate of Interest and the Rate of Technical Progress," *Review of Economic Studies*, XXXVI (July, 1969), 363–379.

—— and ——, "The Factor Price Frontier with Embodied Technical Progress," *American Economic Review*, LX (December, 1970), 807–813.

Matthews, R. C. O., "The New View of Investment: A Comment," *Quarterly Journal of Economics*, LXXVII (February, 1964), 164–172.

Phelps, E. S., "Substitution, Fixed Proportions, Growth and Distribution," *International Economic Review*, IV (September, 1963), 265–288.

R. M. Solow, J. Tobin, C. C. von Weizsäcker and M. Yaari, "Neo-classical Growth with Fixed Factor Proportions," *Review of Economic Studies*, XXXIII (April, 1966), 79–115.

Chapter 12

On Estimation of Production Functions from International Cross-Section Data[1]

"If ever there was a case of looking in a dark room for a black cat that we are pretty certain is not there, it is looking for a static production function in international statistics." – Joan Robinson (1964)

I

In recent years estimation of production functions from international cross-section data has become popular. One of the pioneering attempts has been that of Arrow, Chenery, Minhas and Solow (1961). They have shown that under the assumptions of constant returns to scale and competitive labor markets the elasticity of labor productivity for any industry with respect to the wage-rate is equal to the elasticity of factor substitution along the underlying production function. Therefore, they point out [1961, p. 229], "information about σ (the elasticity of substitution) can be obtained, under these assumptions, from observations of the joint variation of output per unit of labor and the real wage." Once the elasticity of substitution is known, the production function could be derived in their model up to a constant of integration. They take an international cross-section of industries and estimate the coefficient of regression of the logarithm of observed value added per unit of labor on that of observed wage-rate for each of the twenty-four industries in their sample.[2] The value of the elasticity of factor substitution – their regression coefficient b [1961, p. 229] – turns out to be significantly above zero and below unity for most industries. This leads them to reject both Cobb-Douglas and Leontief-type fixed-coefficients production functions.

The underlying production theory of their analysis is clearly static. One might wonder if in a world in which there is continuous growth and technical progress, in which machines "embody" the technology of their date of construction and once a machine is built there is little scope for altering its labor requirement, *b* really gives a reliable estimate of the extent of substitution possibilities along a production function facing the entrepreneur;[3] if not, one might be interested in exploring the nature of bias in the estimate. In the next section we try to do this analytically for one special, albeit interesting, case. We assume that in the "data-generating model" the different countries are in long-run equilibrium (Arrow *et al.* assume their countries to be in *static* equilibrium).[4] We assume that the different countries have similar *ex ante* production functions, the same rate of Harrod-neutral (completely "embodied") technical progress *g* and the same rate of population growth μ. This is done to isolate those aspects of the problem in which we are particularly interested and also to keep the model comparable to the analysis by Arrow *et al.* Physical depreciation is ignored (again for simplicity) and obsolescence takes its toll when rising wages absorb all the output of a particular machine. One of the essential features of this model is that with different wage-rates different countries have different age structures of capital, and this is reflected in the observed joint variation of labor productivity and real wage.

In this world let us find out if the Arrow-Chenery-Minhas-Solow estimate of *b* – the elasticity of average labor productivity with respect to the wage-rate – is an underestimate or overestimate of the elasticity of factor substitution *ex ante*, *i.e.*, at the time when it is being decided what kind of machine should be built.

It should be noted here that the present writer does not necessarily commit himself to the view that the data-generating model assumed in this paper is more "realistic" than the static model of Arrow *et al.* But many people do consider (mostly on grounds of casual empiricism) our model to be a better approximation of reality than the static model, and it is surely worth one's effort to investigate the nature of "error" one would make by assuming the latter rather than the former model.

In order to avoid lots of superscripts and subscripts, we shall use a single-industry model in the next section, although the results are immediately generalisable to the many-industries case.

II

The total labor supply at time *t* is

$$L(t) = L(0) \cdot e^{\mu t} = \int_{t-T}^{t} L(v, t)\, dv \tag{1}$$

where $L(v, t)$ is the labor used at time *t* on a machine of vintage *v* and *T* is the age of the oldest machine in use. From (1) it is easy to show that the equilibrium distribution of labor over the operating vintages of machines is "exponential,"[5] so that labor assigned to new machines is related to total labor supply as follows:

$$L(t, t) = \frac{L(t)\mu}{[1 - e^{-\mu T}]} \tag{2}$$

Similarly, from the exponential growth – at rate $(\mu + g)$ – of output it follows that

$$F(t, t) = \frac{F(t) \cdot (\mu + g)}{[1 - e^{-(\mu+g)T}]} \tag{3}$$

where $F(t, t)$ is output at time t of a machine of vintage t and total output at time t is

$$F(t) = \int_{t-T}^{t} F(v, t) \, dv \tag{4}$$

From the scrapping condition of machines and with entrepreneurs correctly expecting the wage-rate to rise at rate g,

$$\frac{F(t, t)}{L(t, t)} = W(t + T) = W(t) \cdot e^{gT} \tag{5}$$

From (2), (3) and (5) the average productivity of total labor in this economy is

$$v(t) = \frac{F(t)}{L(t)} = \frac{W(t)}{q(T) \cdot e^{-gT}} \tag{6}$$

where

$$q(T) = \frac{(\mu + g) \, [1 - e^{-\mu T}]}{[1 - e^{-(\mu+g)T}]\mu}$$

Now in this model the elasticity of average labor productivity with respect to the wage-rate, denoted by b as in Arrow *et al.* (1961), is given by

$$b = \frac{dv(t)}{dW(t)} \cdot \frac{W(t)}{v(t)} = 1 - \frac{dT}{dW(t)} \cdot W(t) \left[\frac{q'(T)}{q(T)} - g \right]. \tag{7}$$

Let us now find out the sign of $\left[\dfrac{q'(T)}{q(T)} - g \right]$

From the definition of $q(T)$

$$\frac{q'(T)}{q(T)} = \frac{\mu \cdot e^{-\mu T}}{[1 - e^{-\mu T}]} - \frac{(\mu + g) \cdot e^{-(\mu+g)T}}{[1 - e^{-(\mu+g)T}]}$$

$$= \frac{\mu}{e^{\mu T} - 1} - \frac{(\mu + g)}{[e^{(\mu+g)T} - 1]} \tag{8}$$

Hence

$$\left[\frac{q'(T)}{q(T)} - g\right] = \frac{1}{T}\left[\frac{\mu T}{e^{\mu T} - 1} - \frac{(\mu + g)T}{e^{(\mu+g)T} - 1} - gT\right]$$

$$= \frac{1}{T}\left[\frac{1}{Z(\beta)} - \frac{1}{Z(\alpha)} + (\beta - \alpha)\right] \tag{9'}$$

where

$$Z(x) = \frac{e^x - 1}{x}, \quad x = \alpha, \beta$$

and

$$\alpha = (\mu + g)T$$
$$\beta = \mu T$$
$$\alpha - \beta = gT > 0$$

$$= \frac{1}{T}\left[\frac{1 + \beta Z(\beta)}{Z(\beta)} - \frac{1 + Z(\alpha)\alpha}{Z(\alpha)}\right] \tag{9}$$

If $y(x) = \dfrac{1 + xZ(x)}{Z(x)}$, then (9) is positive or negative as $y'(x) \gtreqless 0$. From the definition of $Z(x)$, it can be shown that

$$\frac{Z'(x)}{Z(x)} = \frac{1 + [x - 1]Z(x)}{xZ(x)} > 0 \tag{10}$$

Now from the definition of $y(x)$

$$sgn\, y'(x) = sgn\, [Z^2(x) - Z'(x)] = sgn[x \cdot Z^2(x) - (x - 1)Z(x) - 1]$$
$$= sgn\, [Z(x) - 1][1 + xZ(x)] > 0. \tag{11}$$

since from the definition of $Z(x)$, $Z(x) > 1$. Therefore

$$\left[\frac{q'(T)}{q(T)} - g\right] < 0 \tag{12}$$

Putting (12) in (7),

$$b \gtreqless 1 \quad \text{as} \quad \frac{dT}{dW} \gtreqless 0. \tag{13}$$

Now an important determinant of the sign of dT/dW is the *ex ante* elasticity of factor substitution. It has been shown[6] by Matthews (1964, pp. 169–71) that in a model like ours given the rate of technical progress, a higher wage-rate is associated with a *longer* operating life of capital if the *ex ante* elasticity of substitution is equal to unity,[7] if the latter is zero a higher wage-rate is associated with a *shorter* operating life of capital; and if the *ex ante* elasticity of substitution is sufficiently below unity and above zero the operating life of capital is *invariant* with respect to changes in the wage-rate across steady-state paths. In other words, if σ is the *ex ante* elasticity of substitution,

$$\left. \begin{array}{c} \text{when } \sigma = 1, \dfrac{dT}{dW} > 0; \\[2mm] \text{when } \sigma \text{ is sufficiently below unity and above zero} \\[2mm] \text{say,} \qquad \sigma = \sigma^*, \dfrac{dT}{dW} = 0; \\[2mm] \text{when } 1 > \sigma > \sigma^*, \dfrac{dT}{dW} > 0; \\[2mm] \text{when } \sigma^* > \sigma \geqq 0, \dfrac{dT}{dW} < 0 \end{array} \right\} \qquad (14)$$

Thus, for example, if the production function is Cobb–Douglas, $dT/dw > 0$ and from (13) it immediately follows that the Arrow – Chenery – Minhas – Solow estimate of b will give an *overestimate* of the *ex ante* elasticity of substitution. More generally, it follows from (7), (12) and (14) that when $1 \geqq \sigma \geqq \sigma^* > 0$, b gives an *overestimate* of σ.[8] In case of fixed coefficients of production, *i.e.*, $\sigma = 0$, $b < 1$, but that it once again gives an *overestimate* can be proved as follows.

With fixed coefficients of production and with exponential Harrod-neutral technical progress, (5) will give us

$$W(t) = e^{g(t-T)} \cdot \lambda \qquad (15)$$

where $\lambda = \dfrac{F(0, t)}{L(0, t)}$, a given constant.

From (15), $\quad \dfrac{dT}{dW(t)} \cdot W(t) = -\dfrac{1}{g} \qquad (16)$

Putting (16) in (7),

$$b > 0 \quad \text{if} \quad \dfrac{q'(T)}{q(T)} > 0$$

From (8) and (9'),

$$\frac{q'(T)}{q(T)} = \frac{1}{T}\left[\frac{Z(\alpha) - Z(\beta)}{Z(\beta)Z(\alpha)}\right]. \qquad (16a)$$

Since $\alpha > \beta$ and since from (10), $Z'(x) > 0$, we can say that

$$\frac{q'(T)}{q(T)} > 0$$

Thus when $\sigma = 0$, $b > 0$.

The observation by Arrow et al. (1961) of a value of b greater than zero but less than unity in the majority of industries leads them to reject both the Cobb–Douglas and fixed-coefficients production functions. In the light of our results above such an observed value of b, while strengthening the case against Cobb–Douglas, is not at all incompatible with fixed coefficients production functions.

Thus in the light of the "data-generating model" assumed in this paper[9] we have analyzed the nature of what may be called the "specification error" in the usual estimation of production functions from international cross-section data.[10] While the significance of our result is by no means confined, as is obvious from our analysis, to estimation of international cross-section data, it is of particular import-ance in the latter case, since divergences in wage-rates and operating lives of equipment are often more significant across countries than across, say, regions in the same country.

Having investigated the nature of bias in the estimate of elasticity of substitu-tion, we thought it might be useful to have a rough idea of the *extent* of bias. If the latter is quantitatively insignificant there is not much point in the whole exercise of this paper. So we tried to make some illustrative numerical estimates. Suppose the *ex ante* elasticity of substitution is zero; given some "plausible" values of the rate of growth of labor, the rate of growth of productivity of labor and the economic life of capital, we try to find out the extent of over-estimation of elasticity of substitution that will result from the Arrow–Chenery–Minhas–Solow procedure.

When $\sigma = 0$ we know from our equations (7), (16) and (16a) that

$$b = \frac{[Z(\alpha) - Z(\beta)]}{gT \cdot Z(\alpha) \cdot Z(\beta)} \tag{17}$$

where as before, $\alpha = (\mu + g)T$, $\beta = \mu T$, and $Z(x) = \dfrac{e^x - 1}{x}$, $x = \alpha, \beta$.

Table 12.I gives some numerical estimates of equation (17). A look at Column 5 of the table tells us that the extent of overestimation of σ is significant indeed (particularly when one remembers the values of b observed by Arrow et al.).

III

Two other implications of the analysis above may be pointed out. As has been pointed out by Arrow et al., in the comparative-static case with constant-returns production function and pure competition, the wage-share in national-income

Table 12.I

T (years)*	μ (annual %)	g (annual %)	μ + g (annual %)	b	σ
6	1.5	2.5	4.0	0.50	0
6	1.0	2.5	3.5	0.47	0
6	2.0	2.0	4.0	0.53	0
6	1.5	2.0	3.5	0.50	0
6	1.0	2.0	3.0	0.48	0
8	1.5	2.5	4.0	0.48	0
8	1.0	2.5	3.5	0.49	0
8	2.0	2.0	4.0	0.48	0
8	1.5	2.0	3.5	0.49	0
8	1.0	2.0	3.0	0.51	0
10	1.5	2.5	4.0	0.49	0
10	1.0	2.5	3.5	0.48	0
10	2.0	2.0	4.0	0.44	0
10	1.5	2.0	3.5	0.49	0
10	1.0	2.0	3.0	0.46	0
17	1.5	2.5	4.0	0.42	0
17	1.0	2.5	3.5	0.44	0
17	2.0	2.0	4.0	0.42	0
17	1.5	2.0	3.5	0.43	0
17	1.0	2.0	3.0	0.44	0

* According to the United States Commerce Department calculations, the average age of gross stocks of *equipment* in manufacturing industries (based on data published in the Internal Revenue Service's Bulletin F) was 8.1 years in 1961. Alternative calculations "based on assumed lives 20% shorter" give an average age of 6.2 years.

T in our model is not, however, the average age of capital, but is that of the machine on the margin of obsolesence, which should be longer. But T is certainly shorter than the *physical* life of capital. It may be noted that the total "service life" of manufacturing equipment is 17 years, according to calculations "based on Bulletin F lives." Alternative calculations "based on assumed lives 20% shorter" give a service life of 13 years.

In view of all this the range of T assumed in the table may not be grossly off the mark (in any case the value of b does not seem to be very sensitive to changes in T so far as the range taken in the Table is concerned).

Source: G. Jaszi, R. C. Wasson and L. Grose, "Expansion of Fixed Capital in the U.S.," *Survey of Current Business*, November, 1962. (For this reference I am indebted to Robert Solow.)

increases remains unchanged, or decreases with a rise in the wage-rate as the elasticity of substitution, σ, is less than, equal to, or greater than unity. But if we take a comparative-dynamic view of the world as we have done above, it is easily seen that the wage-share in national income increases, remains unchanged or decreases with a rise in the wage-rate as b, the elasticity of average labor productivity with respect to changes in the wage-rate (and not σ, which in most cases is lower than the corresponding b), is less than, equal to, or greater than unity. This follows from (6) and (12) above.

From (6), the wage-share in national income,

$$Q(t) = \frac{W(t)L(t)}{F(t)}$$

$$= q(T) \cdot e^{-gT}$$

Now from (12) and (13),

$$\frac{dQ}{dW} \gtreqless 0, \text{ as } b \gtreqless 1$$

In the Cobb–Douglas case, for example, the wage-share *decreases* with a rise in the wage-rate. The wage-share is invariant with respect to the wage-rate only in the case when $\sigma = \sigma^*$ (as defined in equation 14).

The other point to note is about the sufficient condition for precluding the "reversal of factor intensities" in a two-sector model. It is easy to show that in the comparative-static model (Arrow *et al.* have shown it for the special case of constant-elasticity production functions) a sufficient condition for non-reversals of factor-intensities is to have the elasticities of substitution in the two sectors of the same value always. In our comparative-dynamic view of the world, *if* we call the sector with the higher wage-share as the more labor-intensive of the two sectors, it can be shown that the corresponding sufficient condition is for the value of b (and not σ) to be the same in the two sectors.

In our two-sector case we can rewrite[11] (7) as

$$b_i = 1 - \frac{dT_i}{dW(t)} \cdot W(t)\left[\frac{q'(T_i)}{q(T_i)} - g\right] \tag{17a}$$

We can rewrite the equation for Q as that for Q_i, the wage-share in *i*th sector; *i.e.*,

$$Q_i(t) = q(T_i) \cdot e^{-gT_i} \tag{18}$$

From (7a) and (18),

$$b_1 = b_2 \text{ implies } \frac{dQ_1}{dW} \cdot \frac{1}{Q_1} = \frac{dQ_2}{dW} \cdot \frac{1}{Q_2}$$

This means that if one sector is more labor-intensive than the other in the sense that one has a higher wage-share than the other to start with, then it will remain so under the sufficient condition that the value of b is the same in the two sectors.

Notes

1. For helpful discussion or comments I am indebted to Christopher Bliss, Franklin Fisher and Paul Samuelson. Needless to add, all errors and opinions in this paper are mine alone. An earlier version of this paper was read in a Harvard-M.I.T. Joint Faculty Seminar on Mathematical Economics and in a seminar in the University of Pennsylvania.
2. For a similar attempt with reference to two-digit industries – instead of three-digit industries considered in Arrow *et al.* (1961) – see the results of Murata and Arrow as reported in Nerlove (1965).
3. This has been one of the most important criticisms of the Arrow–Chenery–Minhas–Solow procedure. Joan Robinson (1964), for example, finds fault with Minhas' work (1963) for, among other things, the following reason:

    > Even if the *ex ante* production function from which choices for current invest-ments are being made were in some sense the same for any one industry in each country, we should not be able to see it in the statistics. The capital equipment in existence at any moment in each country has been built up over a long past during which there has been an accumulation of technical knowledge. . . . The *de facto* relation of cost of capital per man to output per man reflects differences between one country and another in their past history for varying lengths of time (since the age of equipment is not the same in all).

    A similar point was made earlier in another review (Harcourt, 1963) of Minhas' book.
4. In other words, we have a comparative-dynamic version of the comparative-static analysis used by Arrow *et al.*; the former may not be on a higher level of abstraction than the latter. The analysis becomes very messy indeed when one gets off the steady-state path.
5. For an explicit proof, see Phelps (1963), Appendix C.
6. There is a slip in the proof in footnote 9 of Matthews (1964): his use of Taylor series approximation actually gives the wrong result. But it is not difficult to prove that his conclusions are valid. A proof for the Cobb–Douglas case is given in the Appendix (the method of proof was originally suggested by James Mirrlees). The proof for the other cases involves a simple extension of that for the Cobb–Douglas case. See also Phelps (1963).
7. To quote Matthews (1964, p. 171), "With Cobb–Douglas, instead of getting, for a given difference in W between two steady states, an exactly proportional difference in capital-intensity, leaving labour's share on new machines constant (as is the case for a non-vintage model), what happens is that a higher W is associated with a lower r (the rate at which future quasi-rents are discounted), more weight is given to the future (when labour is dearer) and hence there is a somewhat *greater* than proportional difference in capital intensity. The result is that labour's share on new machines is lower, and this leads to a longer T. There will be some value of σ lower than unity at which the above-noted effect of the fall in r will exactly offset the increase in labour's share that would otherwise have occurred, and so will leave labour's share and T unchanged."
8. It is possible to prove a stronger result: b gives always an overestimate of σ in the range $1 \geqq \sigma \geqq 0$. But the small gain in generality seems to be outweighed by the length and cumbersomeness of the proof. Hence I omit it here. For the essential result of this paper this does not matter much. Any reader interested in the general proof may correspond with the writer.
9. It can be checked that exactly the same kind of overestimation will result if the "data-generating model" happens to be Arrow's "learning" model (1962).

10. Samuelson suggests that b in this paper actually estimates the elasticity of substitution along a "surrogate" production function, while σ is the elasticity of substitution reflected in the "book of blueprints."
11. We are assuming that g is the same in both the sectors.

References

K. J. Arrow, "Economic Implications of Learning by Doing," *Review of Economic Studies*, June 1962.

K. J. Arrow, H. B. Chenery, B. S. Minhas, and R. M. Solow, "Capital–Labor Substitution and Economic Efficiency," *Review of Economics and Statistics*, August 1961.

G. C. Harcourt, review of Minhas' book (1963) in Economic Journal, 1963.

R. C. O. Matthews, "The New View of Investment: A Comment," *Quarterly Journal of Economics*, February 1964.

B. S. Minhas, *International Comparisons of Factor Costs and Factor Use* (1963).

M. Nerlove, "Notes on Recent Empirical Studies of the CES and Related Production Functions," Technical Report No. 13, Institute for Mathematical Studies in the Social Sciences, Stanford University, July 19, 1965.

E. S. Phelps, "Substitution, Fixed Proportions, Growth and Distribution," *International Economic Review*, September 1963.

J. Robinson, "Factor Prices Not Equalised," *Quarterly Journal of Economics*, May 1964.

Appendix *The Sign of $\dfrac{dT}{dW}$ for the Cobb–Douglas Case*

If r is the rate of interest at which future quasi-rents are discounted and if it is assumed constant, the present value of the output of a machine of vintage v over its life is given by

$$F(v,\, t) \cdot \frac{[1 - e^{-rT}]}{r} \tag{19}$$

The present value of the cost of labor employed with the machine of vintage v over its life is likewise

$$W(v) \cdot L(v,\, t) \cdot \frac{[1 - e^{-(r-g)T}]}{(r - g)},\ r > g \tag{20}$$

Maximising the excess of (20) over (19) leads to

$$\frac{\partial F(v,\, t)}{\partial L(v,\, t)} = W(v) \cdot \frac{r[1 - e^{-(r-g)T}]}{(r - g)[1 - e^{-rT}]} \tag{21}$$

A machine of vintage v is scrapped when

$$W(v) \cdot e^{gT} = \frac{F(v,\, t)}{L(v,\, t)} \tag{22}$$

Substituting for $W(v)$ from (21),

$$\frac{F(v, t)}{L(v, t) \cdot \dfrac{\partial F(v, t)}{\partial L(v, t)}} = e^{gT} \cdot \frac{(r - g)\,[1 - e^{-rT}]}{r[1 - e^{-(r-g)T}]} = \frac{[e^{rT} - 1]}{r} \cdot \frac{(r - g)}{[e^{(r-g)T} - 1]}$$

Or, $\dfrac{1}{a} = \dfrac{Z(m)}{Z(n)} = N(r, T)$ (23)

where a is the exponent of labor in the Cobb–Douglas production function, Z is as defined before, $m = rT$, $n = (r - g)T$, $m - n = gT > 0$ and N is defined as the ratio of $Z(m)$ and $Z(n)$.

From (23), $\dfrac{dT}{dr} = -\dfrac{\dfrac{\partial N(r, T)}{\partial r}}{\dfrac{\partial N(r, T)}{\partial T}}$ (24)

From (23), $\dfrac{\partial N}{\partial r} \cdot \dfrac{1}{N} = T \left[\dfrac{Z'(m)}{Z(m)} - \dfrac{Z'(n)}{Z(n)} \right]$

and $\dfrac{\partial N}{\partial T} \cdot \dfrac{1}{N} = \dfrac{Z'(m)}{Z(m)} \cdot r - \dfrac{Z'(n)}{Z(n)} \cdot (r - g)$

Let us now find out the sign of $\left[\dfrac{Z'(m)}{Z(m)} - \dfrac{Z'(n)}{Z(n)} \right]$

Define $p(x) = \dfrac{Z'(x)}{Z(x)} = \dfrac{1 + (x - 1)Z(x)}{x\,Z(x)} > 0$

Hence, $\operatorname{sgn} p'(x) = \operatorname{sgn} [-Z + Z^2 - xZ'] = \operatorname{sgn} [Z^2 - (1 + xZ)]$

$$= \operatorname{sgn} \left[\frac{(e^x - 1)^2}{x^2} - e^x \right]$$

Since by expansion in Taylor series it can be shown that $\dfrac{e^x - 1}{x} > e^{\frac{x}{2}}$, $p'(x) > 0$.

Therefore, $\dfrac{Z'(m)}{Z(m)} > \dfrac{Z'(n)}{Z(n)}$ since $m > n$.

Thus $\dfrac{\partial N}{\partial r} \cdot \dfrac{1}{N}$ and $\dfrac{\partial N}{\partial T} \cdot \dfrac{1}{N}$ are positive and from (24), $\dfrac{dT}{dr} < 0$.

Since in this model it can be shown that $\dfrac{dr}{dW} < 0$, we can now say that $\dfrac{dT}{dW} > 0$.

Part III

Factor Markets and Rural Development

Introduction

While the earlier two parts of the book dealt with features of the aggregative economy, in this part we focus more on micro aspects of development, in particular on the imperfect markets for land, labor, and credit in the rural sector of a poor country. Much of the emphasis here is on empirical studies. In recent years there has been a surge in the theoretical literature[1] on rural factor markets, applying contract theory, but the empirical information on the nature of informal contracts in these markets is still rather scanty. Chapters 13, 14, 17, and 18 report on some large-scale surveys carried out in India by the author (in collaboration with Ashok Rudra), which tried to understand the nature of production relations in agriculture. These surveys were unique in at least one respect. They differed both from large-scale household sample surveys carried out by large statistical organizations and the small-scale intensive probing by social anthropologists. The former have the advantage of generating statistically reliable estimates, but the nature of necessary standardization often makes them miss the nuances, complexities, and variabilities of informal economic relations that rural people have with one another. For example, the large land or employment surveys carried out periodically by the Indian National Sample Survey will give you good estimates of the proportion of land that is leased in or the proportion of laborers who work on wage contracts, but will not give you a good understanding of the multilayered variations in the land lease or labor contracts sometimes within the same village or of the qualitatively different kinds of dependence that the tenant–borrower–worker may have with the landlord–creditor–employer. The social anthropologist can give you details of these nuanced relationships in a richly contextualized village or a local community, but the results may not be generalizable. Rudra and I devised an intermediate type survey which is large enough to give us some basis for generalization but intensive enough to probe into the qualitative nature of relationships which the bureaucratically administered surveys often missed. Villages were randomly chosen but a small number of respondents within each village was purposively chosen, and our purpose was less to find out about their own personal characteristics, but more about what they think are the modal types of relations and contracts in the village.[2]

Chapter 13 reports data on terms and conditions of sharecropping contracts in 334 randomly selected villages in four provinces in India, following this survey method. It provides information on distribution of different types of crop shares[3] and cost shares, the nature of other obligations the sharecropper has to his landlord, his credit arrangements, and the nature of the landlord's participation in decision-making in production. Using a similar survey method, Chapter 14 reports data on the detailed terms and conditions of agricultural labor contracts, particularly focusing on the heterogeneity of employer–employee relationships, from a random sample of 110 villages in West Bengal. It covers data on variations in the wage rate both intra-village and inter-village, modes of wage payment and of changes in negotiated wage, the nature and extent of labor dependence on and contract duration with particular employers, highlighting the great variety of labor categories that exist in agriculture but are often overlooked in the usual large-scale surveys.

Chapter 15 is on the measurement of rural unemployment or underemployment, particularly in situations of informal employment in agriculture. The currently used measures applied to large-scale household survey data often ignore the very important phenomenon of involuntary withdrawal from the labor force by potential job-seekers, particularly women, discouraged by bleak job prospects. This chapter suggests a simple alternative measure that goes toward correcting this underestimation.

Chapter 16 is a theoretical as well as an empirical analysis of labor "tied" to particular employers. Contrary to a common characterization of such labor as a feudal relic, it brings out many possible cases of voluntary labor-tying long-term contracts which may even be associated with capitalist agricultural development. The rationale in the two-period model of this chapter is in terms of insurance against wage fluctuations across periods, as in implicit contract theory, taking laborers to be more risk averse than employers. There are, of course, other kinds of rationale for labor tying discussed in the development literature. The employer often puts a high premium on quick and ready availability of labor for some operations in the peak season, when there are various risks and costs of delay. This makes the employer enter into contracts[4] with laborers in the lean season in exchange for a commitment to provide ready labor in the peak season as soon as the employer needs it. (In Chapter 14 we report on some "beck-and-call" contracts in West Bengal.) In both of these rationales for labor-tying mentioned above, casual or untied labor is a residual category with its extent depending on the state of labor demand in the peak season. A. Mukherjee and D. Ray[5] modify these implicit contract cases by introducing an incentive constraint which makes labor-tying optimal if and only if seasonal fluctuations in the labor market exceed a certain threshold level. A third kind of rationale, again depending on seasonality, but now in terms of the efficiency theory of wages, is provided by A. Guha,[6] where there is a one-period lag in the way a nutrition–efficiency link works: only in the peak season can the employer capture the higher productivity effect of paying an efficiency wage to the tied laborer in the lean season. In all the three kinds of rationales for labor-tying discussed so far, tied and casual laborers differ in the duration of their labor contracts but not in the tasks they carry out. M. Eswaran and A. Kotwal[7] provide a two-season model where the rationale involves different tasks and functions.

If Chapter 16 is about two-tiered labor markets on the basis of contract duration, in Chapter 17 we provide some evidence of territorial segmentation of the rural labor market and of limited labor mobility even within adjacent territories. On the basis of a field survey in 80 villages in West Bengal, separated into 5 clusters of 16 neighboring villages, we suggest how personal connections between employers and employees, mutual trust and credit relationships turn out to be more important determinants of labor mobility than short-run wage differences. Economists do not usually analyze the economic implications of what can be called the boundaries of the village "moral community" (which do not always coincide with its geographic boundaries) and the consequent process and pattern of market segmentation. Social anthropologists often refer to the local patron–client relationships in a village as a mark of traditional social systems, but they often ignore the underlying economic rationale of such clientelization, with costs of information, performance monitoring and social control over the labor process rising sharply as one goes outside one's own moral community.

Chapter 18 provides data from 276 randomly selected villages in 3 provinces in India, following the same survey method as in Chapters 13 and 14, on how the terms and conditions of contracts in land, labor, and credit markets are interlinked, with transactions sometimes taking place between the same landlord–creditor–employer and the tenant–borrower–laborer straddling multiple factor markets. There is now quite a bit of theoretical literature[8] on interlinked contracts in the context of a poor agrarian economy, trying to understand their microfoundations and their consequences (for example, in the form of interlinkage itself acting as a barrier to entry by unlinked outsiders). But there is as yet very little empirical work on the subject. Our dataset is one of the earliest and one of the largest that exist in shedding some light on the nature of such interlinked contracts. It also tries to grapple with the traditional descriptions of such relations as "semi-feudal." While not minimizing the possible adverse consequences of such patterns of interlinkage, particularly for the weaker party in such contracts, it tries to locate the rationale of the existence and persistence of such relations even in contexts of ongoing agricultural progress.

Notes

1. For examples of the relevant theoretical models, see P. Bardhan and C. Udry, *Development Microeconomics*, Oxford University Press, Oxford, 1999.
2. For a more detailed discussion of our survey method see A. Rudra, "Field Survey Methods", in P. Bardhan (ed.), *Conversations between Economists and Anthropologists: Methodological Issues in Measuring Economic Change in Rural India*, Oxford University Press, New Delhi, 1989.
3. Recently H. P. Young and M. A. Burke, "Competition and Custom in Economic Contracts", *American Economic Review*, vol. 91, 2001, found our cropshare frequency data useful in making their point about focal shares in a dynamic model of contract formation that takes the role of custom into account.

4. For a discussion of such a rationale see P. Bardhan, *Land, Labor and Rural Poverty*, Chapter 4, Columbia University Press, New York, 1984.
5. A. Mukherjee and D. Ray, "Labor Tying", *Journal of Development Economics*, vol. 47, 1995.
6. A. Guha, "Consumption, Efficiency, and Surplus Labor", *Journal of Development Economics*, vol. 31, 1989.
7. M. Eswaran and A. Kotwal, "A Theory of Two-Tiered Labor Markets in Agrarian Economics", *American Economic Review*, vol. 75, 1985.
8. For a discussion of this theoretical literature, see Bardhan and Udry *op. cit.*, Chapter 9.

Chapter 13

Terms and Conditions of Sharecropping Contracts: An Analysis of Village Survey Data in India*

I

There is now a sizeable theoretical literature[1] on sharecropping tenancy in agriculture. In comparison the literature on the actual nature of sharecropping contracts empirically observed in peasant agriculture is rather small. In India neither the large-scale Land Holdings Surveys carried out by the National Sample Survey Organization nor the small-scale village surveys[2] carried out by the Agro-Economic Research Centres in different parts of India collect data on the contractual details in the land-lease markets. Some field surveys by individual economists[3] or social anthropologists in a handful of purposely chosen villages have sometimes been quite intensive and useful in terms of their coverage of tenancy contracts, but their microscopic nature and purposeful sample inhibit statistically valid generalization. Our present paper is based on what may have been the first[4] intensive and yet fairly large-scale survey of contractual relationships in rural India. We shall be reporting here data collected in 1975–6 from 334 randomly chosen villages in four states in Northern and Eastern India: West Bengal, Bihar, Uttar Pradesh and Orissa.

In these states villages were randomly selected,[5] in each such village four types of questionnaires were canvassed: one to be answered separately, by two purposely chosen and, if possible, different types of tenants, one by two casual laborers (separately), one by two permanent farm servants (separately), and one general village questionnaire to be filled in on the basis of information obtained from all these six respondents and cross-checking them with other people living in the village. Since this paper is concerned with the terms and conditions of sharecropping

Table 13.1*

Number of villages and tenancy patterns in survey

State	Number of villages surveyed	Number of tenancy patterns reported	Crop for which tenancy patterns observed
West Bengal	110	188	Paddy
Bihar	101	106	Paddy
Orissa	22	29	Paddy
Uttar Pradesh	100	90	Wheat

*The source of this Table and all subsequent Tables is the Survey referred to in paragraph 1 of the text.

Notes to Tables
By a tenancy pattern we have understood a combination of crop-sharing and cost-sharing patterns involving one or more crops and several inputs. Whenever any one element in the combination is different we have considered that there are two different patterns. Thus in the same village we have often encountered more than one pattern. We have counted for each village the number of different patterns prevailing there. However, an identical pattern occurring in different villages has been counted not once but as many times as it has occurred. This gives the total number of patterns observed. All the percentages in the Tables numbered 13.2, 13.3, 13.4, 13.5, 13.7, and 13.12 refer to the number of patterns of a certain kind occurring in the total number of patterns defined as above.

contracts, our main focus will be on the tenancy schedules in each village; for some of the other results of the survey, the reader may refer to Bardhan and Rudra (1978). The tenant (and laborer) respondents were asked questions about the contract they themselves have entered into and those others prevailing in the village, and other particulars about themselves; in addition they were asked about the characteristics of their landlords or employers or creditors and about general features, institutions and trends in the village economy as perceived by them. We did not canvas any questionnaire with the village landlords, employers or money lenders as such. We avoided them deliberately as it is our understanding that they are much more inclined towards falsifying information than laborers, poor tenants, etc.

The ultimate unit of investigation is the village. Most of the questions relate to the standard type or types of contracts prevailing in the village, and the answers given by one respondent belonging to a particular category (for example, tenant) about the prevailing contractual type in the village have been cross-checked with those given by the other respondents in the same category. Although villages were chosen randomly, the respondents within a village were selected. This was done deliberately to increase the quality of information. The respondent from a given group was selected by the investigator on considerations of the cooperation that was sought and given as well as that of his knowledgeability.

II

In the overwhelming majority of the villages surveyed sharecropping is the predominant form of tenancy, although there are some signs of increase in the incidence of fixed-rent tenancy in some areas and for some crops (as high as 91 percent of the cases of tenancy reported in West Bengal and Bihar). In our survey 100 percent of tenancies in Orissa and 93 percent in U.P. take the form of share-cropping. An important feature of the sharecropping arrangements is that the share proportion clusters around certain simple rational fractions, the most import-ant of which is, of course, that of 50:50. Table 13.2 presents frequency distributions of the share of the principal crop in crop-sharing arrangements in the four states. While in all the four states more than two-thirds of the cases report 50:50 share, the tenant's share is *less* than 50 percent in 19 percent of cases in West Bengal, 12 percent of cases in Bihar and 16 percent of cases of U.P. In 21 percent of cases in Orissa and 14 percent of cases in West Bengal, the tenant's share is *more* than 50 percent.

Much of sharecropping theory assumes *either* that the (exogenously or endogen-ously determined) crop share is uniform for all tenancy contracts in a village, *or* (less frequently) that the crop share varies from one contract to another in the same village depending on the varying bargaining power of individual lessors and lessees or on their differential risk-aversion or on farm size used as a screening device. Neither of these neat theoretical alternatives seems to fit our data. Table 13.3 shows that while the majority of villages have only one prevailing share pattern, in a significant number of villages more than one share proportion coexists in the same crop in the same village; on the other hand, there is no evidence that the share varies from one pair of lessor–lessee to another or that the share is sensitive to the particu-lar characteristics of individual parties.

In fact it is not very easy to find a definite pattern in the intra-village or inter-village variations in crop shares. But from Table 13.4 it seems that high-yielding varieties (HYV) of grains are more frequently associated with higher tenant share than in the case of ordinary varieties, and in West Bengal and Orissa we encounter a significantly larger incidence of the tenant's share being greater than 50 percent in the case of HYV than for ordinary paddy. In West Bengal it is also observed that the crop sharing proportion is very much more concentrated on the 50:50 share in cases where fertilizer is not used than when it is.

There is also a remarkable association between the crop share and the incidence of cost-sharing by the landlord. As Table 13.5 shows, when the landlord does not share in the costs, the tenant's crop share is in general higher in all the four states; and, when the landlord shares in the costs, the tenant's crop share is 50 percent or lower. The chi-square test, reported in Table 13.6, shows that the association between the landlord's crop share and the existence of cost sharing is significant for all the states except Bihar.

The widespread prevalence of cost-sharing arrangement as a part of the tenancy contract is a strikingly new phenomenon in Indian agriculture.[6] In West Bengal and Uttar Pradesh two-thirds of the cases report some cost sharing by the landlords; in Bihar 58 percent of cases and in Orissa 48 percent of cases do so. The phenomenon is, of course, more frequently observed in the "advanced" villages (where tubewells and pumps are used and use of chemical fertilizers and HYV seeds are highly prevalent and/or spreading) in our data set than in other villages.[7]

Table 13.2

Frequency distribution of crop shares

Crop Shares (Tenant:Owner)

(Percentages)

States	3:1 (75%)	2:1 (66.7%)	10:6 (62%)	3:2 (60%)	9:7 (56%)	1:1 (50%)	18:22 (45%)	7:9 (44%)	2:3 (40%)	6:10 (38%)	7:13 (35%)	1:2 (33.3%)	6:17 (26%)	1:3 (25%)
(1)	(2)	(3)	(4)	(5)	(6)	(7)	(8)	(9)	(10)	(11)	(12)	(13)	(14)	(15)
						Paddy								
West Bengal	6.4	4.7	1.2	1.8		66.9	3.5		3.8		0.6	6.4	0.6	4.1
Bihar		0.5		1.0		86.5		1.6		2.6		6.2		1.6
Orissa	3.4		6.9	6.9	3.4	79.4								
						Wheat								
Uttar Pradesh	0.6					83.8			6.0			6.0		3.6

Table 13.3
Incidence of single and multiple crop shares in the same villages

Number of Villages

States	Number of share patterns in the same village				No crop sharing in paddy/wheat †	Total
	One*	Two	Three	Four		
(1)	(2)	(3)	(4)	(5)	(6)	(7)
West Bengal	63	35	9	1	2	110
Bihar	78	10	2	0	11	101
Orissa	17	4	1	0	0	22
Uttar Pradesh	65	11	0	0	24	100

*In the cases of West Bengal, Bihar and Orissa, all the cases (e.g. 63, 78 and 17) are of 50:50 share. In the case of Uttar Pradesh, out of the 65 cases of mono-share pattern, 62 are cases of 50:50 share.
†In the cases of West Bengal, Bihar and Orissa, the figures refer to sharecropping arrangement in paddy. In the case of Uttar Pradesh the figures refer to share arrangement in wheat.

Table 13.4
Difference in crop shares for ordinary and high yielding varieties

(Percentages)

State	Crops	Tenant's share of crops		
		less than 50%	equal to 50%	more than 50%
(1)	(2)	(3)	(4)	(5)
West Bengal	Paddy (ordinary)	21.4	68.4	10.2
	(H Y V)	22.8	61.4	15.8
Bihar	Paddy (ordinary)	12.0	86.4	1.6
	(H Y V)	4.2	95.0	0.8
Orissa	Paddy (ordinary)		88.0	12.0
	(H Y V)		76.0	24.0
Uttar Pradesh	Wheat (ordinary)	17.9	81.4	0.7
	(H Y V)	15.5	83.8	0.7

As for the extent and the pattern of cost-sharing there are many variations. In the traditional arrangements, the tenant is supposed to provide his own labor and his own bullock and plough; the landlord is expected to pay the land taxes as well as irrigation taxes when they exist. But with the introduction of new inputs, new crops and new irrigation devices, new cost-sharing arrangements have developed. Table 13.7 shows that while in the overwhelming majority of cases in Bihar, Orissa and U.P. and in half the cases in West Bengal, tenants bear all of the costs of seed and manure, 50:50 cost-sharing with the landlord is much more common in the

Table 13.5
Association between cost shares and crop shares

(Percentages)

	West Bengal Cost Sharing			Bihar Cost Sharing			Orissa Cost Sharing			Uttar Pradesh Cost Sharing		
	Exists	Does not exist	Total	Exists	Does not exist	Total	Exists	Does not exist	Total	Exists	Does not exist	Total
1	2	3	4	5	6	7	8	9	10	11	12	13
Tenant's share less than 50%	98.5	0.5	100 (19.0)	65.2	34.8	100 (12.0)				96.2	3.8	100 (15.6)
Tenant's share and owner's share 50:50	69.4	30.6	100 (67.0)	57.8	42.2	100 (86.5)	56.5	43.5	100 (79.3)	61.4	38.6	100 (83.8)
Tenant's share above 50%	10.4	89.6	100 (14.0)	33.3	66.7	100 (2.5)	16.7	83.3	100 (20.7)	0.0	100.0	100 (0.6)
Total	66.7	33.3	100	58.3	41.7	100	48.3	51.7	100	66.5	33.5	100

N.B.: The figures in brackets are the percentages of different crop shares.

Table 13.6
Measures of association between crop shares and cost shares

State	Value of Contingency Chi-square	Degree of freedom	Remarks
West Bengal	98.77**	2	The chi-square is calculated
Bihar	0.45	1	leaving out the two cell frequencies corresponding to tenant's crop share above 50%.
Orissa	6.09*	1	The chi-square is calculated
Uttar Pradesh	11.93**	1	leaving out the two cell frequencies corresponding to tenant's crop share above 50%.

**Significant at 1% level.
*Significant at 5% level.

case of chemical fertilizers, a new input. There is also evidence that in West Bengal (unlike in Bihar) the use of fertilizer is positively associated with cost-sharing not only in fertilizer, but also in seed and manure, the incidence of cost-sharing of seed and manure being much higher when fertilizer is used than otherwise. In West Bengal some (though not many) cases are observed where the sharing of a paddy byproduct – straw – depends on the sharing of fertilizer costs: if any one of the parties pays for the entire cost of fertilizers, they receive the entire output of straw; if the fertilizer cost is shared, the straw is also shared in the same proportion.

III

Let us now look at some of the contractual terms other than those of crop and cost shares. Thus the tenancy contract is predominantly a short-term contract holding good for a year or less than a year (say, for a crop season). There are indications that the practice of lease for a specific crop and for a specific season is on the increase. Tenancy arrangements which leave all decision-making to the tenant, the landlord being interested only in the rent, seems to be far from typical (except possibly in the case of Bihar), as may be seen from Table 13.8. The landlord does not confine himself to supervision of harvesting alone, which, of course, is an activity to which he attaches much importance, but quite frequently he participates in making decisions, singly or jointly with the tenant, about such matters as what crops to grow and what inputs to use. This phenomenon is more often observed in the "advanced" (by our earlier definition) than in the backward villages. Harvest sharing and threshing taking place in the landlord's premises (which usually works to the landlord's advantage) is again not very typical: in West Bengal it is observed in slightly less than

Table 13.7

Frequency distribution of cost shares

Cost Shares (Tenant:Owner)

(Percentages)

States	Inputs	0:1 (0%)	1:3 (25%)	1:2 (33.3%)	8:12 (40%)	18:22 (45%)	1:1 (50%)	2:1 (66.7%)	3:1 (75%)	1:0 (100%)
(1)	(2)	(3)	(4)	(5)	(6)	(7)	(8)	(9)	(10)	(11)
West Bengal	Seed	9.9		1.5	1.2	1.5	36.2			49.7
	Manure	10.2					15.2			74.0
	Fertilizer	9.1					51.7		0.6	24.3
Bihar	Seed	6.2		0.5			16.7			76.6
	Manure	2.1					3.6	6.2	0.5	93.8
	Fertilizer	2.1					40.1			31.2
Orissa	Seed									100.0
	Manure									100.0
	Fertilizer						48.3			37.9
Uttar Pradesh	Seed			1.2			36.5			62.3
	Manure	3.6		1.2			6.6			88.6
	Fertilizer	2.4		1.2			44.3	1.2		50.3

N.B.: The row totals do not necessarily add up to 100.0 as some of the input items, fertilizer in particular, do not get used in all cases for which sharecropping systems have been reported.

Table 13.8
Other particulars of tenancy contracts

Percentages of contracts	West Bengal	Bihar	Orissa	U.P.
(1)	(2)	(3)	(4)	(5)
with duration one year	76	53	98	78
with duration smaller than one year	24	53	20	21
involving crop decisions by owner jointly with tenant or singly	56	29	50	96
involving input decisions by owner jointly with tenant or singly	54	30	46	90
which provide for supervision of harvesting by employer or his representatives	91	89	87	95
which provide for harvest sharing to take place in owner's house	49	58	26	35
which provide for threshing to take place in owner's house	49	61	44	14

half of the cases, in Orissa and U.P. in considerably less than half of the cases; in Bihar, however, it is observed in about 60 percent of the cases. In the remaining cases harvest-sharing and threshing take place either in the field or in the tenant's premises or in some public place.

The terms and conditions of the tenancy contract are often enmeshed in various social relations between landlords and tenants which are of the nature of dominance and dependence. In certain parts of the literature it has become a common practice to treat these relations as characteristics of "feudalism" or "semi-feudalism". Our survey results, however, suggest that the institution of sharecropping tenancy as it has been evolving in India does not at all conform to the stereotype of landlord–serf relationship familiar from European or Japanese history. On the contrary, there is a considerable amount of evidence that the institution has been adapting itself more and more to the needs of increasing production and profit by enterprising farmers, both owners and tenants.

First, on the question of freedom of the tenant to enter into tenancy contracts with other landlords. On the basis of the answers of our tenant respondents, it seems it is indeed very rare in any of the four states that the tenant cannot lease in land from more than one landlord. Such instances of the tenant being tied to a

Table 13.9

Dominance–dependence relations between landlords and tenants

(Percentages of Respondents)

Tenants	States			
	West Bengal	Bihar	Orissa	U.P.
(1)	(2)	(3)	(4)	(5)
1. who cannot lease in land from more than one landlord	4	2	0	8
2. who sell their product to their landlords	9	3	2	2
3. who have to render services to their landlord against				
(a) full payment	18	10	28	0
(b) less than full payment	5	6	2	1
(c) no payment	5	5	0	22
4. who have to render labor services (fully paid, less than fully paid or unpaid) for landlords				
among landed tenants	10	14	19	12
among landless tenants	52	55	57	34
among all tenants	28	21	30	23

particular landlord occur in four percent of tenants surveyed in West Bengal, two percent in Bihar, eight percent in U.P. and none in Orissa (see Table 13.9).

Take again the question of unpaid and obligatory services by the tenant to the landlord, typical of the classic model of feudalism. As seen in Table 13.9, 70 percent or more (in Bihar and U.P. nearly 80 percent) of the tenants in our survey reported rendering *no* (paid or unpaid) labor services to the landlord. Even among entirely landless tenants (who render labor services to the landlord more often than the landed tenants), more than 40 percent (in U.P., about two-thirds) reported rendering *no* labor service to the landlord. Among those tenants who do work for the landlord, nearly all in the case of Orissa, nearly two-thirds in West Bengal and nearly half in Bihar reported being "properly" (in the tenant's judgement) paid for the work. In all, a relatively small proportion (10 percent in West Bengal, 11 percent in Bihar, 2 percent in Orissa and 23 percent in U.P.) of all the tenants in our survey reported rendering "unpaid" or "underpaid" services to the landlord.

Another binding constraint of the tenancy contract may be that of the landlord being the principal marketing channel for the tenant's share of the crop. But in our sample this seems to be quite unimportant. In less than five percent (in West Bengal, less than 10 percent) of the cases do our tenants report selling their product to their landlords (Table 13.9).

IV

A major factor of the tenant's dependence on the landlord works through the former's indebtedness to the latter. The institution of sharecropping tenancy often dovetails in a land-lease contract and a credit contract. This is not unexpected in a situation of inadequately developed credit market: while a poor sharecropper may have few assets acceptable as collaterals in the outside credit market, his landlord would accept the tenancy contract itself as collateral. The landlord has the incentive to supply production credit (since he shares in the outcome of its use) and also is in the best position to enforce repayment (of both production and consumption loans) at the time of harvest sharing.

In our surveyed villages the landlord is undoubtedly an important, though not the only, source of credit to his tenant. Our Tables 13.10 and 13.11 indicate that about half of all the tenants reported taking consumption loans (as well as general-purpose loans for ceremonial expenditures, etc.) from their landlords. In West Bengal nearly

Table 13.10
Incidence of consumption loans to tenants by landlords with and without interest

States	Percentage of tenants taking consumption loans from landlords		
	with interest	without interest	total
(1)	(2)	(3)	(4)
West Bengal	28	23	51
Bihar	48	2	50
Orissa	46	2	48
Uttar Pradesh	48	6	54

Table 13.11
Incidence of general purpose loans to tenants with and without interest

States	Percentage of tenants taking general-purpose loans from landlords		
	with interest	without interest	total
(1)	(2)	(3)	(4)
West Bengal	50	5	55
Bihar	57	1	58
Orissa	35	4	39
Uttar Pradesh	55	3	58

half of these consumption loans are interest free; however, the proportion is much lower in the other States.

Some recent theorists[8] of "semi-feudalism" would have us believe that in the landlord–tenant relationship usury dominates as the mode of exploitation and the landlord's considerations of usurious income from the indebted tenant dampens his incentive to increase production through productive investments. It is obviously difficult to test this hypothesis directly from empirical data: the same phenomenon of adoption or non-adoption of yield-increasing innovations may have various explanations quite different from that implied in the hypothesis. All we can say is that the indirect evidence from our large-scale survey in North India is not at all consistent with this hypothesis.

In our survey, we asked the tenants about the principal occupation (in terms of income source) of their landlords. In our sample of 109 villages reporting tenancy in West Bengal *not one* tenant reported money-lending as a principal occupation of his landlord. In the overwhelming majority of cases the tenant reported self-cultivation as the principal occupation of his landlord. What is more important to note for our present purpose is that in 43 percent of cases in West Bengal, 59 percent of cases in Orissa, 35 percent of cases in U.P. and 29 percent of cases in Bihar the landlord gives advances to the tenant to meet his production needs of seeds, fertilizers, etc. (see Table 13.12). In West Bengal and Orissa about half of these cases of tenants receiving production loans from landlords were reported to be interest-free (see Table 13.13). The common practice is for the advance to be paid by the landlord in kind in the form of fertilizers, seeds, etc. and to be repaid by the tenant in terms of grains at the time of harvest. One also observes in Table 13.12 a positive association between cost-sharing and giving of production loans by the landlord in West Bengal, Bihar and Orissa. A chi-square test carried out on the data suggests a highly significant association in West Bengal and Bihar. Production loan as well as cost-sharing obviously indicate a strong interest on the part of the landlord in productive investment on the tenant farm. On their self-cultivated land 60 to 70 percent of the landlords of our tenant-respondents are reported as using HYV seeds and chemical fertilizers (see Table 13.14). All this is a far cry from usurious landlords uninterested in productive investments.

In the literature on production relations it has become an uncritically accepted habit of thought to equate tenancy with feudalism and indebtedness by poor peasants to their landlords with debt-bondage. This has been a source of considerable confusion in the recent discussion on modes of production. First of all, in most regions tenancy involves only a relatively small part of agriculture – less than 20 percent of all cultivated area is under tenancy in the four states of North India under our consideration, according to estimates from 1970–1 N.S.S. Land Holdings Survey Data. Moreover, a substantial proportion of area under tenancy is leased in by enterprising farmers who already are large owners of land (sometimes leasing in land from small landowners). But even in villages where the institution of tenancy is important and where many poor tenants are entering into land-lease, labor and credit relationships with their landlords, our survey results indicate that the institution as it operates is far from being anything akin to feudalism by most accepted

Table 13.12

Association between cost shares and owners giving production loans to tenants

(Percentages)

	West Bengal Cost Sharing			Bihar Cost Sharing			Orissa Cost Sharing			Uttar Pradesh Cost Sharing		
	Exists	Does not exist	Total	Exists	Does not exist	Total	Exists	Does not exist	Total	Exists	Does not exist	Total
1	2	3	4	5	6	7	8	9	10	11	12	13
Owners giving production loans to tenants	84.4	15.6	100 (42.9)	81.8	18.2	100 (28.7)	55.9	44.1	100 (58.6)	61.0	39.0	100 (35.3)
Owners not giving production loans to tenants	53.3	46.7	100 (57.1)	48.9	51.1	100 (71.3)	37.5	62.5	100 (41.4)	69.4	30.6	100 (64.7)
Total	66.7	33.3	100	58.3	41.7	100	48.3	51.7	100	66.5	33.5	100

N.B.: The figures in brackets are the percentage of cases of owners giving production loans to tenants.

Table 13.13

Incidence of production loans to tenants by landlords with and without interest

States	Percentage of tenants taking production loans from landlords		
	with interest	without interest	total
(1)	(2)	(3)	(4)
West Bengal	21	23	44
Bihar	26	15	41
Orissa	30	27	57
Uttar Pradesh	34	8	42

Table 13.14

Landlords of tenants making productive and unproductive investments

States	Percentage of landlords				
	Using chemical fertilizers	Using H Y V seeds	Principal occupation: self cultivation	Buying grains from tenants	Giving loans to poor peasants other than his own tenants
(1)	(2)	(3)	(4)	(5)	(6)
West Bengal	62	59	62	19	38
Bihar	68	63	72	11	25
Orissa	61	61	72	2	33
Uttar Pradesh	73	68	82	2	56

definitions of the term. It is commonly agreed that one essential feature of feudal relationship is associated with the appropriation of surplus in the form of unpaid labor services and other obligatory payments by primarily rentier landlords through *extra-economic coercion*, that is, through various social and politico-legal compulsions. In our surveyed villages, unpaid and obligatory service by the tenant for the landlord is quite uncommon – even less common is the phenomenon of a tenant being tied to any particular landlord. The landlord quite often (though certainly not always) gives production loans to the tenant, shares in costs of seeds, fertilizers, etc., participates in decision-making about the use of these inputs and in general takes a lot of interest in productive investments on the tenant farm (as well as on his self-cultivated land), quite contrary to the prevailing image of rentier or usurious landlords. Needless to say, desperate conditions of poverty and underemployment often afflict the small sharecropper and push him into unequal relationships of mutual dependence with the landlord–creditor–employer. But surely, unequal contracts giving rise to economic dependence–dominance relationships are not distinguishing features of feudalism as opposed to other modes of production?

Notes

*   University of California – Berkeley and Indian Statistical Institute. Bardhan gratefully acknowledges research support from National Science Foundation Grant no. SOC 78-04022.
1. For a brief summary of the early literature see Johnson (1950). Since then Cheung (1969), Bardhan and Srinivasan (1971), Stiglitz (1974), Newbery (1975). Bell and Zusman (1976), Newbery and Stiglitz (1978), and others have contributed to this literature.
2. See, for example, the detailed anthology of village studies compiled by the IDS, Sussex.
3. See, for example, Bharadwaj and Das (1975), Bell (1977) and Bliss and Stern (1982).
4. Our survey was preceded by a large pilot survey on similar issues carried out in about eighty villages of West Bengal by one of the present authors; see Rudra (1975).
5. It was decided to take about 100 villages in each of the three states other than Orissa. The villages were allocated to the districts in proportion to the agricultural population of the districts; and within each district villages were selected randomly with probability proportional to the village agricultural population. The numbers allocated to West Bengal, Bihar and U.P. were 110, 101 and 100 respectively. The 23 villages of Orissa were not selected by following this procedure or any other strictly defined procedure. On account of the largeness of the state of U.P., we covered by our sample only the districts of Western and Eastern U.P. So, although in our subsequent discussion we refer to U.P. without any qualification, it should be understood that our analysis refers only to West and East U.P.
6. This has been noted by several authors in different parts of India. See, for example, Parthasarathy (1975) for evidence in West Godavari (Andhra Pradesh) and Rao (1975) for evidence in Kota (Rajasthan) and Karnal (Haryana).
7. For detailed evidence the reader may refer to Bardhan and Rudra (1978).
8. See, for example, Bhaduri (1973).

References

Bardhan, P. K. and Rudra, A., 1978, "Interlinkage of Land, Labor and Credit Relations: An Analysis of Village Survey Data in East India", *Economic and Political Weekly, 13,* 6 & 7 February.

Bardhan, P. K. and Srinivasan, T. N., 1971, "Crop Sharing Tenancy in Agriculture: A Theoretical and Empirical Analysis", *American Economic Review, 61,* 1, March.

Bell, C., 1977, "Alternative Theories of Sharecropping: Some Tests Using Evidence from Northeast India" *Journal of Development Studies, 13,* 4, July.

Bell, C. and Zusman, P., 1976, "A Bargaining Theoretic Approach to Crop Sharing Contracts", *American Economic Review, 66,* 4, September.

Bhaduri, A., 1973, "Agricultural Backwardness Under Semi-Feudalism", *Economic Journal, 88,* March.

Bharadwaj, K. and Das, P., 1975, "Tenurial Conditions and Mode of Exploitation: A Study of Some Villages in Orissa", *Economic and Political Weekly, 10,* 6 & 7, February.

Bliss, C., and Stern, N. H. 1982, Palanpur: *Studies in the Economy of a North Indian Village,* Oxford: Oxford Univ. Press.

Cheung, S. N. S., 1969, *The Theory of Share Tenancy,* Chicago: University of Chicago Press.

Johnson, D. G., 1950, "Resource Allocation Under Share Contracts", *J. of Political Economy,* *58*, April.

Newbery, D. M. G., 1975, "The Choice of Rental Contracts in Peasant Agriculture", in Reynolds, L. (ed.), *Agricultural and Development Theory,* New Haven, Conn.: Yale University Press.

Newbery, D. M. G. and Stiglitz, J. E., 1978, Sharecropping, Risksharing and Imperfect Information", Economic Theory Discussion Paper No. 8, University of Cambridge.

Parthasarathy, G., 1975, "West Godavari, Andhra Pradesh", in *Changes in Rice Farming in Selected Areas of Asia,* IRRI, Philippines.

Rao, C. H. H., 1975, *Technological Change and Distribution of Gains in Indian Agriculture,.* Institute of Economic Growth, Delhi.

Rudra, A., 1975, "Sharecropping Arrangements in West Bengal", *Economic and Political Weekly, 10,* 39, September 27.

Stiglitz, J. E., 1974, "Incentives and Risksharing in Sharecropping", *Review Economic Studies, 41,* April.

Chapter 14

Terms and Conditions of Labor Contracts in Agriculture: Results of a Survey in West Bengal 1979*

I. Introduction

Most of the theoretical and empirical work on agricultural labor markets in poor countries relates to the wage rate and unemployment of workers. The question of "surplus labor" has often overshadowed other issues. Information is rather scanty on the actual nature of agricultural labor contracts in these countries and on the details of their terms and conditions. These conditions of the employer–employee relationship involve, apart from the rates of remuneration: (a) duration of contract – day, month, season, period of a particular operation, year, etc., (b) basis of payment – hourly, daily, piece rate, product share, etc., (c) frequency of payment – day, month, year, several irregular instalments during the year, bonus during festivals, etc., (d) medium of payment – cash, kind, meals, snacks, and their different combinations, (e) degree to which work obligations and hours of work are specified or are left unspecified, (f) interlinkage with other contracts with the employer in credit or land relations, or in employment of other members of the laborer's family on the same employer's farm, (g) freedom to work for alternative employers – full freedom, total absence of such freedom, conditional or restricted freedom, etc., and so on. Variations in these conditions in individual contracts often imply types of labor that need to be differentiated; the attendant segmentation of the labor market can be ignored only at the cost of misleading analysis and policy prescriptions.

In this paper we report on the results of a fairly large-scale, yet intensive, survey of a random sample of 110 villages in West Bengal that we carried out in 1979. This survey focuses on the detailed terms and conditions of agricultural labor contracts and emphasizes the heterogeneity of employer–employee relationships. In sections

II–IV we discuss modes of wage payment, intra-village and inter-village variations in wage rates and modes of wage change. In the rest of the paper (sections V–XI) we analyze the employer–employee relationships of attachment and dependence and highlight the variety of labor categories that exist in agriculture but are often overlooked in usual surveys.

In our survey the villages were allocated to the districts in proportion to the agricultural population of the districts, and within each district villages were selected randomly with probability proportional to the village agricultural population. Within each village a questionnaire was canvassed with purposively chosen respondents in each labor category (provided such a category existed in the village): two casual laborers (one landless, one with some land), two fully attached laborers (one with more than 5 years of service with the employer and the other with 5 years or less), and two or more (if possible, different types of) "semi-attached" (see our subsequent definition) laborers; there was in addition a general village questionnaire to be filled in on the basis of information obtained from all these six or more respondents and from a cross-checking of these accounts with other people living in the village. The village questionnaire contained questions on the general economic, demographic, and agricultural conditions of the village as well as questions on types of labor contracts prevailing in the village (and the particulars of these contracts). It may also be noted here that the same sample design and in fact the same set of sample villages for West Bengal were used by us in an earlier (1975–6) survey on terms and conditions of contracts in land, labor and credit markets in 400 sample villages in North India. For some of the results of that survey, see Bardhan and Rudra (1978) and Bardhan and Rudra (1980).

II. Modes of Wage Payment

Our survey records a whole variety of modes of wage payment. Table 14.1 reports the relative incidence of different modes of payment, both for daily and longer-term labor contracts, in our sample villages classified by the extent of agricultural progress in the village. It seems in general that it is quite common for the laborer to receive wages in some combination of cash, kind and some perquisites like meals or snacks. In Table 14.1, so far as daily wage contracts are concerned, about 74 percent of all villages report either cash *plus* meals or cash *plus* meals *plus* kind payment or cash *plus* kind payment. The same combination of modes constitutes a much larger percentage (about 87 percent) of the total number of longer-term wage contracts in our sample. It may be worth noting that in a substantially larger percentage of longer-term contracts than in daily contracts the wage includes meals. This is consistent with the hypothesis that if longer-term contracts enable employers to capture the productivity benefits of the worker's nutrition intake, the employer is interested in ensuring, through payments of wages partly in the form of meals consumed at the work site or in the employer's house, that a larger part of wages is spent directly on nutrition for the worker and less on his dependents and on non-food items of expenditure.

Table 14.1

Modes of wage payment

(1) Type of village	(2) Contract type by duration	(3) No. of villages	Percentages of villages where the following modes of payment are reported								
			(4) Cash only	(5) Cash plus meals	(6) Cash plus meals plus kind	(7) Cash plus kind	(8) Kind only	(9) Kind plus meals	(10) Meals only	(11) Piece rate	(12) Share rate
Highly advanced	Daily contracts	31	26	23	23	16	0	10	0	71	19
	Longer-term contracts	28	5	42	37	5	0	9	2	0	0
Advanced	Daily contracts	50	24	44	8	28	0	2	0	42	8
	Longer-term contracts	36	4	59	33	4	0	0	0	0	0
Semi-advanced	Daily contracts	17	12	64	6	12	12	6	0	18	29
	Longer-term contracts	11	0	64	18	0	0	18	0	0	0
Not advanced	Daily contracts	12	25	66	0	0	0	25	0	17	8
	Longer-term contracts	6	0	50	0	0	0	50	0	0	0
All	Daily contracts	110	23	44	11	19	2	7	0	44	15
	Longer-term contracts	81	3	53	30	4	0	9	1	0	0

Notes: Modes of wage payment reported here for daily contracts are only for major agricultural operations. We have classified the whole sample of villages into four mutually exclusive categories of villages: (1) "highly advanced" villages where more than half of the cultivated area is (a) irrigated *and* (b) is under chemical fertilizers for some season or crop *and* (c) is under HYV seeds in some season; (2) "advanced" villages where (a) *or* (b) *or* (c) obtains; (3) "semi-advanced" villages where there is (d) any use of chemical fertilizers *or* (e) any use of HYV seeds *or* (f) any irrigation from canals, tubewells or pumps; and (4) "not-advanced" villages where *neither* (d) *nor* (e) *nor* (f) obtains.

The percentages in column (4) to (12) add up in each row to more to more than 100 percent as the same village may report more than one mode of wage payment.

It is interesting to note that wage payment in the form purely of cash applies to only 23 percent of all villages for daily contracts and 3 percent of all villages for longer-term contracts in our sample. Putting together the "highly advanced" and "advanced" villages in one category and the "semi-advanced" and "not advanced" in another, the evidence in Table 14.1 suggests that monetization of wage payments seems to increase with technical advance in agriculture (for the definition of the categories of villages classified by agricultural advance, see the note to the table).

Table 14.1 also suggests that in about half of all sample villages piece-rate daily wage payment (for a job done, like the ploughing of a given plot) or, somewhat less frequently, a share-rate system (payment to the laborer of a fraction of the total number of bundles harvested by him, for example) prevail, along with other forms of wage payment. The rationale for such forms of incentive payment is clear when supervision and monitoring of work effort is costly for the employer. It is particularly important when the speed of completion of a given job is crucial and the time rate of payment may lead to costly delays. It is not surprising, therefore, to note from Table 14.1 that the relative incidence of piece-rate wage system is significantly higher in agriculturally more advanced than in backward villages. Sixteen villages in our sample reported that the incidence of piece or share rates is increasing.

III. Wage Variations within the Village

There are certain remarkable variations and equally remarkable uniformities when one looks at the wage rates received by different laborers in the same village agricultural labor market. For annual-contract laborers there is no uniform wage or salary in the village; it varies from one contract to another. We have been able to locate at least one factor that may partly explain the variation. Table 14.2 shows that in at least 60 percent of all the villages where we have two or more annual-contract labor respondents in our sample, the laborer with longer years of service with a given employer receives a higher wage. Apart from experience (or learning by doing) enhancing a laborer's productivity, long years of service usually imply his dependability for the employer, which gets reflected in the higher wage.

While there is no uniformity in the wages received by annual-contract laborers in a village, there is a remarkable uniformity in the wage rate received by a daily contract adult laborer (of a given sex) for a given agricultural operation within the village. Very few daily contract laborers in our sample reported receiving a wage rate different from the prevailing market wage in the village for their sex and for a given operation.

One possible case of variation of the daily wage rate arises when laborers migrating from other areas may get a different wage rate compared to local laborers. But this is not an important source of wage variation in our sample. Out of our sample of 110 villages, 46 villages reported in-migration of labor, but only 7 of them reported migrant laborers receiving wage rates different from local laborers (in 4 villages receiving *less*, in 3 receiving *more*). Of course, even when migrants receive the same wage as the local laborers, the cost of hiring a migrant is larger for an employer, since he often has to pay costs of transportation from the migrant's place

Table 14.2

Wage variations with longer service for annual-contract laborers

Types of villages	With two or more annual contract laborers	Where the respondent with longer service reports getting higher wage	Where the respondent with longer service reports getting same wage	Where the respondent with longer service reports getting lower wage
		Number of Villages		
(1)	(2)	(3)	(4)	(5)
Highly advanced	26	17	2	2
Advanced	25	14	2	3
Semi-advanced	8	5	0	1
Not advanced	3	1	0	0
All villages	62	37	4	6

Notes: Only in 62 out of our total sample of 110 villages did we have two or more annual-contract laborers among our sample respondents so that we could compare their respective wages. Even among these villages the wages of the annual-contract labor respondents were not comparable or available in some villages, so that the figures in columns (3), (4), and (5) do not add up to the figure in column (2).

of origin and also for his temporary accommodation near the farm. The employer is prepared to pay a higher cost for a migrant laborer in such cases because the latter may have specialized skills (for special operations like ploughing or transplantation) or because he is easier to discipline and less likely to get involved in labor agitation.

Another possible case of variation of the daily wage rate is when the laborer has some leased-in land and he also works for the landlord as a wage laborer. In our sample, out of six respondents with leased-in land, two reported being paid a wage rate lower than the prevailing market wage rate.[1]

A more frequent case of variation of the daily wage rate from the prevailing market rate arises when the laborer is repaying a loan in terms of labor to the employer-creditor. Table 14.3 shows that in 86 out of our sample of 110 villages the system of loans against labor exists, a system known as *Dadan* in many villages, by which a laborer takes cash or grains in the lean season from a potential employer against commitment of future labor when the latter needs it. In 58 of these villages the number of labor days in which the loan is repaid by the laborer is calculated at an imputed wage rate which is below the market wage rate prevailing at the time of repayment. This imputed wage rate is sometimes pre-fixed at a given level (however high the market wage rate is) as reported in 28 of our sample villages, or is at a level which is below the market wage rate by a fixed differential as reported in 34 of our sample villages. The difference between the ruling wage rate and the imputed or accounting wage is the implicit interest cost of the loan. Since along with the implicit interest, the principal is also paid in labor, it is obvious that the accounting

Table 14.3

Loan repayment in terms of labor

		Number of villages			
Types of villages	In sample	Where the system of loan against labor exists	Where loan repayment is at implicit wage rate below the market rate	Where the implicit wage rate is at a pre-fixed level	Where the implicit wage rate is below the market rate by a fixed differential
(1)	(2)	(3)	(4)	(5)	(6)
Highly advanced	31	28 (90)	25 (81)	11 (35)	15 (48)
Advanced	50	37 (74)	21 (42)	8 (16)	14 (28)
Semi-advanced	17	14 (82)	9 (53)	7 (41)	4 (24)
Not advanced	12	7 (58)	3 (25)	2 (17)	1 (8)
All villages	110	86 (78)	58 (78)	28 (25)	34 (31)

Notes: In eight villages both the systems indicated in columns (5) and (6) exist; in four villages neither does, even though the implicit wage rate at loan repayment is below the market rate. The figures in parentheses represent percentage of villages of each type.

wage rate is *not* the rate at which the laborer is actually paid during the days of loan repayment. If, for example, a laborer has borrowed Rs 20 and if his stipulated accounting wage rate is Rs 4 per day, then he may work for 5 days with no wages paid, or work for 10 days at the actual payment of Rs 2 per day or work for 20 days at the actual payment of Rs 3 per day.

Apart from the case of loan repayment in terms of labor, departures from the prevailing market wage rate in the case of individual adult daily laborers for a given operation are quite infrequent. Some employers have been reported as willing to pay a higher wage for quick completion of some jobs. Our labor respondents were specifically asked if they ever offered to work for lower than the ruling wage rate to get more work. About 95 percent of our daily contract labor respondents replied in the negative. The majority cited "no need" or that "earnings from lower wages will be insufficient" as reasons; a small group articulated the class consciousness that such action would have led to a lowering of the ruling wage rate to the detriment of all laborers. The different reasons cited by our respondents suggest to us that the principle of a uniform daily wage rate is a matter that has been well established in the consciousness of both employers and employees in the village.

The wage rate, as usual, varies with the sex of the laborer. Female laborers usually get a lower rate. Out of 80 sample villages where women work as agricultural laborers, only 15 report equal wage rates for men and women. For our whole sample the simple average harvesting wage rate per day for women is 17 percent below that for men. Even in the case of transplantation of paddy, which is widely regarded in this area as particularly "suited" to women workers and for which women are often preferred, they get lower wage rates than men. In 60 out of 75 of our sample villages for which we had comparable wage rates for male and female laborers in transplantation, women got a lower rate.

The other clear case of intra-village variation is between different seasons (with associated operations) of the agricultural year. The wage rates are usually higher for operations like harvesting, transplanting, or ploughing. It is however, remarkable that in 42 percent of our sample villages the daily wage rate is reported to be invariant to different operations for the same paddy crop. This invariance is also more marked in backward than in advanced villages. This suggests that in the backward villages there is significant unemployment or underemployment even during the so-called busy seasons whereas in the more advanced villages this is less of a problem.

IV. Inter-Village Wage Variations

Wage variations across our sample villages are more marked than within the same village. For each village we have estimated the hourly wage rate for daily laborers in harvesting the main (*aman*) paddy crop in terms of rice equivalent, from our data on cash wages, kind wages, meals and snacks at work,[2] village price of paddy in the harvesting months, number of hours worked per day, paddy-rice conversion ratio, etc. The mean value of this wage rate for male laborers in our sample villages is 469 g of rice per hour and the standard deviation is 112 g.

One would expect the more advanced villages to have higher wages than the less advanced. This is indeed so but only to a mild extent; putting together our "highly advanced" and "advanced" villages in one category and our "semi-advanced" and "not advanced" villages in another, the mean hourly wage rate for male laborers in the former category is 471 g of rice and 451 g in the latter. In fact the differences in the variation within each of the two categories as measured by the variance are statistically significant (the more advanced having a wider dispersion), so that it is not possible to carry out the usual Fisher test of significance for the differences in the means of the two categories of villages.

One would also expect the wage rate to be relatively low in villages with excess supply of laborers. If we crudely define two categories of villages from this point of view, one where during the harvest months 100 percent (or almost) of male laborers reportedly get work, and the other containing the rest of the villages, we find our expectation confirmed: the former set of villages has a higher wage rate. The mean harvesting wage rate per hour of male labor is estimated to be 476 g in the former set of villages and 378 g in the latter.

We have discussed in section III how loans against labor often involve repayment at an accounting wage rate below the market rate. There is some weak evidence that in villages where this system of repayment at a lower accounting wage rate exists, the market wage rate itself is somewhat depressed (the lower accounting wage possibly indicating the weaker bargaining power of laborers in the village). The mean harvesting wage rate per hour of male labor is estimated to be 455 g of rice in such villages, whereas it is 480 g in villages where loan repayment does not introduce this constraint or where the system of loan against labor does not exist. We may also note here our finding, in Table 14.3, that the incidence of loan repayment in labor at lower than market wage rate is significantly higher[3] in more advanced villages (again putting together "highly advanced" and "advanced" villages in one category and "semi-advanced" and "not advanced" villages in another). This suggests that any wage-depressant effect on this account may counteract the wage-boosting effect of agricultural advance itself, and this may be a partial explanation of the weak relation between the mean wage rate and agricultural advance noted in the beginning of this section. Another explanation may be that advanced villages draw more in-migration of labor (for which there is evidence in our sample) and that the consequent wage-depressant effect counteracts the wage-boosting, effect of agricultural advance itself.

V. Modes of Wage Change

In the preceding two sections we have discussed intra-village and inter-village variations in the agricultural wage rate at a point of time. The rate, of course, changes over time. In 46 out of our 110 sample villages there was a reported rise in the daily agricultural wage rate between the previous agricultural year and the time of our survey. This upward revision in the wage rate was brought about in different ways in different villages; in many villages more than one way prevailed. Table 14.4 shows three different ways in which wage changes took place in the sample villages: the wage rate was raised by the employer on his own, different laborers asked for a rise individually or in small groups, and there were cases of labor agitation. It seems that labor agitation has been the single most important way of bringing about wage

Table 14.4
Modes of wage change

	Number of villages			
Type of villages	In sample	Where the employer raised the wage rate on his own	Where laborers asked for a wage rise in small groups	Where labor agitation took place
(1)	(2)	(3)	(4)	(5)
Highly advanced	31	5 (16)	6 (19)	11 (35)
Advanced	50	15 (30)	11 (22)	14 (28)
Semi-advanced	17	4 (24)	6 (35)	6 (35)
Not advanced	12	2 (17)	2 (17)	1 (8)
All villages	110	26 (24)	25 (23)	32 (29)

Notes: For three highly advanced villages and one semi-advanced village information was not available on the question relating to column (4). One should note that in many villages more than one mode of wage change prevailed. The figures in parentheses represent percentage of villages of each type.

changes, and that the relative importance of agitation has been greater in advanced villages (putting "highly advanced" and "advanced" types together) than in the others. Almost all the cases of labor agitation in our sample villages have been led by political parties, principally the CPI(M), the ruling Left Party with the largest mass organization.

VI. Types of Labor Attachment

Apart from the wage rate, one of the most important conditions of labor contracts is obviously that relating to the nature and extent of labor tying or attachment to the employer. Many surveys of rural labor (for example, the Rural Labor Enquiries in India in 1963–5 and 1974–5) completely overlook this aspect, some others (for example, the Agricultural Labour Enquiries in India in 1950–1 and 1956–7) recognize it but use only a simple dichotomy of fully attached laborers and casual laborers. As our subsequent discussion shows, this leaves out a whole range of labor relations in agriculture. The data collected by us in our West Bengal survey suggest the following more elaborate scheme of classification of agricultural laborers:

(1)   totally unattached laborers (or "casual laborers")
(2)   totally attached laborers (or farm servants)
(3)   semi-attached laborers (Type 1) – they are attached to an employer for part of the year, but for the major part of the year they have the freedom to work for other employers
(4)   semi-attached laborers (Type 2) – they are obliged to work for the employer whenever called, for a stipulated number of days in a stipulated period
(5)   semi-attached laborers (Type 3) – they are obliged to work for the employer whenever called, for an unstipulated number of days over an unstipulated period

In addition, we have to recognize a category of workers who are very similar to fully attached laborers but who get paid in terms of a share of the produce (as in the case of the *Kirsheni* system in Birbhum district). These *Kirshens*, however, should be distinguished from sharecropping tenants, since the former work fully under the direction of the employer and work on the employer's land with the employer's means of production (like bullock and plough). It may be noted that we do not include "bonded laborers" as a category. Such laborers are obliged to work for a *single* employer over an indefinite period mostly at less than market wage rates or at no fixed wage rate at all. These laborers, who may have been numerically important in the past and who may still exist to some extent in localized pockets in other parts of India, do not seem to be at all significant in West Bengal.[4]

Let us now provide some explanations for the categories distinguished above. By "totally unattached laborer" we mean what is commonly called a daily or casual laborer. Such a laborer, in his pure form, is one who enters into an agreement or a contract with a particular employer for a single day at a time, different contracts being negotiated on different days, in principle with possibly different employers, the contract for one day with one employer not having any influence on the contract with another employer on another day. Normally he gets paid at the end of the day's work, but he may take an advance payment or it may be withheld to make possible a loan repayment.

By a "fully attached laborer" we mean one who has a usual contract duration of one year, although there are occasional cases of more-than-one-year or slightly-less-than-one-year contracts. Thus for almost the whole year the attached laborer has to work full time exclusively for his employer (members of his family are usually allowed as proxy when he has to be absent). Such a laborer receives his payments partly at the end of the year and partly in irregular instalments spread over the year (including some kind of a bonus during festival times).

While casual and fully attached laborers as described above dominate among the agricultural laborers, there is a rich variety of labor contracts that fall somewhere between the two polar cases of daily contracts with casual workers and annual contracts with fully attached workers. They are intermediate not merely in contract duration but also in the degree of attachment to the employer. Most of the village surveys as well as the Agricultural Labour Enquiries have overlooked this class of contracts, and hence a major focus of our West Bengal survey has been deliberately directed on them. In our survey we have called this intermediate set of contracts as that applying to "semi-attached" labor. We have defined a laborer as semi-attached if, (a) he has or is expected to have some continuity of association with a particular employer (or employers), (b) the contract is for more than just a few days, and (c) he has the freedom to work for other employers for the major part of the year. The majority of our sample villages (nearly 60 percent) report the existence of such intermediate contracts. It is also worth noting from Table 14.5 that our estimates of semi-attached farm labor families in West Bengal turn out to be as large as 60 percent of the total number of attached farm labor families.

Broadly speaking, semi-attached laborers in our sample can be divided into two categories, depending on two aspects of attachment in which the semi-attached laborers' attachment falls short of that of the fully attached laborer. One is that of the duration of contract and the other is that of the freedom of choice of employer. The first broad category of semi-attachment is like full attachment in that workers do not have the freedom to work for other employers during the contract duration but the restriction applies to shorter periods, coinciding with the busy periods in agriculture. Such laborers are employed for a month or a few months at a time or for the period required for completing an important operation for a certain crop. It is important to note that such laborers are usually paid every day (occasionally even at a higher rate than the ruling market wage rate or at the usual rate plus a bonus). We call this kind of laborer "semi-attached laborer" of Type 1.

The second category of semi-attachment involves more freedom for the worker to work for other employers than does full attachment. The typical stipulation in such a relation is that the laborer has to work for the employer whenever the latter calls on him; but on those days when the employer does not have any work for the laborer he is free to work for any other employer. A semi-attached laborer of this kind is usually paid on a daily basis. He is paid by the employer only for the days on which he is employed.

These semi-attached laborers of the second broad category can be divided into two sub-categories. The first sub-category is what we call semi-attached laborer of Type 2. Such a laborer has to work for a given employer whenever the latter needs his services, but normally his commitments are clearly defined and understood on both sides in terms of the number of days of labor he has to provide, the period during which his labor may be demanded in this way and the rates at which he is paid during his days of work. These rates are sometimes lower than the market wage rates. This kind of semi-attachment arises out of a particular loan taken from the employer to be repaid in terms of labor.

We call semi-attached laborers of Type 3 those for whom an arrangement of the above type has no specified duration. The relationship is often an informal one in the nature of an understanding rather than that of an explicitly stipulated contract. As the payment is made on a daily basis it is not necessary on either side to make any commitment about duration. Such a relationship typically involves the laborer taking consumption loans from the employer whenever he needs them and repaying them by working for the employer when the latter needs his work in a continuing process of exchange with not too clearly kept accounts, as distinguished from a single loan taken and liquidated during a specified period in terms of a specified number of days' labor. Such a relation of attachment is often strengthened when the laborer receives an allotment of land from the employer. Semi-attached labor of Type 3 is sometimes described as a "beck-and-call" relationship, an expression used by Thorner (1975) following some earlier authors.

Table 14.5 shows the estimated proportions of total farm labor families that are casual, fully attached, or semi-attached for our sample villages in West Bengal

Table 14.5

Proportional importance of different types of labor families in sample villages of West Bengal, 1979

Type of village	No. of sample villages of each type	Casual labor families as proportion of total labor families in sample villages	Attached labor families as proportion of total labor families in sample villages	Semi-attached labor families as proportion of total labor families in samples villages
	(1)	(2)	(3)	(4)
Highly advanced	31	77	18	5
Advanced	50	85	8	7
Semi-advanced	17	90	6	4
Not advanced	12	97	2	1
All villages	110	84	10	6

classified by the extent of technical advance in the village. While for all villages taken together, 84 percent of all farm labor familes are casual, 10 percent are fully attached, and about 6 percent are semi-attached, the contrast between "highly advanced" and "not advanced" villages is quite sharp: the relative importance of attached and semi-attached labor is much higher in the former than in the latter. It is quite likely that with agricultural progress there is an increased need on the part of employers for non-casual committed labor supply over a sequence of days, or the period of an operation, or a crop season, or an agricultural year, particularly on account of the larger emphasis on timeliness of operations as well as a larger number of shorter-duration crops raised in the year. Fully attached labor on year-round contracts may be too expensive to maintain except for very rich farmers and the intermediate semi-attached labor contract may be increasingly found more convenient by a larger set of employers. In any case Table 14.5 is inconsistent with the notion lingering in some circles that attachment of labor is a sign of pre-capitalist relations or of stagnation.

VII. Bases of Attachment

Full or partial attachment relations between laborers and employers are usually based an certain arrangements, the most important among which are the following; (a) allotment of land, (b) current consumption loans, and (c) old debts. It is not at all uncommon, however, for a long duration attachment to exist without any such specific factors.

Allotment of land as a means of tying a laborer to an employer works in the following way. The employer allots a tiny piece of land to the laborer who cultivates it with the help of the employer's bullock and plough and receives the total or a fraction of the crop output. He sometimes receives even other kinds of help from the employer, e.g. in the form of supplies of seeds and fertilizers. In exchange, the laborer gets committed to work for the employer at whatever time might suit the latter. It may be the case that the laborer works exclusively for the employer right through the year. This is the case of a fully attached laborer receiving a part of his payment from the employer in the form of the produce of the allotted land. But somewhat more often, allotment of land goes with semi-attachment (18 percent of semi-attached labor families in our sample villages are reported to have land allotment as a basis of attachment; the same is reported for 11 percent of attached labor families). Under these conditions the laborer works for the employer only on those days when the employer requires his services and he receives payment only for those days of work. The employer thus ensures for himself a supply of labor of a requisite kind and quality for any time that he may need it, but does not have to pay him for the entire year.

Hereditary or outstanding long-term debt as an obligatory basis of long-term attachment and the coercive role it exercises over the laborer is a phenomenon frequently talked about. We may note from Table 14.6 that in our random sample *not a single* labor respondent in any of the 110 villages in West Bengal reported

Table 14.6
Credit and attachment in sample villages in West Bengal, 1979

Type of labor	Number of respondents			
	In Sample	Reporting hereditary debt as basis of attachment	Reporting outstanding loan taken by laborer himself as basis of attachment	Reporting that it is easier to get consumption credit as attached or semi-attached than as totally unattached
(1)	(2)	(3)	(4)	(5)
AB. Totally attached	128	0	2	115
C. Semi-attached (Type 1)	24	0	0	20
D. Semi-attached (Type 2)	18	0	0	10
E. Semi-attached (Type 3)	25	0	0	24
F. *Kirshen*	15	0	0	15

Notes: For definition of Attached, Semi-attached, and *Kirshen* see text. Answers to question on Column (5) were unavailable for five respondents in the category of semi-attached of Type 2.

an ancient hereditary debt as the basis of his long-term attachment to an employer, and only two out of 138 fully-attached labor respondents reported an outstanding loan taken by the laborer himself some years back as the basis of attachment.

A hereditary or outstanding debt should be distinguished from another basis of attachment which is that of the employer being a common and frequent source of consumption loans, currently taken and liquidated by the end of the current crop year. This basis is more important for semi-attached than for attached labor. Sixty-five percent of semi-attached labor families in our sample villages are reported to have such loans as the basis of attachment; the same is reported for only 3 percent of attached labor families.[5] The overwhelming majority of fully attached labor families are reported to have no special reason for their attachment. The employer and the employee each may find it convenient to work continuously with a party with whom there is an understanding and familiarity over a long time, without any binding obligation. It may happen that such a laborer frequently takes consumption loans from such an employer. Yet it may not be correct to say that the consumption loan necessarily forms the basis of attachment. It may be the other way around. It may be that it is the long-running attachment which is the reason (providing a kind of "collateral") for the loan relationship. In our sample, if one takes those respondents who have been fully attached (including *Kirshens*) to an employer for more than 5 years, out of 75 such respondents only 27 reported consumption loans as a basis of their attachment, even though 60 reported taking consumption loans from the employer.

VIII. Duration of Association

The duration of association between a laborer and his employer can be and frequently is much longer than the duration stipulated in the contract or agreements. In most cases it is a matter of the contract or agreement being renewed on the termination of the contract period, which would be a perfectly reasonable thing to happen if the arrangement is convenient to both parties.

As one may see from Table 14.7, most of the fully attached laborers in our sample have worked for the same employer for periods of 2–10 years. The sample of fully attached laborers was chosen with a stratification drawn at 5 years of working for the same employer. As the population lying between two strata are not known we cannot form any idea about what proportion of fully attached laborers have worked for the same employer more than 5 years and what proportion have worked for 5 years or less. But among those who have worked with the same employer for more than 5 years, only 19 percent report having worked for more than 10 years. Among those who have worked for 5 years or less for the same employer, 22 percent have worked for 1 year or less. The conclusion that we draw on the basis of these figures is that fully attached laborers tend to renew their annual contracts and that there is no tendency for rapid changes of employment to occur. But there is no strong tendency towards indefinite extensions of the relationship either. The same conclusion holds for *Kirshens*.

Semi-attached laborers, in contrast to fully attached laborers, tend to retain their association with the same employer for much shorter periods. In our sample of 67 semi-attached laborers of all three types, only one has had an association with the same employer for more than 5 years. Out of 42 semi-attached labor respondents who report attachment to a single employer, 21 have been with their current employer for 1 year or less and 38 have been with their current employer for 5 years or less. It is important to understand clearly what an association over several years for a semi-attached laborer means: obviously it is no association of continuous working, for that would have marked these laborers as fully attached. It is an association of the laborer working intermittently or periodically for the same employer.

IX. Freedom in Choice of Employers

For fully attached laborers the question of freedom to work for other employers during their period of work contract does not arise. It does happen, however, that such a fully attached laborer sometimes works for other parties with the permission of his own employer when the latter does not have enough work for him. In our West Bengal survey only 4 out of a total of 138 attached labor respondents indicated that they could work for other employers when their own master did not have

Table 14.7

Duration of association with current employer for attached and semi-attached laborers

Type of labor	In sample	Currently attached to one employer	Number of Respondents				Who have worked for more than one employer in the current crop season
			Attached to current employer for years				
			≤1	2–5	6–10	10+	
(1)	(2)	(3)	(4)	(5)	(6)	(7)	(8)
A. Totally attached to same employer for more than 5 years	64	64 (100)	– (–)	– (–)	52 (81)	12 (19)	0 (0)
B. Totally attached to same employer for 5 years or less	74	74 (100)	16 (22)	58 (78)	– (–)	– (–)	0 (0)
C. Semi-attached (Type 1)	24	19 (79)	11 (46)	7 (29)	0 (0)	0 (0)	7 (29)
D. Semi-attached (Type 2)	18	11 (61)	5 (28)	5 (28)	1 (6)	0 (0)	10 (56)
E. Semi-attached (Type 3, Beck-and-Call)	25	12 (48)	5 (20)	5 (20)	0 (0)	0 (0)	18 (72)
F. *Kirshen*	15	15 (100)	0 (0)	7 (47)	6 (40)	2 (13)	3 (20)

Notes: For definitions of Attached, Semi-attached, and *Kirshen*, see text. Columns (4)–(7) are reported only for those Semi-attached who belong to column (3), i.e. those who report attachment to one employer. Answers were not available for two respondents in labor category D and one respondent in labor category E for questions relating to columns (4)–(7). Figures in parentheses represent percentages of laborers of type as shown in column (1).

enough work. (The number having this freedom may be somewhat larger in other areas in India.)[6]

We have already noted that 65 percent of semi-attached labor families in our sample villages are reported to have loans from the employer as *the* basis of their attachment. Contrary to the popular impression of the coercive role of the debt to the employer, it does not seem to inhibit the semi-attached laborer's freedom to work for more than one employer for the major part of the agricultural year.

While semi-attached laborers especially of Types 2 and 3 are in principle free to work for as many employers as they like, it is interesting to note that a considerable proportion of them prefer to work for a single employer during a period of time. From Table 14.7 we can see that out of 67 semi-attached labor respondents in our sample, only 35 reported having worked with more than one employer during the current crop season. There are no indications whatsoever in our data that this phenomenon of working for a single employer during a season and that of working continuously or intermittently for the same employer over a number of years implied any *extra-economic* coercion exercised by the employer over the laborer, robbing the latter of his freedom to terminate his services with the employer. There is in our sample hardly any case of special obligations (like unpaid labor or *begar*) reported by our labor respondents. While the fact of *economic* dependence of the laborer on the employer is a part of the universal phenomenon of the unequal relation between the poor and the rich, it is well to remember that any employer or employee may find it more convenient to work in an environment of mutual understanding and familiarity over a long time and prefer working with the same opposite party rather than changing parties too often. That long association with an employer is not one of unrequited obligation for the attached laborer is also borne out by the evidence, already referred to in Table 14.2 and section III, that attached laborers with longer years of service with a given employer receive a *higher* wage.

Thorner (1957) has described the "beck-and-call" relationship – our semi-attached labor of Type 3 – as unfree. He suggests that quite often long-term outstanding loans which the laborer is not in a position to repay bind him (or his family members) to the employer in such a relationship. In our West Bengal sample *none* of the beck-and-call laborers reported hereditary debt or a long-term debt incurred by the laborer as a basis for his attachment to the employer (Table 14.6). But the overwhelming majority of them reported the periodic taking of consumption loans or wage advances from the employer as the basis of their attachment. It is arguable that a laborer who is at the beck and call of his employer for an unspecified length of time is not an entirely free participant in the labor market. His relationship with the employer is more often an informal one in the nature of a vague understanding or a personalized obligation than that of an explicit contract.

X. Interlinkage of Credit and Labor Attachment

We have already noted that while indebtedness to the employer does not form the basis of attachment for most fully attached laborers, taking consumption loans from the employer is quite common for them. Out of 138 fully attached labor respond-

Table 14.8

Loan against labor commitment for different types of labor in sample villages

Type of labor	Number of respondents		
	In sample	Who have taken loan against commitment of labor	Who report that loan will be repaid by labor at lower than market wage rate
(1)	(2)	(3)	(4)
AB. Totally attached	128	21 (16)	2 (2)
C. Semi-attached (Type 1)	24	19 (79)	7 (29)
D. Semi-attached (Type 2)	18	13 (72)	5 (28)
E. Semi-attached (Type 3)	25	12 (48)	8 (32)
F. *Kirshen*	15	6 (40)	1 (7)
G. Casual laborers with land cultivated	109	6 (6)	4 (4)
H. Casual laborers without land cultivated	109	27 (25)	12 (11)

Notes: Answers to question on column (4) were unavailable for two respondents in category of Semi-attached labor of Type 1. Figures in parentheses represent percentages of laborers of type as shown in column (1).

ents in our sample, 77 percent reported usually taking consumption loans from the employer. Most of these loans in West Bengal are interest-free[7] and, in general, the overwhelming majority of our labor respondents agree that attachment to an employer makes it easier to get consumption credit (see Table 14.6). For the creditor-employer not merely is recovery of loans far easier from one's own attached laborers, but the loan also helps cement the labor-tying relationship.

In section III we have already referred to the widespread system of *Dadan* in West Bengal villages, that of taking loans against future commitment of labor. Such loans are uncommon for fully attached laborers since their labor is already fully committed to the employer; but on occasions when they do take *Dadan*, repayment is usually in the form of an extension of the work period in their contract. Since commitment of labor in return for loans (or other favours) from a potential employer is part of the essential nature of the semi-attached labor relation, it is not surprising that nearly two-thirds of the semi-attached laborers in our sample take *Dadan* from their employers, whereas this is the case for only 15 percent of the purely casual laborers in our sample (Table 14.8).

XI. Dependence

In all the aspects of labor relations discussed above we have emphasized the absence of extra-economic coercion by the employer and the mutual advantage of the employer–employee contracts. It is interesting to note from Tables 14.9, 14.10, and

Table 14.9

Preferred contract duration for attached labor respondents

| | Number of respondents | | | |
| | In sample | Who prefer | | |
		Yearly contract	Daily contract	Contracts of intermediate duration
	(1)	(2)	(3)	(4)
Totally attached to same employer for more than 5 years	64	61 (95)	3 (5)	0 (0)
Totally attached to same employer for 5 years or less	74	66 (89)	8 (11)	0 (0)
Kirshen	15	10 (67)	2 (13)	2 (13)

Notes: For 1 *kirshen* respondent information regarding preferred duration is not available. Figures in parentheses represent percentages of laborers of type as shown in column (1).

Table 14.10

Preferred contract duration for casual labor respondents

| | Number of respondents | | | |
| | In sample | Who prefer | | |
		Yearly contract	Daily contract	Contracts of intermediate duration
	(1)	(2)	(3)	(4)
Casual laborers with land cultivated	109	1 (1)	108 (99)	0 (0)
Casual laborers without land cultivated	109	15 (14)	93 (85)	1 (1)

Notes: Figures in parenthesis represent percentages of laborers of types as shown in column (1).

14.12 that most laborers of different categories in our sample seem not to desire any change from the existing contract duration to any other. More than 90 percent of the fully attached workers report their preference for their present yearly contracts over other types of contracts. Similarly, more than 90 percent of laborers in daily contract (casual or semi-attached) prefer their present daily contracts to other types of contract. As we have noted before, the attached labor contract, far from involving relations characterized by a total lack of freedom in the case of feudal serfs or bonded laborers, is more often like one in which the employer provides cheaper

Table 14.11

Existing contract duration of semi-attached laborer respondents

	In sample	Number of respondents			
		With contract duration			
		Yearly	Daily	Half a year or crop season	Quarter of a year or a month or a sequence of days or for a specific operation
	(1)	(2)	(3)	(4)	(5)
Semi-attached (Type 1)	24	0 (0)	0 (0)	6 (25)	15 (63)
Semi-attached (Type 2)	18	2 (11)	5 (28)	3 (17)	4 (22)
Semi-attached (Type 3)	25	– (–)	– (–)	– (–)	– (–)

Notes: Information on current contract duration is unavailable for three Semi-attached labor respondents of Type 1 and 4 of Type 2. For Semi-attached laborers of Type 3 columns (2)–(5) are left blank, since by the definition of this labor category they do not have any specified contract duration. Figures in parentheses represent percentages of laborers of type as shown in column (1).

Table 14.12

Preferred contract duration of semi-attached labor respondents

	In sample	Number of respondents with preferred contract duration			
		Yearly	Daily	Half a year or crop season	Quarter of a year or a month or a sequence of days or for a specific operation
	(1)	(2)	(3)	(4)	(5)
Semi-attached (Type 1)	24	3 (13)	8 (33)	3 (13)	9 (38)
Semi-attached (Type 2)	18	10 (56)	4 (22)	3 (17)	0 (0)
Semi-attached (Type 3)	25	2 (8)	23 (92)	0 (0)	0 (0)

Notes: Information on preferred contract duration is unavailable for one Semi-attached labor respondent of Type 1, and one of Type 2. Regarding the figure of 23 in column (3) for Semi-attached laborers of Type 3, it should be noted that it does not necessarily imply a preference for the casual labor category, since our question here was strictly regarding the duration of contract irrespective of attachment conditions. Figures in parentheses represent percentages of laborers of type as shown in column (1).

credit, land allotment, and some job security in return for the worker's voluntary assurance of a dependable and readily available source of labor supply over the year, their mutual advantage contributing often to the continuity of attachment. Similarly, the more intermittently used semi-attached labor contract is mutually convenient for some employers and employees.

But a relation based on mutual convenience or advance is not necessarily, and in this case not usually, one of equal exchange. The employer–employee relations discussed above are asymmetric in the highly unequal bargaining power of the two sides. In a situation of low wages, severe unemployment or underemployment particularly in the lean seasons and low availability of cheap or convenient institutional sources, of credit, most relations of attachment are also conditions of "dependence". Land allotment by the employer and loans and jobs given during the desperate lean seasons, of course, serve the needs of the poor worker,[8] but they also effectively emasculate his bargaining strength. In our survey we found that in villages where some form of labor agitation for agricultural wage increase took place, about three-fourths of our fully attached labor respondents reported non-participation in the movements and the majority of them cited their ties with the landlord as the primary reason for their non-participation (Table 14.13). Out of a total of 20 semi-attached labor respondents from our sample villages where similar agitation took place, 12 participated in it and 8 did not. Thus, as expected, the proportion of our semi-attached respondents in *such* villages participating in wage agitation is between that for our fully attached labor respondents (about one-fourth) and that for our casual labor respondents (about three-fourths). It is clear that attachment relations with laborers and their careful interlocking with personalized transactions in credit or land allotment serve the interests of the rich farmers not merely in getting assured sources of labor supply, but also in enhancing their social control over laborers and in restraining the development of class solidarity among laborers.

XII. Conclusions

In conclusion, instead of summarizing the various points of detail in the preceding pages regarding the terms and conditions of labor contracts, let us focus on some of the major theoretical issues arising out of these that might be of interest in the analysis of rural labor markets in development theory. In spite of various socio-economic constraints on participation in the labor market (caste-determined aversion to manual work or taboos against female work outside, etc.), in most villages there is a fairly vigorous market for daily agricultural labor, particularly for operations like ploughing, sowing, transplantation, and harvesting. Within a village the market wage rate for any one of these operations for a daily-contract laborer (of a given sex) is remarkably uniform. It does not seem to vary with the worker's social background, amount of land ownership, or any recognizable proxy for his "ability". With some exceptions, migrant laborers in these villages seem to be paid at the same rates as local laborers. A much more frequent case of intra-village variation in the daily wage rate arises when the laborer is repaying a loan in terms of labor to the employer-

Table 14.13

Participation in labor agitation by types of labor

Type of Labor	In sample	Number of respondents			
		In village where some agitation for wage increase took place	Who participated in such agitations	Have participated who have borrowed from employer	Who attribute their non-participation to dependence on employer
(1)	(2)	(3)	(4)	(5)	(6)
A. Totally attached to same employer for more than 5 years	64	14 (22)	3 (5)	2 (3)	9 (14)
B. Totally attached to same employer for 5 years or less	74	19 (26)	6 (8)	1 (1)	10 (14)
C. Semi-attached (Type 1)	24	8 (33)	5 (21)	4 (17)	3 (13)
D. Semi-attached (Type 2)	18	4 (22)	2 (11)	2 (11)	2 (11)
E. Semi-attached (Type 3, beck-and-call)	25	8 (32)	5 (20)	3 (12)	3 (12)
F. *Kirshen*	15	8 (53)	2 (13)	2 (13)	4 (27)
G. Casual laborers with land cultivated	109	31 (28)	22 (20)	0 (0)	0 (0)
H. Casual laborers without land cultivated	109	31 (28)	24 (22)	0 (0)	0 (0)

Notes: Figures in parentheses represent percentages of laborers of type as shown in column (1).

creditor at an imputed wage rate which is below the market wage rate (the difference presumably is part of the implicit interest cost on the loan) prevailing at the
time of repayment. Such interlinked credit-cum-labor contracts[9] help out workers
who are desperately in need of grain loans for consumption in the lean season, who
do not have the collateral to raise loans from professional money-lenders, and who
find it much easier to pay back the interest as well as the principal in terms of labor
(which may not be acceptable as a means of payment to creditors other than employers
– a standard problem of "double coincidence of wants" in non-monetized transactions).
For the employer such interlinked contracts ensure a guaranteed supply of labor just
when he needs it (an important benefit in view of the weather-dependent uncertainty of the timing of various operations and the considerable risks and costs of
delay) and also act as a kind of barrier to entry for other employers or creditors who
operate only in the labor market or in the credit market.

The inter-village variations in wage rate seem to be sensitive to differences in
demand and supply conditions. The mean harvesting wage rate is significantly higher
in villages where almost all laborers reportedly get work during the harvest months
than in other villages. The mean harvesting wage rate is positively, though weakly,
related to the degree of agricultural advance in the village. The weakness of the
relation may partially be due to the fact that advanced villages draw more in-
migration of labor. The advanced villages show also a larger incidence of wage
payment in the form of piece rates, since quick completion of jobs is presumably at
a premium there.

Unlike in the case of laborers on daily contracts, the wage rates for laborers
on long-term (say, annual) contracts vary from one contract to another within the
same village. There is some evidence that workers attached to the same employer
for a longer duration get a higher wage rate. Apart from farm-specific experience
(or learning by doing) enhancing a laborer's productivity, long years of service
usually imply his dependability for the employer, which gets reflected in the higher
wage.

In general, the actual duration of association between a laborer and his employer
is much longer than the duration stipulated in the contract, and the majority of
workers prefer their existing contract duration. This suggests that under the present
circumstances and constraints the existing contracts are convenient to both parties.
There are no indications whatsoever in our data that the phenomenon of working
continuously (or intermittently) for the same employer over a long period implies
any *extra-economic* coercion exercised by the employer over the laborer as in pre-
capitalist relations of obligatory labor service. In fact our inter-village cross-section
evidence shows that the incidence of attached and semi-attached labor contracts
is significantly higher in the agriculturally more advanced than backward areas.
While agricultural development weakens the institution of "bonded labor" (of
which there was no trace in our sample villages), it at the same time increases the
need for durable labor contracts on account of a general tightening of the labor
market and the larger emphasis on timeliness of operations (as well as a larger
number of shorter-duration crops raised in the year) involved in new agricultural
technology.

But to point to a relation based on mutual convenience or advantage is not to deny the undoubted asymmetry in the bargaining power of the two sides in the employer–employee contracts in these villages. The attachment relations with laborers and their careful interlocking with personalized transactions in credit or land allotment enable the employer to increase his social control over them. Our survey illustrates this by showing that in villages where some form of labor agitation for agricultural wage increases took place, a much smaller fraction of attached and semi-attached than of fully unattached laborers participated in these movements.

Notes

*   Research support by National Science Foundation under Grant No. SES-7804022 A01 to the Institute of International Studies, University of California at Berkeley is gratefully acknowledged. Prem Thapa provided valuable research assistance.

1. In our earlier (1975–6) survey of villages in four states in northern India we found that 10 percent of tenants in Bihar, 2 percent in Orissa and 23 percent in Uttar Pradesh reported rendering unpaid or underpaid services to the landlord. See Bardhan and Rudra (1980).

2. On an approximation basis meals only have been assumed to contain the equivalent of 1 kg of rice, snacks only that of 0.50 kg of rice and meals *plus* snacks that of 1.25 kg of rice.

3. The most likely reason for this phenomenon is that in more advanced villages with a larger need for timely application of labor and sharper rises in peak wage rates, the employers are keener to provide consumption loans against commitment of labor in times of need at lower than market wage rate.

4. In our earlier (1975–6) survey of a random sample of villages in North India we found that the percentage of attached laborers who were obliged to work for the employer for an indefinite period till a loan from him was repaid was 2, 14 and 11 in West Bengal, Bihar, and Uttar Pradesh, respectively. See Bardhan and Rudra (1978).

5. These figures are exclusive of those families who report land allotment by the employer as a basis of attachment; in other words, the figure would be somewhat larger if we also took cases where consumption loans were *one* of the bases of attachment.

6. In our earlier (1975–6) survey of villages we found that the population of attached laborers who were permitted to work for other employers when their own master did not have enough work was much higher for Bihar than for West Bengal or Uttar Pradesh.

7. As many as 37 out of 41 fully attached labor respondents and *Kirshens* in our sample who were currently indebted to their employers (not to be repaid in terms of labor) reported their loans to be interest-free. In our earlier (1975–6) survey also we found that more than 85 percent of consumption loans by employers to attached laborers were interest-free; but such interest-free loans were found to be less common in Bihar and Uttar Pradesh than in West Bengal.

8. There is some evidence in our survey that relatives of attached workers are given priority in hiring by the employer when in the lean season agricultural work opportunities are scarce. This is clearly of some advantage to the laborer; at the same time the entire family's depending on a single employer for employment increases its vulnerability.

9. For a more detailed analytical discussion on interlinked contracts, see Bardhan (1980).

References

Bardhan, P. (1980). "Interlocking Factor Markets and Agrarian Development: A Review of Issues", *Oxford Economic Papers*, Vol. 32, March.

Bardhan, P. and Rudra, A. (1978). "Interlinkage of Land, Labor and Credit Relations: An Analysis of Village Survey Data in East India", *Economic and Political Weekly*, Vol. 13, February.

Bardhan, P. and Rudra, A. (1980). "Terms and Conditions of Sharecropping Contracts: An Analysis of Village Survey Data in India", *Journal of Development Studies*, Vol. 16, April.

Thorner, D. (1957). "Employer–Laborer Relationships in Agriculture", *Indian Journal of Agricultural Economics*, Vol. 12, April–June; reprinted in Thorner, D. and Thorner, A. (eds.) (1962), *Land and Labor in India*, Asia Publishing House, Ch. 3.

Chapter 15

On Measuring Rural Unemployment

Poverty is usually associated with unemployment. Yet in the rural economies of many developing countries, while poverty, by any standard, is quite rampant, most estimates of unemployment (and underemployment) yield extremely low figures. In India, depending on one's definitions and data, poverty (in the sense of a level of living below a bare minimum) is estimated to afflict between 40 and 60 percent[1] of the rural population; and yet, from the latest employment and unemployment survey data (for 1972–73) of the National Sample Survey (N.S.S.) the most careful estimate of the rural unemployment rate turns out to be less than 7 percent.[2] There are, of course, several well-known explanations of this apparent paradox. First of all, in an economy with the State paying no unemployment benefits, the poor cannot afford to be unemployed in the sense of being in the process of job-search for any significant period. They take whatever jobs or activities they can lay their hands on (wage-paid or self-employed either in own farm/enterprise or in various collection activities from village common property). Secondly, poverty and unemployment figures are not likely to be similar, since unemployment is, after all, only one factor contributing to poverty. Others are low earnings per worker and high dependency ratios. While these undoubtedly provide the major parts of the explanation, the present note focuses on several sources of underestimation bias inherent in the current procedures of measuring rural unemployment, and in one respect provides an alternative measure which substantially raises the unemployment estimates, particularly for women. Our comments and methods used should be generally applicable, but all illustrations in this note will be made with the help of estimates derived from detailed data for about 8,500 workers belonging to nearly 4,900 sample households from over 500 sample villages in rural West Bengal, collected by N.S.S. in their 1972–73 employment and unemployment survey to which we had access.

In several attempts[3] that have been made at measuring rural unemployment the most common factor is that of finding the *intersection* of two basic sets of workers: (a) those who are fully or partially idle in terms of working days or hours in the reference period and (b) those who report willingness to work (presumably at the going market wage). In cases where day-to-day time disposition data for the reference period (usually a week) are available and where different households are surveyed in different weeks in the year, from the averages of different weekly situations one can construct an aggregate *time rate* of unemployment, computed as the ratio of the total number of (idle) person days seeking or being available for work to the total number of person days reported to be in the labor force (i.e. working in "gainful" activities or seeking or being available for work). In our subsequent discussion we shall refer to this time rate as the unemployment rate (UR) and most of our comments will be focused on the limitations of this measure. For rural India in 1972–73 UR has been estimated[4] to be about 6.8 percent, and being an average of weekly situations, it is, of course, much higher than the estimated one percent of the rural labor force being chronically (roughly, over the preceding year) unemployed. Apart from open unemployment, UR clearly takes into account underemployment in a time sense, but not in the sense of low earnings or unsuitable occupations; the latter involve the specification of arbitrary norms (or cut-off points) of income, productivity or consumption or of some matching of skills and occupations that introduce issues qualitatively different from those involved in a time measure. In this note we shall confine our attention to the problem of time measures alone.

UR counts only those idle days as unemployed when a person reports actually seeking or being available for work. It is quite likely that when job prospects are bleak a respondent to a survey investigator may not care to report his availability; in other words, the expected frustration about its outcome may discourage the process of job-seeking (particularly, its public reporting) itself.[5] Labor supply thus depends on its own demand, especially when the labor markets are unstable and fragmentary. This is particularly important in the rural economy where the major economic activities are often irregular and sporadic with pronounced seasonal fluctuations leading to periodic entry and withdrawal from the labor force, especially on the part of marginal laborers, often women, who shift back and forth between what is reported as "domestic" work (usually taken as outside the labor force) and "gainful" work. According to our estimates from the rural West Bengal survey data for 1972–73 referred to earlier, 16 percent of self-employed male farmers and 39 percent of self-employed female farmers report *not* working regularly throughout the year; 27 percent of male family helpers on the farm and 22 percent of female farm helpers report *not* working regularly throughout the year because there was not enough work. Taking the farm family helpers, a category of workers more likely to be among marginal laborers, we notice distinct seasonal fluctuations in their entry and withdrawal from the labor force. For instance, for the workers who are usually farm helpers (the *usual* status of a laborer has been defined in the survey as one which prevailed over, say, the preceding one year and which is also likely to continue in the future) those who had *domestic work* as the principal (i.e. the single most important) occupation in the reference week in the relatively slack six-month period of January–June were nearly eight times as many as those among them who had domestic work as the current principal occupation in the relatively busy six-month period of July–December. For women in the 15–44 age group, only about eight percent of *usual* farm helpers had domestic work as the current principal occupation in the busy period of July–December, whereas in the slack period of January–June it was as high as 58 percent. Taking all women laborers by *usual* status in the 15–44 age group, those who had domestic work the current principal occupation in the slack period of January–June were more than four times as many as those usual women laborers in the same age group having domestic work as current principal occupation in July–December.

Table 15.1 presents the data from another, earlier (1970–71), survey by N.S.S. for women (in the 15–44 age group) in small cultivator and wage earning house-holds in different states in rural India on the percentage of total person days in the reference week spent in domestic work in different quarters in the year. It shows a great deal of fluctuation in the proportion of time spent in domestic work in most states across the four quarters of the year. Such an extent of fluctuations in the intensity of domestic work cannot be explained merely by fluctuations in necessary household chores.[6] They may have more to do with fluctuations in opportunities for gainful work leading to periodic entries and involuntary withdrawals from the labor force.

Since the UR measure overlooks this phenomenon of discouraged dropouts from the labor force in the reference week, we have devised an alternative measure which might go towards correcting this. This measure starts with the presumption that if a person is in the labor force by our earlier definition of the *usual* status, any withdrawal by him (more often, by her) from the labor force in the reference week is more due to the perceived lack of opportunities, and days actually spent in domestic work by him/her in the reference week should more properly be counted as unemployed days, even though he/she may not have explicitly reported his/her availability for work to the survey investigator. So our alternative measure of (poten-tial) underemployment, called PUR is defined as:

$$PUR = \frac{A + D + X}{E + A + D + X}$$

where E = number of days in the reference week spent in all kinds of gainful activities

A = number of days spent in the reference week in seeking work or in being available for work

D = number of days spent in domestic work by a person who was in the labor force in the reference week

X = number of days spent (assumed to be seven per person) in domestic work by a person who was in the *usual* labor force but in the refer-ence week was in domestic work (and hence outside the current labor force).

Table 15.1

Percentage of total person – days in reference week spent in domestic work by rural women in 15–44 age group in 1970–71

States	Small Cultivator Households				Wage-earning Households			
	July–Sept	Oct–Dec	Jan–March	April–June	July–Sept	Oct–Dec	Jan–March	April–June
Andhra Pradesh	29.29	24.35	36.96	42.06	28.27	32.08	41.21	43.58
Assam	76.51	78.26	78.54	81.63	89.42	91.82	85.45	82.78
Bihar	43.64	55.57	63.58	67.60	48.26	53.01	52.29	60.83
Gujarat	35.80	48.60	54.48	70.74	29.10	34.97	34.16	65.66
Haryana	76.30	66.67	77.76	73.39	70.36	50.00	80.95	95.65
Karnatak	28.25	25.24	31.62	21.84	24.91	25.53	23.36	25.04
Kerala	50.48	42.13	47.95	47.00	77.85	54.76	49.26	45.06
Madhya Pradesh	29.97	33.84	47.08	53.98	27.28	52.72	41.88	44.48
Maharashtra	22.48	25.72	27.65	37.57	20.49	15.28	19.40	35.39
Orissa	57.17	54.28	68.50	70.43	63.08	54.39	66.02	73.35
Punjab	87.22	74.36	77.68	79.89	47.00	60.00	70.93	81.67
Rajasthan	16.20	30.40	39.43	50.07	53.58	36.11	54.84	37.50
Tamil Nadu	33.40	36.48	35.97	35.98	22.74	16.35	45.53	49.05
Uttar Pradesh	52.45	57.79	59.44	67.62	61.23	52.89	56.17	67.36
West Bengal	71.91	74.08	76.17	81.30	66.13	73.05	75.22	75.54
India	46.27	46.54	52.24	57.26	45.42	42.57	46.90	54.93

Source: National Sample Survey (25th Round), Report Nos. 230/1, 242, 245 and 246.

The admissible set over which *PUR* is defined is that of all persons in the labor force by *usual* status. Contrast this with the standard measure of $UR = A/(E + A)$, defined over the set of persons in the current labor force in the reference week.[7] Table 15.2 presents the estimates of *UR* and *PUR* for rural West Bengal in 1972–73 for males and females in different occupational groups.[8] For all groups taken together, the *UR* for males is 9.8 percent, while *PUR* is 10.6 percent: not a very significant difference. But there is a substantial difference for women; *UR* is 18.1 percent and *PUR* is 32.9 percent. As mentioned before, the phenomenon of periodic entry and withdrawal from the labor force is much more striking in the case of women. In the case of female farmers or farm helpers, the unemployment measure of *PUR* is about *four* times that of *UR*: for female farmers *UR* is 7.6 percent and *PUR* is 29.6 percent; and for female farm helpers *UR* is 11.1 percent and *PUR* is 43.7 percent.

One immediate objection to the use of *PUR* as opposed to *UR* may be that the withdrawal by a *usual* laborer from the labor force and into domestic work may not be involuntary at all, it may be simply due to lower wage rates in slack seasons. While this may be valid for some workers, the significant amount of withdrawal even by very poor groups (whose propensity to substitute leisure for income may not be very strong) suggests that for them it may be more due to a lack of work opportunities. Of the total number of days spent in domestic work $(D + X)$ by those women who are self-employed farmers by *usual* status, 83 percent is accounted for by women belonging to households having less than 2.5 acres of cultivated land. *PUR* for these small cultivator women is about 30 percent, four times as large as their *UR*, which is 7.7 percent. Of the total number of days spent in domestic work $(D + X)$ by those women who are family farm helpers by *usual* status, 43 percent is accounted for by women belonging to households having less than 2.5 acres of cultivated land. *PUR* for these women helpers in small cultivator households is 44.4 percent, about four times as large as their *UR*, which is 10.9 percent.

Similarly, of the total number of days spent in domestic work $(D + X)$ by those women who are family farmers or farm helpers, 43 percent is accounted for by women belonging to households having less than Rs. 30 per capita per month consumer expenditure at 1972–73 prices. *PUR* for these women farmers or farm helpers in poor households is 42.8 percent, nearly three times as large as their *UR*, which is 15 percent. Again, for women who are casual agricultural laborers by *usual* status, another poor labor group, *PUR* is 39.5 percent, significantly higher than their *UR*, which is 30.6 percent.

It is quite possible that not *all* the days spent in domestic work in the reference week by a person in the usual labor force should strictly be counted as involuntary unemployment, and as such *PUR* may in some cases overestimate unemployment. On the other hand, to ignore the phenomenon altogether as in the case of the *UR* measure, is to underestimate unemployment seriously. Besides, *PUR* itself may be an underestimate to the extent that discouraged dropouts withdraw not merely from the *current* labor force (i.e. in the reference week) but also from the *usual* labor force. A woman facing bleak job opportunities may have opted for being a housewife by *usual* status and will be counted out of the admissible set for our measure of

Table 15.2

Alternative unemployment rates (in percentage) for different rural occupational groups in West Bengal, 1972–1973

			July–Sept	Oct–Dec	Jan–March	April–June	Annual
(A)	Casual Agricultural Laborers	UR male	13.55	8.05	21.93	23.99	16.89
		female	21.01	18.76	43.69	43.19	30.56
		PUR male	14.61	9.11	22.90	24.38	17.74
		female	24.76	31.42	53.37	52.64	39.51
(B)	Self-employed Farmers	UR male	2.30	3.11	7.60	3.80	4.20
		female	0	2.00	6.27	15.92	7.57
		PUR male	3.18	3.88	9.04	5.10	5.30
		female	27.61	29.81	36.44	25.69	29.62
(C)	Farm Helpers	UR male	5.23	3.09	7.02	5.61	5.31
		female	7.03	9.29	4.60	22.80	11.10
		PUR male	5.23	3.43	7.64	5.61	5.57
		female	11.68	30.24	69.84	63.25	43.70
(D)	All Laborers by Usual Status	UR male	8.45	6.09	11.58	13.06	9.77
		female	14.90	13.77	21.78	23.03	18.07
		PUR male	9.24	6.82	12.65	13.88	10.62
		female	24.87	29.96	39.59	38.61	32.94

Source: N.S.S. 27th Round, author's tabulation.

PUR. Another related reason why *PUR* may give an underestimate (so does *UR*, *a fortiori*) is the way in which the survey investigator's question about "seeking work or being available for work" is usually interpreted. Quite often the respondent interprets this question as one of availability for *wage* employment outside. There are large numbers of self-employed or family workers (particularly women), who may be available for extra work at home or on their own farm, but do not report availability for wage employment outside. In this way a woman may be classified as a housewife (and hence outside the *usual* labor force because of her negative answer to the question), even though she would have really been available for gainful work *at home*. As a solution to this problem, we have suggested elsewhere[9] that the standard survey question about availability be rephrased in two parts: one asking about availability for work *outside* (example: wage employment) and another for availability *if work is brought to the household* (examples: sewing and tailoring, handicrafts, animal husbandry, etc.) in case the respondent is not available for work outside.

It is interesting to note from our survey data that for casual agricultural laborers, even among those who report *not a single* day (or half day) in the reference week seeking work or being available for work, the majority (60 percent for men and 52 percent for women) answer "yes" to the probing question about their availability for a hypothetical job (wage or salaried employment) *in* the village. The latter probably is more an index of current job dissatisfaction than of unemployment. For the laborers who report both a current farm wage received and an acceptable wage for the hypothetical job in the village, the value of the ratio of the latter to the former is estimated to be about 1.6. Sixty percent thus seems to be on an average the desired margin of wage on a hypothetical job in the village over their current one.

Finally, both *UR* and *PUR* as measures of unemployment are subject to the varying limitations of time-disposition data for different groups of workers. For hired laborers, time disposition data in terms of standardized days or hours are more meaningful. But for the self-employed even the most precise count of time spent in different activities may at times be misleading. In particular, neither of the two measures can take account of underemployment disguised in the form of work-spreading. When there is not much work, self-employed workers may reduce the intensity of work effort but spread it over the whole day or week – the survey investigator will count it as a full day or week worked. This is a difficult problem to handle in large-scale surveys. In serious cases of this sort time measures of unemployment fail, and we may have to resort to more indirect measures with pre-specified norms of productivity or consumption.

Notes

1. For a collection and assessment of these estimates see Srinivasan and Bardhan (*1974*).
2. See, for example, Raj Krishna (*1976*).
3. For a survey of the various concepts used in the literature, see Raj Krishna (*1976*). See also Sen (*1975*), Hauser (*1974*) and ILO (*1974*).

4. See N.S.S. (*1976*). Since work in agriculture and many other unorganized activities cannot be easily reduced to a standard hourly pattern and since many respondents find it rather difficult to report hourly disposition of their time, intensity of work by "full" or "half" day has been adopted as a better measure. It is also to be noted that the standard definition of work or "gainful" work excludes purely domestic work. Domestic work is a catch-all category; quite often, it includes, apart from household chores, various collection activities (like collecting fish, small game, wild fruits and vegetables, firewood, cowdung, etc.), which, in our opinion, should be classified as "gainful" work.

5. This problem in generating rural employment estimates from survey data was noted by P. C. Mahalanobis in his preface to the first N.S.S. report on employment and unemployment in India: "Persons who are idle, especially in rural areas would not be seeking work simply because they know that no work would be available" (*N.S.S., 1959*). The present paper is an attempt to provide an alternative estimate, as a partial solution to the problem, on the basis of recent N.S.S. data.

6. Of course, there is some seasonality in social and ceremonial activities which are part of domestic work, but they are in many areas bunched in the October–December quarter when many of the major Indian festivals take place; in any case they cannot fully explain the significant rise in incidence of domestic work in the lean seasons in most states.

7. Dantwala (*1976*) has suggested an alternative measure of $(A + D)/(E + A + D)$ for all those who are in the labor force in the reference week. While we regard this as a better measure than UR, it does not seem to take into account the phenomenon of *usual* laborers

Table 15.3

Alternative unemployment rates (in percentage) in different districts in rural West Bengal, 1972–73

Districts	UR		PUR	
	male	female	male	female
Darjeeling	4.57	7.60	4.57	17.59
Jalpaiguri	11.01	15.39	11.11	34.16
Cooch Bihar	1.61	25.10	1.62	34.17
West Dinajpur	10.95	23.56	11.55	44.27
Malda	11.65	7.11	11.65	16.16
Murshidabad	11.45	19.31	11.45	28.11
Nadia	5.29	9.51	5.76	37.34
24 Parganas	9.74	8.63	12.86	30.57
Howrah	14.79	16.78	16.27	24.36
Hooghly	7.58	10.77	8.09	29.28
Burdwan	9.00	20.35	9.54	32.34
Birbhum	6.22	13.54	6.51	18.65
Bankura	14.45	40.58	14.86	50.31
Midnapur	10.57	17.86	10.88	30.59
Purulia	11.49	16.28	12.55	40.55

Source: N.S.S. 27th Round, author's tabulation. In most of the districts the sample size of males or females exceeds 100, except in the case of females for the districts of Cooch Bihar, Murshidabad, Nadia, and Howrah, where the small sample size makes the estimates for female unemployment less reliable.

Table 15.4

Alternative unemployment rates (in percentage) for farmers and farm helpers by size groups of cultivated land in rural West Bengal, 1972–73

Size Class of Land Cultivated by Household (in acres)		UR		PUR	
		male	female	male	female
(1) up to 0.1	Self-employed Farmers	12.01	0	12.01	15.62
	Farm Helpers	17.04	0	19.83	19.80
(2) 0.1–2.49	Self-employed Farmers	6.21	9.22	8.01	32.43
	Farm Helpers	7.81	11.76	8.04	45.99
(3) 2.5–7.49	Self-employed Farmers	2.99	6.91	3.45	28.00
	Farm Helpers	5.31	12.29	5.61	44.61
(4) 7.5 and above	Self-employed Farmers	0.48	–	2.10	–
	Farm Helpers	1.03	0	1.03	23.88
(5) All	Self-employed Farmers	4.20	7.57	5.30	29.62
	Farm Helpers	5.31	11.10	5.57	43.70

Source: N.S.S. 27th Round, author's tabulation. On account of small sample size the estimates for size-class (1) for both males and females and for female farmers in size-class (3) and for female helpers in size-class (4) are less reliable than the others.

Table 15.5

Alternative unemployment rates (in percentage) for workers in family-farm or non-farm enterprise by household expenditure groups in rural West Bengal, 1972–73

Household per Capita per Month Consumption Expenditure Group (in Rupees at 1972–73 prices)		UR		PUR	
		male	female	male	female
(1) up to Rs. 14.99	Family Farm Workers	9.75	18.05	9.75	39.86
	Family Non-Farm Workers	7.47	21.58	9.84	44.03
(2) Rs. 15–Rs. 29.99	Family Farm Workers	4.97	14.78	5.95	43.02
	Family Non-Farm Workers	4.64	8.54	6.92	25.34
(3) Rs. 30–Rs. 49.99	Family Farm Workers	5.02	7.04	5.85	38.33
	Family Non-Farm Workers	2.16	1.44	3.61	26.69
(4) Rs. 50–Rs. 74.99	Family Farm Workers	2.85	3.59	3.78	33.64
	Family Non-Farm Workers	2.23	0	3.98	30.54
(5) Rs. 75 and above	Family Farm Workers	4.40	3.21	4.96	34.85
	Family Non-Farm Workers	0.96	0	1.00	59.12
(6) All	Family Farm Workers	4.52	9.92	5.38	39.54
	Family Non-Farm Workers	3.13	5.99	4.85	28.37

Source: N.S.S. 27th Round, author's tabulation. Family farm or non-farm workers include helpers. On account of small sample size and estimates for expenditure group (1) for both males and females and for expenditure groups (4) and (5) for females are less reliable than the others.

withdrawing into domestic work and therefore out of the labor force in the reference week.
8. To bring out the contrast of *UR* and *PUR* in detailed regional disaggregation we provide the alternative estimates for the 15 districts of rural West Bengal in Table 15.3. Table 15.4 presents the alternative estimates disaggregated for size groups of household cultivated land for farmers and farm helpers, and Table 15.5 presents them disaggregated for household per capita expenditure groups for family farm and non-farm workers.
9. See Bardhan [*1976*].

References

Bardhan, P. K., 1976, "Underemployment Characteristics of the Rural Poor: An Analysis of N.S.S. 25th Round Data for Punjab, Haryana and Uttar Pradesh", paper presented to the Symposium on Concepts and Measurement of Rural Unemployment held at Trivandrum, July 1976.

Dantwala, M., 1976, "Some Issues in the Discussion of Concepts and Measurement of Unemployment", paper presented to Symposium, *ibid.*, July 1976.

Hauser, P. M., 1974, "The Measurement of Labor Utilisation", *The Malayan Economic Review*, vol. 19, April.

I.L.O., 1974, "Measuring the Adequacy of Employment in Developing Countries", *Journal of Development Planning*, vol. 5.

N.S.S., 1959, *Report on Employment and Unemployment*, 9th Round.

N.S.S., 1976, *Employment-Unemployment Profile for India*, March.

Raj Krishna, 1976, "Rural Unemployment – A Survey of Concepts and Estimates for India", paper presented to Symposium, *op. cit.*, July 1976.

Sen, A. K., 1975, *Employment, Technology and Development*, Clarendon Press, Oxford, 1975.

Srinivasan, T. N. and P. K. Bardhan, (eds.) 1974, *Poverty and Income Distribution in India*, Statistical Publishing Society, Calcutta.

Chapter 16

Labor-Tying in a Poor Agrarian Economy: A Theoretical and Empirical Analysis*

I

The terms of agricultural labor contracts in poor countries are often characterized by varying degrees of labor-tying or "attachment" to particular employers. Yet much of the standard development literature assumes demand and supply functions of labor that fail to take into account these ties and bonds and the labor market segmentation they involve. This leads sometimes to inappropriate policy prescriptions (like those for the creation of employment opportunities of a type for which the tied laborers cannot make themselves a available). Economic historians, who do consider tied labor, have a tendency to equate it automatically with "feudal" or "semi-feudal" relations and treat it as a symptom of economic stagnation. The purpose of this paper is to contribute toward a clarification of this question, to construct a theoretical model to show how even capitalist agricultural development may involve a strengthening of the institution of labor-tying, and to test empirically some economic hypotheses explaining regional variations in the incidence of tied labor contracts on the basis of some fairly large sample surveys of agricultural laborers in India.

Historically, agrarian labor-tying brings to mind the blatant cases of obligatory service by the tenant-serf to the lord of the manor (as in the classic instances of European feudalism) or those of debt-peonage to moneylender-cum-landlord as what prevailed in many parts of the world. These are clearly cases where tying involves continuing lack of freedom on the part of the laborer and the sanctions underlying the employer's authority are based primarily on social or legal compulsion or what Marxists often call extra-economic coercion. This is to be distinguished from the case where the laborer voluntarily enters long-duration contracts with his employer and reserves the right to leave unconditionally at the end of the specified period. In situations of widespread poverty and unemployment, this freedom to choose one's employer may sometimes be perilously close to the freedom to starve, yet conceptually the distinction between extra-economic coercion and economic exploitation on the basis of unequal but voluntary contracts is important.

While circumstances obviously vary from country to country, it is probably correct to say that today in most parts of the world labor-tying in the sense of bonded and unfree labor is quantitatively not very important or is on the decline. In India a survey[1] of agrarian relations carried out by the author (jointly with A. Rudra) in 1975–1976 in a random sample of more than 300 villages in Eastern India (a region where the problem has been alleged to be acute) suggested that debt bondage of labor is currently rather infrequent. On the other hand, the incidence of varying degrees of tying in voluntary contracts in agriculture is quite significant. This is particularly true if one includes not only the laborers under annual contracts (usually called "attached" laborers in India), but also those under other contract durations, like a season or a period of a given agricultural operation or a specified sequence of days. These labor-tying arrangements are often cemented by the provision of consumption credit or homestead by the employer.

There are alternative theoretical ways of rationalizing these voluntary tying arrangements. In the theoretical model developed in the next section, we emphasize the rationale in terms of risk-sharing in the face of wage uncertainty for peak operations. The employer in the beginning of the year contracts with some tied laborers, feeding them at a steady rate across the seasons (i.e., giving them consumption credit to survive the lean season) in exchange for their delivering a committed labor supply in the peak season; if the peak labor demand is higher than that supplied by the tied laborers, the employer then enters the spot or casual market hiring the additional labor at the uncertain wage rate of that time.

II

We have two stylized periods, the "lean" and the "peak," with no work in the lean period, followed by a peak period in which the employer requires a random amount of labor. The labor requirement (say, for harvesting) per unit of output in the peak period is given by a fixed coefficient β. Mean output level is given by x, while the actual yield is Ax, where A is a random variable (representing weather and other production uncertainties) with an expected value of unity. If the total labor requirement in the peak period βAx exceeds the amount of tied labor L_t hired in the lean period, the employer needs to hire some casual labor, which will be paid at the (random) rate W in the peak period.

The employer's profits π are thus given by

(1) $\pi = \pi_1 = Ax - (2 + \rho)cL_t$ if $\beta Ax \lessgtr L_t$

(2) $\pi = \pi_2 = Ax - (2 + \rho)cL_t - (\beta Ax - L_t)W$ if $\beta Ax > L_t$,

where c denotes the minimum consumption level in each period that will induce workers to accept the labor-tying contract and ρ is the unit interest cost to the employer for paying out the consumption amount c to each tied laborer in the lean period. Note that c is the same in both periods. If the workers are risk-averse, but the employer has sufficient wealth and portolio-diversification opportunities to be assumed risk-neutral, and if for simplification for the time being, we assume that the workers discount utility at the same rate ρ as the employer discounts profits,[2] the optimal risk-sharing considerations will imply labor-tying contracts that smooth worker consumption over the two periods.

Let us now look more closely into the labor supply side and the alternative opportunity costs of workers. Take the case of a worker who does not enter into labor-tying contracts. Suppose that such a worker obtains a consumption of y_0 in the lean period, and $y \geq y_0$ in the peak period, say, through production on his own plot of land or other activities. Assume that y_0 is identical for all such workers, but they differ with respect to y. Let $G(\cdot)$ be a cumulative distribution of workers by their alternative opportunities. Thus, $G(\bar{y})$ is the proportion of workers such that $y \leq \bar{y}$.

Of course, if the spot wage in the peak period is W, then a type y worker will enter the spot market if $W > y$. When the utility function is normalized so that $U(y_0) = 0$, the expected utility of a casual worker is $EU[\max(y, W)]$. We assume that workers cannot work part of the time for spot wages and the remaining part in their own farms. A worker will thus choose to work on a labor-tying contract if the discounted utility from the stable income from tied work exceeds the expected utility from casual work; i.e.,

(3) $(2 + \rho)U(c) > EU[\max(y, W)]$.

It is easy to see that if a worker of type y accepts the labor-tying contract, then the contract will be accepted by any worker of type $y' < y$. So it is clear that a contract involving a consumption level of c will attract all workers of a type below some critical value $y(c)$.

Suppose that $H(W)$ is a cumulative distribution function of the spot wage W and assume point expectation; i.e., there is a unique W for each state A, so that the spot wage is a function $W^e(A)$ in workers' expectation. Under the above specifications, the supply of contract workers is $G[y(c, W^e(A))]N$, where N is the total number of workers and the supply to the spot market, given any wage W, is $N \max[0, G(W) - G[y(c, W^e(A))]]$, where $[y(c, W^e(A))]$ is given by

(4) $(2 + \rho)U(c) = U(y)H(y) + \displaystyle\int_y^\infty U(W)\,dH(W)$

This is the margin in determining the choice between tied and casual work from the worker's supply point of view.

The demand for tied labor is given by the landlord's maximization of the expected value of his profits $E\pi$ or by

$$\max_{L_t} x - (2 + p)cL_t - \int_z^m (Ax - L_t)W^e(A)\,dF(A),$$

where $z \equiv L_t/\beta x$ is the proportion of total labor employed that is tied, m is the maximum value taken by A, $W^e(A)$ is the spot wage function in the landlord's expectations and $F(A)$ is the cumulative distribution of A. We shall assume that A is never high enough to lead to excess demand or nonharvesting of some part of the field. A sufficient condition for this is $m < G(\beta^{-1})/b$, where $b \equiv \beta x/N$ is the employment rate of average output.

Tied labor demand $L_t(c, W^e(A))$ is given by the first-order condition of landlord's maximization:

$$(5) \quad (2 + p)c = \int_z^m W^e(A)\,dF(A).$$

In the equilibrium, demand for tied labor equals supply, so that

$$(6) \quad L_t(c, W^e(A)) = NG[y(c, W^e(A))],$$

and the actual distribution of W is

$$(7) \quad W(A, W^e(A), W^e(A)) = \begin{cases} y(c, W^e(A)), & \beta Ax \le L_t(c, W^e(A)) \\ G^{-1}(Ab), & \beta Ax > L_t(c, W^e(A)). \end{cases}$$

In rational expectations equilibrium, $W^e(A) = W^e(A) = W(A)$. For $A > z$, the distribution function of W is given by

$$\begin{aligned} (8) \quad H(W) &= Pr(G^{-1}(Ab) \le W) \\ &= Pr(A \le G(W)/b) = F(G(W)/b). \end{aligned}$$

Thus, we can write in equilibrium

$$H(W) = \begin{cases} 0, & W < y(c, W) \\ F(G(W)/b), & W \ge y(c, W). \end{cases}$$

From (4), (7), and (8) the worker's equilibrium condition reduces to

$$(9) \quad (2 + p)U(c) = U(y)F(G(y)/b) + \int_z^m U(G^{-1}(Ab))\,dF(A).$$

The three equations (5), (6), and (9) may be solved to get the equilibrium values of $y(b)$, $z(b)$, and $c(b)$. In the Appendix we prove that dz/db is positive, under the sufficient condition that $G'(y)$ is large, or alternatively that y is uniformly distributed and the utility function is logarithmic.

The intuitive reasoning for dz/db positive is that as b rises, the effect on marginal rates of substitution between contract and spot work is such that the supply price of risk-averse workers rises more slowly for assured contract jobs than for spot labor, favoring employment of contract workers; but at the same time employment of more contract workers raises equilibrium y, the opportunity cost of the marginal contract worker, and hence makes hiring of contract workers more expensive. Our sufficient condition on $G'(y)$ makes sure that this latter effect on changing the *type* of worker at the margin of contract jobs is not strong enough to upset the more familiar effect through marginal rates of substitution. If $G'(y)$ is not large, the alternative sufficient condition ensures that the effect through marginal rates of substitution dominates when the workers' risk-aversion is strong enough for the utility function to be logarithmic. This sufficiently strong *relative* risk-aversion on the part of labor suppliers (preferring stable income from tied work to unstable income from spot work) coupled with risk neutrality on the part of labor demanders explain the dominance in the equilibrium outcome in favor of tied contracts with increasing b.

z indicates the importance of tied labor as a proportion of total labor employed. From the definition of b it is increasing in x and β and decreasing in N. So we can now interpret our result of dz/db positive as follows:

a. Yield-increasing improvements (raising x) increase the importance of tied labor as a proportion of total labor employed.
b. Labor-saving technical progress, like some kinds of agricultural mechanization (lowering β) *reduces* the importance of tied labor as a proportion of total labor employed.
c. The larger the total number of workers (N), the *smaller* is the importance of tied labor as a proportion of total labor employed.

In general, the more is the demand pressure in the labor market relative to supply (indicated by b), the larger is the proportional importance of tied labor. We have not explicitly introduced unemployment in our model, but if a high rate of unemployment is associated with low demand pressure in the labor market relative to supply, it will lead to a smaller proportional importance of tied labor. (Note that this result is similar to the positive association of tied labor with tightness of the labor market derived in Bardhan [1979], where there is labor tying not because of risk-sharing, but because the employer wants to save on his recruitment cost in the peak season.)

III

In the theoretical model of the preceding section, we have assumed lean and peak periods of given duration. But improved agricultural technology (particularly that using HYV seeds, chemical fertilizers, and more privately controlled irrigation) may change the duration and periodicity of the agricultural crop cycle itself, apart from increasing the importance of timeliness of each operation and the requirement of labor at short notice (raising recruitment costs and sharpening wage peaks in the busy season). With a larger number of shorter-duration crops raised in the year, the seasonality of the labor demand profile may be more evened out with a corresponding effect on the composition of hired labor. With the consequent decline in the seasonal underutilization of tied labor and hence in the costliness of "labor-hoarding" from the point of view of the employer, his optimal labor mix is likely to shift in favor of tied labor.[3]

Two additional reasons, not captured in our theoretical model, may reinforce our result about the increase in the relative importance of tied labor with agricultural development. One is that the employer often finds it riskier to entrust animals to casual workers over whom he has less continued control. The other reason has to do with the general problems of labor supervision and control that the employer faces. With agricultural development, as the hired labor force grows in size, the landlord finds it useful to mobilize the services of his attached laborer in overseeing the work of casual laborers and reporting on cases of delinquency or rebelliousness. In general, the two-tiered labor system on a farm is an important check on the development of class solidarity of farm workers. This divide-and-rule policy is particularly effective for the employer when labor-tying is carefully interlocked with personalized credit transactions and provision of homestead or cultivable land allotment by the employer. In a survey of 110 sample villages in 1979 in West Bengal,[4] we found that in villages where some form of group bargaining or labor agitation for an agricultural wage increase took place, most of our tied labor respondents reported nonparticipation in the movements, and the majority of them cited their ties with the landlord as the primary reason for their nonparticipation.

We now turn to some empirical information on the incidence of labor-tying and its relationship with agricultural development and tightness of the labor market. In the above-mentioned 1979 survey in West Bengal, the estimated proportion of tied labor families to total farm labor families was almost twice as large in agriculturally more advanced villages than in backward villages. Bhalla [1976] shows in her study of the prime Green Revolution area of the State of Haryana that, compared with other less developed regions of the same State or with the same region earlier, a much larger proportion of agricultural laborers are employed on rather long-term (two-year and sometimes even three-to-five-year) contracts.

Bent Hansen has drawn my attention to the fact that even in Danish agriculture, for more than a century after the emancipation of serfs, voluntary but long-term contract laborers were the major part of the agricultural workforce, and their importance declined only after the large-scale introduction of mechanization in recent decades. For Sweden, Eriksson and Rogers [1978] report how during the late eighteenth and early nineteenth centuries commercialization of the agricultural sector and the attendant reorganization of the large landed estates in central and southern Sweden resulted in a replacement of *corvée* labor by the growth of a new proletarian group, the *statare*, year-round workers. This system rapidly expanded during the nineteenth century in Sweden. Richards [1979], in his comparative study of estate labor systems in East Elbian Germany (1750–1860), the Egyptian Delta (1850–1940), and Central Chile (pre 1930), has noted that in all three cases, periods of intensification of agriculture and introduction of new crops and new crop rotations have been associated with an *increase* in the relative importance of year-round workers – the *Instleute* in Prussia, the *tamaliyya* in Egypt, and the *inquilinos* in Chile.

We now provide some econometric evidence from a variety of cross-sectional data in rural India on the correlates of labor tying. First, let us take the data from the 1956–57 Agricultural Labor Enquiry Survey in India. In this survey data were collected from agricultural labor households in nearly 3,700 sample villages in the whole of rural India, divided into 38 zones. The proportion (*ATTP*) of attached,[5] usually annual-contract, agricultural labor households to the total number of agricultural labor households in our sample data set from this source has a mean value of 31.23 percent with a standard deviation of 19.35 percent. Table 16.1 presents the results of a regression equation explaining the variations in *ATTP*.

The importance of attached labor in a zone seems to be *negatively* associated with the quantitative importance of total labor households in a zone (a labor supply indicator) and the extent of average unemployment.[6] Attached labor is also more important in areas where the maximum-to-minimum wage ratio across seasonal operations is higher (i.e., where the wage rate shoots up particularly sharply in the peak season relative to that in the lean season, indicating especially tight labor markets in the peak season). All this shows, consistently with our theoretical models, that tighter labor markets lead to more tied labor contracts, contrary to the common presupposition that it is the need for unemployment insurance for workers in areas of larger unemployment that primarily determines the incidence of tied labor contracts. In slack labor markets with high unemployment, the employer often does not bother to have long-term contracts with labor, since he is surer of his labor supply for peak operations.

The importance of attached labor is positively (though weakly) associated with the land productivity factor (as is consistent with our theoretical model). The positive coefficient of *DEBTEMP* implies that attached labor contracts are frequently associated with credit provided by the employer. The employer has a special incentive to lend to his attached laborers, not only because recovery of loans is easier, but also because it helps cement the labor-tying arrangements or makes it easier to enforce implicit contracts. (In the Bardhan-Rudra 1979 survey of West Bengal villages, the overwhelming majority of labor respondents indicated that they would find it easier to get consumption credit as a tied laborer than as a casual laborer.)

Our next set of econometric evidence is from the N. S. S. 1972–73 Employment and Unemployment Survey data and the Reserve Bank of India 1971–72 Debt and Investment Survey data across 60 agroclimatic regions in rural India. Let us denote by *ATTMP* our estimate for each region what the N.S.S. called "regular"[7] (as opposed to casual) farm laborers as a percentage of total farm laborers (male, 15–59 age group). In our sample, *ATTMP* has a mean value of 33.54 percent with a standard deviation of 19.27 percent. Table 16.2 presents the results of a regression equation explaining variations in *ATTMP*. Consistent with our previous discussion, the proportional importance of tied labor is again negatively associated with the

Table 16.1

Linear regression analysis of variations in the percentage of attached agricultural labor households across 36 zones in rural India, 1956–1957

Explanatory variables	Regression coefficient	Standard error	Significant at percent level
1. Percentage of agricultural labor households to all rural households (*AGLABP*)	−0.4634	0.2373	6.0
2. Average number of days unemployed in the year for adult male agricultural laborers (*UNEMD*)	−0.1680	0.0995	10.2
3. Maximum to minimum agricultural wage ratio across seasonal operations (*MAXMINW*)	8.7088	4.9922	9.1
4. Index of land productivity (*PRINDEX*)	0.2205	0.1512	15.5
5. Percentage of total debt of an indebted labor household borrowed from employers (*DEBTEMP*)	61.8663	17.7262	0.2
Constant term	10.4227	20.2874	61.1

$R^2 = 0.5163$; $F = 6.4$; no. of observations = 36

Dependent variable = the percentage of attached agricultural labor households to the total number of agricultural labor households (*ATTP*)

Mean = 31.23 percent

Standard deviation = 19.35 percent

Notes: MAXMINW is the ratio of the daily wage rate for casual adult male laborers in the agricultural operation for which this rate is the highest in a zone to that in the operation for which this rate is the lowest. The data for *AGLABP, UNEMD, MAXMINW,* and *DEBTEMP* for 36 (ALE) zones are all from the N.S.S. Report relating to the Second Agricultural Labor Enquiry. *PRINDEX,* estimated by Sharma [1973] for each district, is a weighted average of gross irrigated area as a proportion of gross sown area in 1959–1961, average annual rainfall in 1959–1961, net sown area as percentage of geographical area in 1959–1961, intensity of cropping in 1959–1961, gross sown area per head of the total rural population in 1961, and the soil index rating. Our zonal estimates of *PRINDEX* are simple averages of the estimates of Sharma for the districts each zone consists of (with the all-India average taken as 100). Since we did not have data for *PRINDEX* for one zone in Assam and one in Bombay, we had to exclude these two zones from the total of 38 (ALE) zones.

Table 16.2

Linear regression analysis of variations in the percentage of attached male farm laborers across 60 regions in rural India, 1972–1973

Explanatory variables	Regression coefficient	Standard error	Significant at percent level
1. Proportion of rural households who are asset-poor (ASTPOOR)	−0.9004	0.2169	0.0
2. Average rural unemployment rate in the region (UR)	−0.0058	0.0043	18.1
3. Coefficient of variation of cultivated land across size classes of land holdings (CVLC)	19.5034	9.6822	4.9
Constant term	31.1527	12.0666	1.2

$R^2 = 0.3831$; $F = 11.6$; no. of observations = 60

Dependent variable = "Regular" (as opposed to casual) farm male laborers in the 15–59 age group as a proportion of total farm male laborers in that age group (ATTMP)

Mean = 33.54 percent

Standard deviation = 19.27 percent

Notes: *ASTPOOR* is the proportion of rural households in each region who possess assets of Rs. 1,000 or less as of June 30, 1971. The source of *UR* is the N.S.S. 27th Round data and that for *ASTPOOR* is the Reserve Bank of India ALL-India Debt and Investment Survey of 1971–72. The latter is also the source of data from which *CVLC* has been estimated for each region. The data for *ATTMP* are from the N. S. S. 27th Round.

Table 16.3

Logit analysis of the probability of any male member (in the 15–60 age group) of an agricultural labor household being a "regular" farm laborer by usual status in rural West Bengal, 1977–1978

Explanatory variables	Estimated coefficient	Standard error
1. Normal annual rainfall in the district in meters (*RAIN*)*	0.2417	0.1123
2. Village irrigation level (*VILIRR*)*	0.4130	0.0825
3. Dummy for scheduled caste (*SCHCASTE*)*	0.9551	0.2014
4. Dummy for unowned homestead (*HMUNOWN*)*	0.4775	0.2672
5. Dummy for indebtedness to employer (*EMDEBT*)	0.3969	0.2830
Likelihood ratio index = 0.6735; no. of observations = 2,195.		

Notes: The data for *VILIRR, SCHCASTE, HMUNOWN*, and *EMDEBT* are from N. S. S. 32nd Round for rural West Bengal. *VILIRR* represents four levels of irrigation in the village: (1) not irrigated at all, (2) the percentage of village cultivated area irrigated is positive but does not exceed 10 percent, (3) it is between 10 and 25 percent, and (4) it exceeds 25 percent. The data for *RAIN* are from the *Statistical Abstract of West Bengal*. (*) denotes a coefficient at the 5 percent level of significance.

indicator (as we interpret the variable *ASTPOOR* to be) of plentiful labor supply in a zone and with the rate of unemployment. It is positively associated with an indicator of inequality in the distribution of land cultivation, possibly indicating that in areas where land is concentrated in fewer hands, more people can afford to hire year-round or long-term laborers than where land is more equally distributed and the average size of farm is smaller. Larger farms also need more attached workers who would oversee and supervise the work of casual laborers.

Our third set of econometric evidence is from the detailed household-level N.S.S. 1977–78 Employment and Unemployment Survey data for rural West Bengal. Table 16.3 presents the results of a Logit analysis of the probability that an agricultural labor household has some male member (in the 15–60 age group) who is a "regular" farm laborer by usual status. It seems that this probability is significantly higher if the household is located in a village with better irrigation or in a district where the normal rainfall is higher (indicating association of labor-tying with areas of higher agricultural productivity). It is also not unexpected that this probability is positively associated with households belonging to low castes, or with unowned homestead or indebtedness to employers (as we have mentioned before, labor-tying agreements are often cemented by provision of credit or homestead by the employer).

IV

In this paper we have shown how tied labor, contrary to its common characterization as a feudal relic and as a symptom of economic stagnation, may actually be strengthened by capitalist agricultural development. We construct a simple two-period theoretical model of a two-tiered labor market to show how the proportional importance of voluntary labor-tying contracts may increase with yield-increasing improvements and with a tightening of the labor market. We then provide in support of these hypotheses some general historical as well as more detailed econometric evidence from a variety of cross-sectional data in rural India.

We should, however, note that our theoretical model in Section II also suggests that there are certain types of agricultural development which may *reduce* the incidence of labor-tying. Agricultural progress in a particular region may involve mechanization of some operations, or may induce seasonal immigration of labor from poorer areas, both resulting, consistent with our model, in a reduction in the employer's need for tied labor. Apart from these theoretical reasons, there may be data-related problems that may vitiate the relevance of the empirical evidence used in testing the hypotheses on labor-tying enumerated in this paper. As an illustration, let us refer to two kinds of such data problems. One relates to regions where pockets of bonded labor or semi-serfdom still exist. Here the data on tied labor will often lump together both free and unfree laborers, and with agricultural progress the former may go up in importance while the latter decline in numbers, canceling or dampening the observed trends in the estimates of tied labor.[8] The second kind of data problem arises because data collectors, particularly in large-scale surveys, often miss out on a variety of *implicit* contracts of labor-tying, or confuse between the concepts of duration of contract and frequency of wage payment (a laborer whose duration of contract is the whole crop season may still be paid on a daily basis like casual laborers), or fail to count as tied laborers the whole class of "semi-attached" laborers whose contract duration does not extend beyond, say, a fortnight or a month, and who are free to work for other employers for the rest of the year.

Appendix

When (5), (6), and (9) are totally differentiated with respect to b and the terms are combined,

$$(10) \quad \frac{dz}{db} = \int_z^m [U'(c) - U'(G^{-1}(Ab))] \frac{Af(A)\,da}{G'(G^{-1}(Ab))} - \frac{U'(y)F(z)z}{G'(y)} \bigg/ U'(c)f(z)y + \frac{U'(y)F(z)b}{G'(y)}.$$

The second terms in the numerator and the denominator in (10) measure the effect of changing b on y. As y is the initial minimum wage rate at which the spot market just opens, we can unambiguously sign dz/db if we assume that the effect of b on this minimum wage is small (a sufficient condition for which is that the cumulative distribution function $G(y)$ is sloped in the relevant range in such a way that $G'(y)$ is very large). Under this sufficient condition all we have to prove for dz/db to be positive is

$$(11) \quad \int_z^m [U'(c) - U'(G^{-1}(Ab))] \frac{A}{G'(G^{-1}(Ab))} f(A)\,dA > 0.$$

If we define $G^{-1}(\bar{A}b) = c$, it is easy to see that

$$A[G^{-1}(Ab) - c] \gtreqqless \bar{A}[G^{-1}(Ab) - c] \text{ for } A \gtreqqless \bar{A}.$$

Use this and equations (5) and (7) to obtain

$$(12) \quad \int_z^m A[(G^{-1}(Ab) - c]f(A) \, dA > 0.$$

By similar logic, $\{U'(c) - U'[G^{-1}(Ab)]\}/\{G^{-1}(Ab) - c\}$ is nonnegative for $G^{-1}(Ab) \gtreqless c$. Multiplying the integrand in (12) by this, (11) is proved. This means that dz/db is positive.

If $G'(y)$ is not very large, an alternative set of sufficient conditions for dz/db positive is that y is uniformly distributed and that the utility function is logarithmic. If y is distributed uniformly on, say, $[0, k]$, $G(y) = y/k$, and $G'(y) = 1/k$. If the utility function is logarithmic, the numerator in (10) then reduces to $(1 + \rho)/b$, which is positive.

Notes

*   I have benefited from comments on earlier drafts by S. Devarajan, R. Lee, T. N. Srinivasan, and two referees and an editor of this *Journal*. Valuable research assistance was provided by T. Paynter, M. Riordan, N. Singh, and P. Thapa. Partial research support by the National Science Foundation, under Grant No. SES-7804022 A01, is gratefully acknowledged.

1. For details of survey design and results, see Bardhan and Rudra [1978]. We define "bonded labor" as a person who is tied to a particular creditor as a laborer for an indefinite period until some loan received in the past is repaid. We found that in West Bengal less than 2 per cent (in Bihar 14 per cent and Uttar Pradesh 11 per cent) of all farm servants (i.e., those who were working for an employer on a long-term contract) – and hence a much lower percentage of *all* agricultural laborers – reported such cases of bondage. The 1977–78 Employment and Unemployment Survey carried out by the National Sample Survey Organization in all of India defined a bonded laborer as a person who is with an employer under obligation on work not specifically compensated by any wage; according to this definition, only about 0.28 per cent of males in the labor force in rural India were estimated to fall into the category of bonded labor.

2. The more realistic case of a difference in the discount rates can be introduced with a slight increase in cumbersomeness of the subsequent equations.

3. For an application of the literature on the choice of base and peak load capacities for an electric utility to the choice of the optimal labor mix for an employer, see Kotwal [1981].

4. For details of this survey see Bardhan and Rudra [1981]. In this survey we included in our definition of tied laborers not merely the annual-contract attached workers but also those whose contract periods were parts of the year (like a month, a fortnight, or some sequence of days).

5. In this survey attached laborers have been defined as those who are "more or less in continuous employment." For a critique of the concepts and definitions used in the Agricultural Labor Enquiry and a reference to the possibility of their varying interpretations by field investigators in different areas of the country, see Thorner and Thorner [1962], Ch. 13. We should also note that a household whose major source of *income* is attached labor has been described as an attached labor household, even though some members of the household may have other occupations.

6. Given the numerical preponderance of casual laborers in most areas, it is unlikely that the cross-section variations in the extent of unemployment are themselves significantly affected by variation in the incidence of attached labor.

7. In the survey schedules no rigorous definition of "regular" as opposed to "casual" laborers has been given. In practice the term "regular" has been applied mostly to cover annual-contract attached workers.
8. The problem is sometimes made worse by the further lumping in the data of disguised tenants whom the landlords may report as attached laborers merely to avoid land reforms that take the form of protective tenancy legislation.

References

Bardhan, P. K., "Wages and Unemployment in a Poor Agrarian Economy: A Theoretical and Empirical Analysis," *Journal of Political Economy*, LXXXVII (June 1979), 479–500.

——, and A. Rudra, "Interlinkage of Land, Labor and Credit Relations: An Analysis of Village Survey Data in East India," *Economic and Political Weekly*, XIII (Feb. 1978), 367–84.

——, and ——, "Terms and Conditions of Labor Contracts in Agriculture: Results of a Survey in West Bengal 1979," *Oxford Bulletin of Economics and Statistics*, XLIII (Feb. 1981), 89–111.

Bhalla, S., "New Relations of Production in Haryana Agriculture," *Economic and Political Weekly*, XI (March 27, 1976), A23–A30.

Eriksson, I., and J. Rogers, *Rural Labor and Population Change: Social and Demographic Developments in East-Central Sweden During the Nineteenth Century* (Uppsala: Almqvist and Wilksell, 1978).

Kotwal, A., "The Impact of Green Revolution on Labor Contracts and Rural Poverty," University of British Columbia Economics Working Paper, 1981.

Richards, A., "The Political Economy of Gutswirtschaft: A Comparative Analysis of East Elbian Germany, Egypt, and Chile," *Comparative Studies in Society and History*, XXI (Oct. 1979), 475–510.

Sharma, P. S., *Agricultural Reorganization of India* (New Delhi: Allied, 1973).

Thorner, A., and D. Thorner, *Land and Labor in India* (New York: Asia Publishing House, 1962).

Chapter 17

Labor Mobility and the Boundaries of the Village Moral Economy*

I

Most of the existing literature on labor mobility within a country relates either to rural–urban migration or, less frequently, to seasonal migration to rural jobs like harvesting. Very seldom has there been any analysis of the range of inter-village mobility of a *resident* peasant laborer in a village and the factors that may restrain such mobility. The presumption has been that within easy daily commuting distance from a village the wage rate that an agricultural laborer receives for similar operations is roughly uniform and hence the question of inter-village mobility within that range is of not much importance. One striking observation from our survey of West Bengal villages that we report here is that there are sometimes considerable wage differences on similar work across even neighboring villages; and yet laborers often do not walk across to the next village to take advantage of higher wages. On the other hand, laborers occasionally go out to work in villages where the wage rate is not significantly higher. The boundaries of labor mobility across neighboring villages are sometimes significantly defined by territorial affinities and the relationships of trust and credit between the laborers and their employers. These relationships may be stronger than the stimulus of short-run wage differences. The employers in one village often do not think they possess enough information about the work ability and particularly dependability characteristics of laborers in other villages, and in hiring "outsiders" they cannot draw upon the considerable reservoir of village loyalty and goodwill they utilize in maintaining their social control over the entire labor process for "insiders". The laborers on their part often look up to their local employers as providers of sustained job opportunities, regular credit and emergency help over the years, and may even forego higher short-term wages in nearby villages in order to maintain their long-term ties.

Development economists have seldom analyzed the economic implications of such moral boundaries of the village community and how the consequent process of market segmentation brings up analytical issues[1] similar to those following from the important distinction of "customer" from "auction" markets made in the literature[2] relating to industrially advanced countries. Anthropologists often refer to the local patron-client relationships in villages as a mark of traditional social systems, but occasionally ignore the underlying economic rationale of such clientelization, with costs of information, performance monitoring and social control over the labor process rising rather sharply as one goes outside the moral community of one's village.

In all we surveyed 80 villages in West Bengal in 1981–82, separated into five clusters of neighboring villages in five districts.[3] If one describes a village as agriculturally advanced when half or more of its cultivated land is under modern irrigation facilities like canals, pumps or tubewells, the five clusters in our surveys are characterized by varying degrees of agricultural advance. As Table 17.1 indicates the most advanced is our cluster of 16 villages in the Bardhaman district where 15 out of them are agriculturally advanced by our definition; next is the cluster in the Hooghly district where 11 out of the 16 villages are advanced; next is the cluster in the Murshidabad district where exactly half of the 16 villages are advanced; then comes the cluster in the Bankura district where seven out of 16 villages are advanced; and last is the cluster in the Jalpaiguri district where none of the 16 villages is agriculturally advanced. Questionnaires were canvassed with six respondents in each village, two casual laborers, two employers, one landlord and one sharecropper. The questions asked of each respondent related to general socio-economic conditions of the village, the nature of inter-village labor movement and hiring patterns and the terms of prevailing land, labor and credit contracts, as well as specific information on these matters pertaining to the particular respondent.

II

As Table 17.2 indicates, in four out of 16 villages in the Bardhaman[4] and Jalpaiguri clusters and three out of 16 villages in the Hooghly cluster, laborers are reported as *not* going to work to any other village, whereas this is the case for none of the villages in either the Bankura cluster or the Murshidabad cluster. In eight out of 16 villages in the Bardhaman[5] cluster and in six out of 16 villages in the Jalpaiguri cluster, employers in the village are reported as *not* hiring laborers from any other village in the area, whereas this is the case for none of the villages in the Bankura, Hooghly or Murshidabad clusters. While in all the villages in the Bankura or Murshidabad clusters, laborers are reported to go to at least *some* adjacent village, this is true for only nine out of 16 villages in the Hooghly or Jalpaiguri cluster and

Table 17.1
Village identification, level of agricultural development and the farm wage-rate

Serial Number	Name of Village	Level of Agricultural Development	Male Wage–Rate (Rs. per day)
Bardhaman Cluster in Figure 17.1:			
1	Basantapur	A	6.70
2	Purampur	A	7.70
3	Berenda	A	7.20
4	Beluti	A	7.70
5	Joyknishnapur	A	7.25
6	Srikrishnapur	A	7.70
7	Sora	A	6.92
8	Nabagram	B	7.70
9	Samaipur	A	6.80
10	Mallickpur	A	7.70
11	Dangal	A	7.20
12	Punnagar	A	7.58
13	Nripatigram	A	7.20
14	Bijoypur	A	7.20
15	Kurumba	A	6.70
16	Selut	A	6.70
Jalpaiguri Cluster in Figure 17.2:			
1	Uttar Baraiguri	B	7.60
2	Madhya Baraiguri	B	4.90
3	Khaluigram	B	4.53
4	Purba Shalbari	B	4.90
5	Paschim Shalbari	B	7.50
6	Jhar Shalbari	B	4.80
7	Kazipara	B	6.08
8	Purba Dangal	B	4.47
9	Dangal	B	5.80
10	Kothapara	B	5.40
11	Kothapara Gadam	B	5.95
12	Bairatikuri	B	6.72
13	Malipara	B	4.40
14	Mallickpur	B	4.90
15	Bhotepara	B	6.20
16	Cadham	B	4.65
Bankura Cluster in Figure 17.3:			
1	Nikunjapur	A	6.70
2	Pindhruhi	A	8.86
3	Bamandihi	A	9.58
4	Belatikuri	A	9.58

Table 17.1 (*cont'd*)

Serial Number	Name of Village	Level of Agricultural Development	Male Wage–Rate (Rs. per day)
5	Digha	A	9.59
6	Nischintapur	A	7.78
7	Down Shalbari	B	9.04
8	Up Shalbari	B	9.04
9	Muktapur	B	8.10
10	Guinnandan	B	8.10
11	Itapanzara	B	8.64
12	Kotalpur	A	9.22
13	Ramnagore	B	9.04
14	Shayer Bakri	B	9.04
15	Chandipur	B	7.78
16	Choukimura	B	7.78

Hooghly Cluster
in Figure 17.4:

1	Duipa	B	5.30
2	Dalapatipur	B	8.00
3	Kamrajpur	A	4.75
4	Jagjeevanpur	A	5.30
5	Kanakpur	A	5.25
6	Narayanpur	B	8.00
7	Mallickpur	A	8.00
8	Panchgachia	A	8.00
9	Gopinathpur	B	8.00
10	Noapara	B	8.00
11	Baramallabpur	A	8.00
12	Gaja	A	5.30
13	Taldaw	A	5.30
14	Kamdebpur	A	5.30
15	Dashatta	A	5.30
16	Gopalprasadpur	A	5.30

Murshidabad Cluster
in Figure 17.5:

1	Biltelkar Dafarpur	B	3.50
2	Basudevpur	B	3.50
3	Mahadevpur	A	3.50
4	Fathepur	A	3.50
5	Bhimpur	A	3.50
6	Shibpur	A	3.50
7	Bahala	B	3.50
8	Dakhingram	A	3.50
9	Kanfala	B	3.50
10	Amat	A	3.50

Table 17.1 (*cont'd*)

Serial Number	Name of Village	Level of Agricultural Development	Male Wage–Rate (Rs. per day)
11	Chanak	B	3.50
12	Bhudaidanga	B	3.50
13	Jurulia	B	3.50
14	Palsanda	B	3.50
15	Barabatham	A	3.50
16	Narayanpur	A	3.50

Notes: A village is agriculturally advanced (marked A) if half or more of its cultivated land is under
modern irrigation facilities like canals, pumps or tubewells; all other villages are taken as backward
(marked B).

   The wage rate, converted into rupees, is the maximum of two average wage rates, one is modal
wage rates averaged over the months of Ashad and Sravan nearest to the date of the survey and the
other averaged over the months of Agrahayan and Poush nearest to the date of the survey.

   In the Hooghly cluster in all cases of daily wages being Rs.5.30 or Rs.5.25, the wage figure does
not include some payments in *muri* (rice crispies).

for only five out of 16 villages in the Bardhaman cluster. Similarly, while in all the
villages in the Bankura or Murshidabad cluster employers are reported as hiring
labor from at least *some* adjacent village, this is true for only 12 out of 16 villages in
the Hooghly cluster, six out of 16 villages in the Jalpaiguri cluster and three out of
16 villages in the Bardhaman cluster. The rest of Table 17.2 and Table 17.3 give
more details of the pattern of inter-village labor mobility in terms of the numbers of
adjacent and non-adjacent villages to which laborers go out to work. In general it
seems labor mobility is the highest in the Murshidabad and Bankura clusters and
lowest in the Bardhaman and Jalpaiguri clusters, with Hooghly indicating a mixed
or intermediate position.

   This pattern of inter-village mobility is significantly associated with territorial
segmentation in regular consumption credit transactions, in the offering of wage
advances (called *dadan* in this region) by employers to their laborers to support their consumption in lean seasons. As Table 17.3 column (5) shows, in most
villages in the Bardhaman cluster, in all villages in the Jalpaiguri cluster and in the
majority of villages in the Bankura cluster employers of the village are reported as
not providing wage advances to laborers from *other* villages (even though the *dadan*
system is quite prevalent within the village). The major reasons cited for this phenomenon include difficulties of enforcing loan repayment and getting work in time
from laborers of other villages. On the other hand, in the majority of villages in the
Hooghly cluster (nine out of 16) and in the Murshidabad cluster (14 out
of 16), employers do provide wage advances to laborers from some of the neighboring
villages. Similarly, in almost none of the villages in the Bardhaman and Jalpaiguri
clusters laborers in the village are reported as getting wage advances from employers

Table 17.2
Labor mobility among villages

From Where Laborers	Number of Villages	To Which Laborers	Number of Villages
1	2	3	4
Cluster: Bardhaman			
(1) Do not go to any other village	4	Do not come from any other village in the area	8
(2) Go to some adjacent villages	5	Come from some adjacent villages	3
(3) Go to some non-adjacent villages in the cluster	11	Come from some non-adjacent villages in the cluster	8
(4) Go to distant villages in the area	4	Come from distant villages in the area	3
(5) Go only to some adjacent villages	0	Come only from some adjacent villages	0
(6) Go to all adjacent villages	0	Come from all the adjacent villages	0
(7) Go to some of both adjacent and non-adjacent villages	5	Come from some of both adjacent and non-adjacent villages	3
(8) Go only to distant villages in the area	1	Come only from distant villages in the area	0
(9) Go to some non-adjacent but not to any adjacent ones	6	Come from some non-adjacent villages but not from adjacent ones	5
Cluster: Jalpaiguri			
(1) Do not go to any other village	4	Do not come from any other village in the area	6
(2) Go to some adjacent villages	9	Come from some adjacent villages	6
(3) Go to some non-adjacent villages in the cluster	10	Come from some non-adjacent villages in the cluster	9
(4) Go to distant villages in the area	1	Come from distant villages in the area	0
(5) Go only to some adjacent villages	2	Come only from some adjacent villages	1
(6) Go to all adjacent villages	2	Come from all the adjacent villages	2
(7) Go to some of both adjacent and non-adjacent villages	7	Come from some of both adjacent and non-adjacent villages	5

Table 17.2 (*cont'd*)

From Where Laborers	Number of Villages	To Which Laborers	Number of Villages
1	2	3	4
(8) Go only to distant villages in the area	0	Come only from distant villages in the area	0
(9) Go to some non-adjacent villages but not to any adjacent ones	3	Come from some non-adjacent villages but not from adjacent ones	4
Cluster: Bankura			
(1) Do not go to any other village	0	Do not come from any other village in the area	0
(2) Go to some adjacent villages	16	Come from some adjacent villages	16
(3) Go to some non-adjacent villages in the cluster	5	Come from some non-adjacent villages in the cluster	7
(4) Go to distant villages in the area	0	Come from distant villages in the area	0
(5) Go only to some adjacent villages	11	Come only from some adjacent villages	9
(6) Go to all adjacent villages	4	Come from all the adjacent villages	4
(7) Go to some of both adjacent and non-adjacent villages	5	Come from some of both adjacent and non-adjacent villages	7
(8) Go only to distant villages in the area	0	Come only from distant villages in the area	0
(9) Go to some non-adjacent villages but not to any adjacent ones	0	Come from some non-adjacent villages but not from adjacent ones	0
Cluster: Hooghly			
(1) Do not go to any other village	3	Do not come from any other village in the area	0
(2) Go to some adjacent villages	9	Come from some adjacent villages	12
(3) Go to some non-adjacent villages in the cluster	7	Come from some non-adjacent villages in the cluster	8
(4) Go to distant villages in the area	0	Come from distant villages in the area	4
(5) Go only to some adjacent villages	6	Come only from some adjacent villages	5

Table 17.2 (*cont'd*)

From Where Laborers	Number of Villages	To Which Laborers	Number of Villages
1	2	3	4
(6) Go to all adjacent villages	0	Come from all the adjacent villages	0
(7) Go to some of both adjacent and non-adjacent villages	5	Come from some of both adjacent and non-adjacent villages	7
(8) Go only to distant villages in the area	0	Come only from distant villages in the area	3
(9) Go to some non-adjacent villages but not to any adjacent ones	2	Come from some non-adjacent villages but not from adjacent ones	1
Cluster: Murshidabad			
(1) Do not go to any other village	0	Do not come from any other village in the area	0
(2) Go to some adjacent villages	16	Come from some adjacent villages	16
(3) Go to some non-adjacent villages in the cluster	10	Come from some non-adjacent villages in the cluster	13
(4) Go to distant villages in the area	8	Come from distant villages in the area	6
(5) Go only to some adjacent villages	2	Come only from some adjacent villages	1
(6) Go to all adjacent villages	5	Come from all the adjacent villages	5
(7) Go to some of both adjacent and non-adjacent villages	10	Come from some of both adjacent and non-adjacent villages	13
(8) Go only to distant villages in the area	0	Come only from distant villages in the area	0
(9) Go to some non-adjacent villages but not to any adjacent ones	0	Come from some non-adjacent villages but not from adjacent ones	0

Notes to Table 17.2

An adjacent village has been defined as one within 3 km. of distance and that does not require crossing a river to reach it. A distant village is defined as one that is not in the cluster. The Table is based on the answers from six respondents in each village. On the question of labor going to other villages (or employers hiring labor from other villages), a village has been counted as sending out (or bringing in) labor even if only a single respondent in the village answered affirmatively. This is true for both Tables 17.2 and 17.3.

Table 17.3

Number of villages with which a village has connections of labor mobility

Cluster: Bardhaman

Number of Villages	Frequency of Villages			
	to which laborers go for work	out of villages in col. (2) laborers get wage advance from employers in other villages	from which laborers come for work	out of villages in col. (4) employers give wage advance to incoming laborers
(1)	(2)	(3)	(4)	(5)
0	4	–	8	–
1	3	–	1	–
2	4	–	1	1
3	3	–	4	1
4	2	2	–	–
5	–	–	1	1
6	–	–	1	–
7	–	–	–	–

Note: In column (3) row (5), and in column (5) rows (3) and (6), the villages have been counted only on the basis of a minority of respondents answering affirmatively to the question of wage advances.

Cluster: Bankura

Number of Villages	Frequency of Villages			
	to which laborers go for work	out of villages in col. (2) laborers get wage advance from employers in other villages	from which laborers come for work	out of villages in col. (4) employers give wage advance to incoming laborers
(1)	(2)	(3)	(4)	(5)
0	–	–	–	–
1	3	2	2	1
2	4	1	4	–
3	2	–	2	1
4	3	2	5	2
5	1	–	2	1
6	2	2	–	–
7	1	–	1	–

Note: In column (3) and row (2), and in column (5) row (4), one village has been counted only on the basis of a minority of respondents answering affirmatively to the question of wage advances.

Table 17.3 (*cont'd*)
Cluster: Jalpaiguri

Number of Villages	Frequency of Villages			
	to which laborers go for work	out of villages in col. (2) laborers get wage advance from employers in other villages	from which laborers come for work	out of villages in col. (4) employers give wage advance to incoming laborers
(1)	(2)	(3)	(4)	(5)
0	4	–	6	–
1	2	–	3	–
2	3	–	1	–
3	4	–	1	–
4	1	–	2	–
5	2	–	1	–
6	–	–	2	–
7	–	–	–	–

Cluster: Hooghly

Number of Villages	Frequency of Villages			
	to which laborers go for work	out of villages in col. (2) laborers get wage advance from employers in other villages	from which laborers come for work	out of villages in col. (4) employers give wage advance to incoming laborers
(1)	(2)	(3)	(4)	(5)
0	3	–	–	–
1	3	–	5	2
2	6	4	6	4
3	3	2	5	3
4	1	–	–	–
5	–	–	–	–
6	–	–	–	–
7	–	–	–	–

Table 17.3 (*cont'd*)
Cluster: Murshidabad

Number of Villages	Frequency of Villages			
	to which laborers go for work	out of villages in col. (2) laborers get wage advance from employers in other villages	from which laborers come for work	out of villages in col. (4) employers give wage advance to incoming laborers
(1)	(2)	(3)	(4)	(5)
0	–	–	–	–
1	–	–	–	–
2	–	–	–	–
3	5	5	6	6
4	7	7	7	6
5	3	2	1	1
6	–	–	1	–
7	1	1	1	1

in other villages; in the majority of villages in the Bankura and Hooghly clusters, laborers in the village do not get wage advances from employers in other villages; but in the Murshidabad cluster almost all villages report availability of wage advances from employers in other villages.

Apart from credit and risks of default, one very important factor in inter-village labor transactions is the degree of knowledge the employer in one village has of the qualities of laborers in another village, particularly in terms of work capacity, reliability and trustworthiness. Such knowledge about outside labor from some of the neighboring villages is reported only by six out of 36 of our individual employer respondents in the Bardhaman cluster and only by 11 out of 32 individual employer respondents in the Jalpaiguri cluster. But the majority of such respondents in the other clusters (25 out of 31 in Bankura, 28 out of 32 in Hooghly and 28 out of 31 in Murshidabad) do report such knowledge.

In general low mobility of laborers across neighboring villages in Bardhaman and Jalpaiguri clusters seems to be associated with both the system of wage advances by employers being largely restricted to laborers of the same village and lack of knowledge of outside laborers on the part of employers. In the Murshidabad cluster neither of these constraints applies and, accordingly, labor mobility seems quite high. The cases of Bankura and Hooghly clusters fall in between these polar cases. In both these clusters the system of wage advances to outside laborers is restricted, but it is somewhat compensated by the reported knowledge of employers about the qualities of laborers in neighboring villages.

III

In discussing mobility across villages in the preceding Section we have not paid attention to inter-village wage differences. First, a word about the calculation of the daily wage rates reported in Table 17.1 and used in our subsequent analysis. The kind payment of wages has been converted into cash at the prevailing rate of Rs. 1.80 per kg. of rice, and one meal has been taken as the equivalent of 1 kg. of rice and tiffin as that of 1/2 kg. of rice. Since much of the labor mobility relates to the peak agricultural seasons, we have taken the average of the reported modal daily wage rates of the two nearest peak periods in this region, one in the Bengali months of Ashad and Sravan and the other in the months of Agrahayan and Poush. The wage rate we have used for each village for our discussion is the greater of these two averages.

Figures 17.1 to 17.5 show the direction of reported movements of laborers from one village to another in each cluster. To sharply distinguish the wage differences in each cluster, we have described in each figure the high-wage villages as those where the wage rate is below the mean by at least half the standard deviation for the cluster. The coefficient of variation of wage rates is the highest in the Hooghly cluster (0.2143), next highest in Jalpaiguri (0.1863), next in Bankura (0.0963), next in Bardhaman (0.0542) and the lowest in Murshidabad where the wage rate is uniform across all the villages in the cluster.

In each figure the heavily marked arrows indicate the movement of laborers in the expected direction of low-wage to high-wage villages. In Figures 17.1 to 17.4 there are many movements in the expected wage-induced direction, but there are many others where the movements must have been induced by other factors. The polar case is that of Murshidabad in Figure 17.5 where laborers in all villages go to at least some adjacent villages and often also to non-adjacent villages even though wage rates are identical.

There are some, though not many, wage-wise "perverse" cases, where labor goes from high-wage to low-wage villages for work. From Figures 17.1 to 17.4 one can see that such uni-directional "perverse" movement of labor reported by the majority of respondents in a village occur in four cases in the Jalpaiguri cluster, two in Hooghly, two in Bankura and one in Bardhaman. There are some other cases (in Bankura) where the "perverse" movement from a high-wage village to a low-wage village is also matched by some "normal" movement in the opposite direction between the same two villages. It is not always easy to explain all the individual cases of "perverse" movements, nor have we explored in our survey all the possible reasons that may have motivated these movements. But in most of these cases ties of familiarity, personal connections and trust, apart from the related credit nexus, may have been stronger than wage differences in influencing the direction of labor movement. There is also some evidence that the equilibrium wage in a village labor market may not have the smooth flexibility of adjustment assumed in textbook economics. Take, for example, the case of village nos. 12 and 2 in the Jalpaiguri cluster in Figure 17.2. Labor goes from high-wage village no. 12 to low-wage

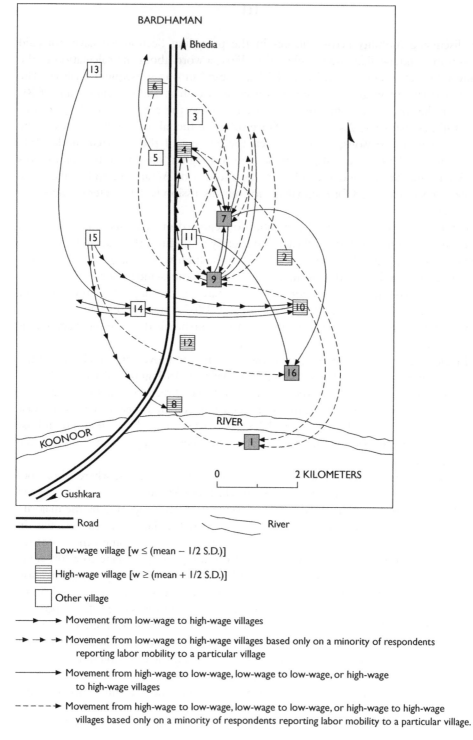

Fig. 17.1

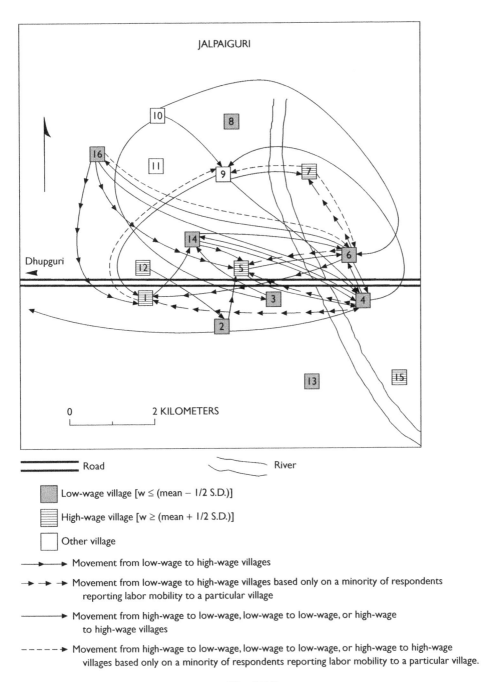

Fig. 17.2

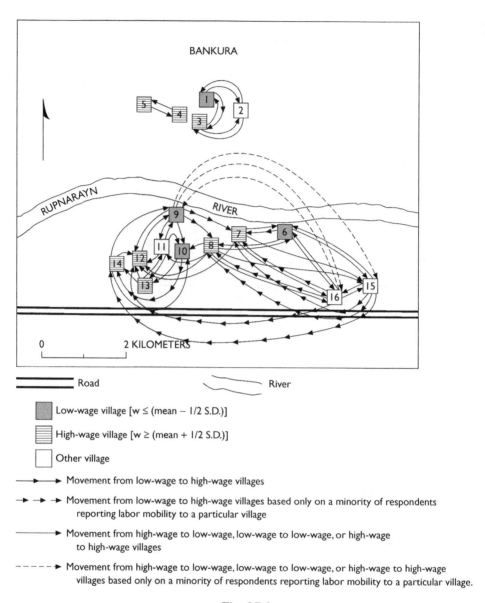

Fig. 17.3

village no. 2 (where the average wage rate is estimated to be 27 percent lower) for work. But looking into the details of these villages we find that the number of agricultural labor families is twice as high in village no. 12 compared to the other village, whereas the latter has two large "jotedar" farmers (the ones who hire laborers in a big way) as compared to none in the former. It seems the higher average wage in village no. 12 does not reflect the relative scarcity or demand for wage labor compared to the other village. We found similar possibilities of maladjustments in

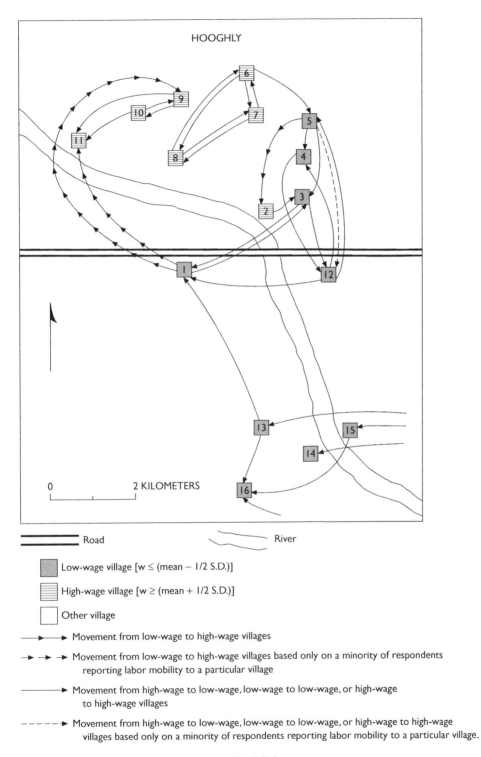

HOOGHLY

Road

River

Low-wage village [w ≤ (mean − 1/2 S.D.)]

High-wage village [w ≥ (mean + 1/2 S.D.)]

Other village

→ Movement from low-wage to high-wage villages

→ → → Movement from low-wage to high-wage villages based only on a minority of respondents
reporting labor mobility to a particular village

→ Movement from high-wage to low-wage, low-wage to low-wage, or high-wage
to high-wage villages

----→ Movement from high-wage to low-wage, low-wage to low-wage, or high-wage to high-wage
villages based only on a minority of respondents reporting labor mobility to a particular village.

Fig. 17.4

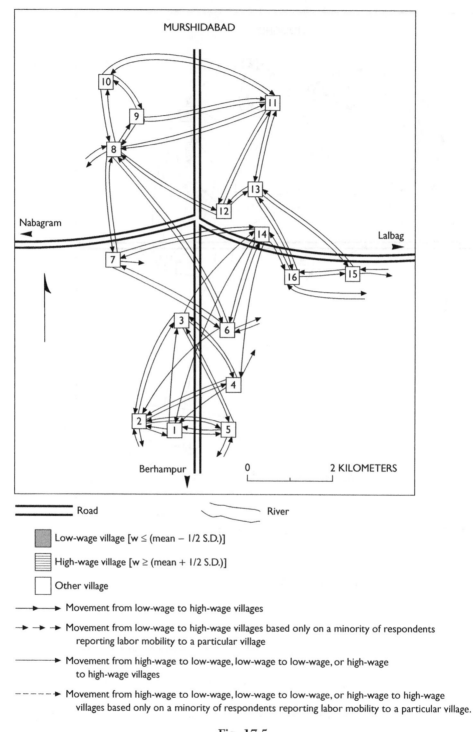

Fig. 17.5

the village wage labor market in a few, though certainly not all, other cases of "perverse" labor movement (in some cases the averaging process in estimating the wage rates may have hidden the "normal" adjustments).

There is a much larger number of cases where laborers reportedly do not move from low-wage to high-wage villages even though they are quite adjacent. Take, for example, the Bardhaman cluster in Figure 17.1. The low-wage village no. 16 is quite near the three high-wage villages nos. 8, 10 and 12, and yet laborers do not report going from the former to the latter for work. The reason cited by our respondents in these villages for this lack of labor mobility is that employers in these high-wage villages give priority to local laborers. We also observe that in the high-wage villages wage-advances are not given to outside laborers. Sometimes labor from a low-wage village goes out for work, not to an adjacent high-wage village, but to a village much farther away even when the wage rate is not always higher there. Personal connections established over time play an important role here. In Figure 17.2 for the Jalpaiguri cluster, for example, labor from village no. 4 goes, not to nearby high-wage village no. 15, but crossing the river to village nos. 9, 14, 5 and 1; similarly, employers in high-wage village no. 1 do not bring labor from nearby low-wage village no. 2, but from village nos. 9, 16, 6 and 4.

In the high-wage village no. 2 in Bardhaman in Figure 17.1, employers do not hire labor from nearby low-wage villages like nos. 7 and 9, and one reason cited by respondents is that this will lead to discontent among local laborers whose loyalty the employers clearly do not want to lose. The same reason has been cited in many cases in other clusters for employers' reluctance to hire laborers from neighboring villages, or for restricted outward mobility of labor from low-wage villages.

It is at the same time interesting to note that in the majority of villages in the Bardhaman and Bankura clusters (but not in the other clusters) the employers hire temporary migrant laborers from distant places in certain (peak) seasons. In four villages in the Bardhaman cluster employers do not reportedly hire any labor from neighboring villages, and yet seasonal migrants come for agricultural work in these villages. The explanation does not usually lie in wage differences: taking account of the recruitment, transportation and temporary shelter requirements of migrant laborers from distant areas, the total cost to the employer of hiring them is not always lower (often much higher) than the wage he would have to pay to labor from a neighboring low-wage village. Yet the employer sometimes finds it worthwhile to bring migrant laborers from a great distance because they are usually much easier to control and to extract work from, at a time when quickness and timeliness of labor on certain peak operations are at a premium. The cost of enforcement of labor contracts with workers residing in nearby villages may be significantly higher than with temporary migrants, residing in employer-provided sheds and more dependent on the employer in unfamiliar surroundings and eager to go back after a quick completion of the job. It also seems that the laborers within the village resent the influx of these temporary migrants somewhat less than that of their year-round competitors from neighboring villages.

Taking the five clusters it seems that intra-cluster labor mobility is most limited in Bardhaman and Jalpaiguri clusters. It is interesting that in terms of the degree of agricultural advance, as we have seen in section 1, the former is the most advanced and the latter is the least advanced among all the clusters. One would have thought that agricultural development would dissolve the barriers insulating the village labor markets in Bardhaman. A part of the explanation of low mobility may have to do with the fact that the inter-village wage differences are relatively small in Bardhaman (as we have seen above from the coefficient of variation of wage rates) so the wage incentives for mobility are not very strong and that a high degree of seasonal migration to this district from distant areas acts as a partial compensating mechanism in periods of peak operations.

IV

Thus we have found that there is a significant territorial segmentation of the labor market in some, though not all, clusters of villages. Laborers often do not go to work in adjacent villages where the wage rate may be higher, or do go to work to villages where the wage rate is not higher, or sometimes go to villages which are farther away than adjacent high-wage villages. Personal connections between employers and employees within a village or established personal contacts with residents of another particular village, even if distant, are often far more important to labor mobility than short-run wage differences. Personal knowledge of the employers in relation to the work capacity, reliability and trustworthiness of particular laborers plays a crucial role in these connections. These affinities are often cemented by relationships of regular consumption credit and wage advances. In the absence of formal collaterals, territorial affinites often serve as guarantees of non-default of loans and repayment in terms of labor at the right time when the employer-creditor needs it. Territorial loyalty also plays an important role in matters of emergency help: employers providing credit and protection at times of crisis in the family of local laborers, and laborers providing labor (and even political support) at short notice as and when the employer family in the village needs it. In the absence of any developed markets for credit and insurance, these relationships of unequal dependence between employers and laborers act as an imperfect substitute and perpetuate the territorial segmentation of the labor market even in adjacent areas.

In the literature on the "moral economy" of peasant societies,[6] there is a lot of emphasis on customary relationships between landlords and peasants embodying the ethics of sharing and the principle of "subsistence rights" of the poor. In West Bengal, the region of our survey, the moral economic system in ensuring a subsistence wage for all the poor peasants is no longer (if ever) operative and the old patron–client *yajmani* relationship of sharing based on the caste system is largely obsolete. But there are significant forms of patron–client relationships between employers and employees based on considerations of trust, credit, familiarity and dependability which may seriously constrain the development of an open, large, competitive labor market over contiguous villages, and structure the nature of inter-village labor mobility in isolated, fragmented patterns not always induced by inter-village wage differences. These relationships, viewed in a long-run perspective are not necessarily economically irrational and may even be regarded as a rational response to imperfect information on worker characteristics, costs of enforcement of contracts with unfamiliar people, and the general absence of credit and insurance markets. Similar qualitative considerations have been extensively cited in the literature on "Internal labor markets" of restricted mobility in industrially advanced countries and on credit rationing everywhere. Of course, the extent of fragmentation and the power asymmetry of unequal relationships are much deeper in a poor agrarian economy where large-scale capitalist farms have not made inroads, but the economic principles involved are not dissimilar.

Notes

* Fieldwork in the survey was carried out by Prasanta Choudhury and Gautam Sinha. We have been helped in data processing by Sobhan Sarkar at Santiniketan and Dilip Dutta at Berkeley. Our thanks are due to all of them.
1. For a discussion of these issues in relation to land, labor and credit contracts in poor agrarian economies, see Bardhan [1980] and Bardhan [1983].
2. See, for example, Okun [1981].
3. In a previous year one of the present authors, Rudra, carried out a similar survey in two clusters in another district (Birbhum) in West Bengal. His results, not very dissimilar to those in this article, are reported in Rudra [1982].
4. These four villages are only those where *none* of the respondents in the village reported that laborers go out to work to any other village. If one includes those villages where the *majority* of the respondents in a village reported that laborers do not go out to work to any other village, the number would be six out of 16 villages in Bardhaman.
5. If one includes those villages where the *majority* of respondents in a village reported that employers do not hire laborers from any other village in the area, the number would be nine out of 16 villages in Bardhaman.
6 See Scott [1976] for exposition and Popkin [1979] for a critique, both with respect to South-east Asian peasant society.

References

Bardhan, P., March 1980, "Interlocking Factor Markets and Agrarian Development: A Review of Issues," *Oxford Economic Papers*.

Bardhan, P., 1983, *Land, Labor and Rural Poverty: Essays in Development Economics*, New York: Columbia University Press; and New Delhi: Oxford University Press.

Okun, A. M., 1981, *Prices and Quantities*, Oxford: Basil Blackwell.

Popkin, S. L., 1979, *The Rational Peasant: The Political Economy of Rural Society in Vietnam*, Berkeley: University of California Press.

Rudra, A., August 1982, "Extra-economic Constraints on Agricultural Labor: Results of an

Intensive Survey in Some Villages near Santiniketan, West Bengal," Asian Employment Programme Working Paper, Bangkok: ILO–ARTEP.

Scott, J. C., 1976, *The Moral Economy of the Peasant: Rebellion and Subsistence in Southeast Asia*, New Haven: Yale University Press.

Chapter 18

Interlinkage of Land, Labor and Credit Relations:
An Analysis of Village Survey Data in East India

This paper presents the results of an intensive and yet fairly large-scale survey, of nearly 275 randomly chosen villages in West Bengal, Bihar and some of the eastern districts of Uttar Pradesh, made in 1975–76, with the primary focus on the terms and conditions of land, labor and credit contracts.

Large-scale studies, such as the present one, of the relevant contractual interrelationships are important not merely for settling pedantic debates on the dominant mode of production, but also for shaping basic directions in agrarian policy and in designing the broad outlines of political programs for the peasantry.

In a village economy, the terms and conditions of contracts in tenancy, wage labor, and credit transactions are sometimes inter-related, and the imperfections in the relevant factor markets might get reinforced by such interlinkages. The landlord-cum-employer may get underpaid labor services on his own farm by means of his dominance in the land-lease market. The creditor-landlord may rob his tenant of his freedom in decision-making and effectively inflate the rent by realising exorbitant interest on loans at the time of harvest-sharing. The loan-giving employer may get away with cheaper labor as well as various labor-tying arrangements. The large-scale surveys quite often do not capture the intricacies of these inter-relationships. For example, the land holdings surveys by the National Sample Survey do not at all focus on the linkages of land-ownership or land-lease patterns with wage labor or credit contracts; the rural labor enquiries by the NSS do not link up with information on conditions in land or credit markets; the rural credit surveys by the Reserve Bank of India are not sufficiently integrated with data on land and labor markets. The village surveys carried out by the Agro-Economic Research Centres in different parts of India are more intensive, but they do not focus on the inter-relationships of contracts; besides, the villages being purposively chosen (in time as well as in space) do not provide an adequate basis for any generalization. Some field surveys by individual economists or social anthropologists in a handful of purposively chosen villages have sometimes been quite intensive and useful in terms of their coverage of these inter-related contracts, but their extremely small-scale nature inhibits (as a matter of fact, in the case of the social anthropologic studies they are not even meant for) wider generalizations.

Yet, at some levels of discussion, generalizability on matters of agrarian relations, despite all its methodological limitations (which the anthropologists never tire of pointing out), is important, not merely for settling pedantic debates on the dominant mode of production, but also in shaping basic directions in agrarian policy and in designing the broad outlines of political programs for the peasantry. Pet theories, based on casual empiricism or worse, can be quite harmful in this respect. Take for instance the idea, popular in some radical circles, of "semi-feudalism" as the prevailing production relation and of usury as the dominant form of exploitation acting as a "fetter" on agricultural progress in Eastern India, if not in other parts of the country. This idea focuses on a possible type of inter-relationship between usury in the credit relation and the contractual constraints in tenancy and labor, inhibiting innovations on the part of the tenant-debtor and creating conditions of bonded labor for the indebted. Recent proponents of this generalization have, however, provided either no evidence at all (as in the case of Bhaduri[1]) or what amounts to highly inadmissible evidence (as in the case of Prasad[2]). It is precisely because such cavalier generalizations, when empirically unwarranted, may be politically quite misleading, that it is imperative to have a large-scale study of the relevant contractual inter-relationships. Our present paper is based on one such study. As an intensive and yet fairly large-scale survey, of nearly 275 randomly chosen villages in three regions, viz, West Bengal, Bihar, and some of the Eastern districts of UP, made in 1975–76 with primary focus on the terms and conditions of land, labor and credit contracts, it may have been the first of its kind in India.[3]

In each of these three states, villages were randomly selected;[4] in each such village four types of questionnaires were canvassed: one to be answered by two (purposively chosen and if possible, different types of) tenants separately, one by two casual laborers separately, one by two permanent farm servants separately, and one general village questionnaire to be filled in on the basis of talking to all these six respondents and cross-checking with other members in the village. Thus, in all, we have tried to get seven schedules filled in for each village. The tenant and laborer respondents were asked questions not merely about the contracts they themselves have entered into but also about the characteristics of their landlords or employers or creditors and about general features and trends in the village economy and institutions as perceived by them. We did not canvass any questionnaire with the village landlords, employers or moneylenders as such.

The ultimate unit of investigation is the village. Most of the questions relate to the standard type or types of contracts prevailing in the village, and the answers

Table 18.1

Distribution of sample villages in more and less advanced areas in the three states

Areas States	Highly Advanced Areas	Moderately Advanced Areas	Not Advanced Areas	All Areas
West Bengal	40	56	14	110
Bihar	38	32	31	101
East UP	6	36	23	65
East India	84	124	68	276

given by one respondent belonging to a particular category (say, tenant) about the prevailing contractual type in the village have been cross-checked with those given by the other respondents in the same category.

Before we discuss the inter-relationships of various contracts, it is interesting to note one general feature of the villages in our sample. Contrary to popular impression, it seems that a majority of the villages in Eastern India show definite signs of technical advance in agriculture. Let us define, for the purpose of this paper, a village as "advanced" when tubewells and pumps are used *and* use of chemical fertilizers and HYV seeds are highly prevalent and/or spreading. We define a village as "moderately advanced" when (a) tubewells and pumps are used *or* use of (b) chemical fertilizers *or* (c) HYV seeds is highly prevalent and/or spreading, *or* a combination of any two of (a), (b) and (c) prevails. We define a village as "not advanced" or "backward" where neither (a), nor (b), nor (c) prevails. In our random sample for West Bengal, there are in all 110 villages. Out of them 40 are "advanced", 56 are "moderately advanced", and only 14 are "backward" by our definition (Table 18.1). In most villages, the big and middle-sized farmers are, obviously, the major users of new inputs. In 59 percent of West Bengal villages, chemical fertilizers are reported to be used more or less by all big and middle sized farmers, and for HYV seeds this is the case for 39 percent of West Bengal villages. Out of a sample of 101 villages in Bihar, 38 are "advanced", 32 are "moderately advanced", and 31 are "backward" by our definition. In 58 percent of Bihar villages, chemical fertilizers are reported to be used more or less by all big and middle farmers, and for HYV seeds it is the case for 55 percent of Bihar villages. Out of a sample of 65 reporting villages in East UP, 6 are "advanced", 36 are "moderately advanced", and 23 are "backward". In very few villages in East UP are the new inputs used by all the big and middle farmers (Table 18.2).

Let us now take the tenancy contract and see how its terms and conditions are affected, if at all, by credit contracts. There is no doubt that the landlord is an important though not the only source of credit to his tenant. In our sample of villages in West Bengal, 51 percent of tenants[5] reported taking consumption loans from the landlords. These consumption loans are all repayable in grains from the harvest share of the tenant. In Bihar, on an average, in 50 percent of the cases the tenants reported taking consumption loans from the landlord. In East UP, in 55

Table 18.2
Prevalence of the use of chemical fertilizers and HYV seeds
(in villages grouped according to level of development)

Level of Development	States	Percentages of Villages				Total Number of Villages
		Use of Chemical Fertilizers		Use of HYV Seeds		
		Highly Prevalent	Moderately Prevalent	Highly Prevalent	Moderately Prevalent	
Highly	West Bengal	78	22	62	38	40
Advanced	Bihar	79	16	63	32	38
Areas	East UP	–	100	33	67	6
	East India	73	25	61	37	84
Moderately	West Bengal	54	43	28	42	56
Advanced	Bihar	56	44	59	33	32
Areas	East UP	6	86	29	71	36
	East India	40	56	36	48	124
Not	West Bengal	18	18	8	17	14
Advanced	Bihar	20	55	10	20	31
Areas	East UP	–	100	–	95	23
	East India	11	67	5	55	68
All	West Bengal	59	23	39	37	110
Areas	Bihar	58	34	55	31	101
	East UP	3	92	20	78	65
	East India	45	48	39	45	276

percent of cases the tenant borrowed from the landlord for consumption purposes (Table 18.3). But the recent theorists of "semi-feudalism" would have us believe that, in the landlord-tenant relationship, usury dominates as the mode of exploitation and the landlord's considerations of usurious income from the indebted tenant hamper the former's incentive to encourage production and productive investment. Evidence in Eastern India is quite contrary to this hypothesis.

In our survey, we asked the tenants about the principal occupation of their landlords. In our sample of 109 villages reporting tenancy in West Bengal, *not a single* tenant reported moneylending as the principal occupation of his landlord.[6] Only in 4 out of 95 Bihar villages reporting tenancy, and 13 out of 53 East UP villages reporting tenancy, did *any* tenant report moneylending as a principal occupation of his landlord. In the majority of cases (62 percent in West Bengal, 72 percent in Bihar, and 72 percent in East UP) the tenant reported self-cultivation as the principal occupation of his landlord (Table 18.4).

There are no doubt professional moneylenders in some villages. In our sample, professional moneylenders operate in 30 percent of West Bengal villages, 53 percent

Table 18.3

Incidence of tenants taking consumption loans with and without interest

Level of Development	States	Percentage of Tenants	
		Who Take Consumption Loan from the Landlord	Who Take Consumption Loan from the Landlord Without Interest
Highly	West Bengal	51	23
Advanced	Bihar	50	1.5
Areas	East UP	50	8.3
	East India	50	13
Moderately	West Bengal	55	25
Advanced	Bihar	62	–
Areas	East UP	51	–
	East India	56	12
Not	West Bengal	38	12
Advanced	Bihar	35	4.3
Areas	East UP	64	–
	East India	45	4.8
All Areas	West Bengal	51	23
	Bihar	50	1.7
	East UP	55	1.0
	East India	52	11

of Bihar villages, and 57 percent of East UP villages (Table 18.5). Only in a small percentage of the sample villages are there professional moneylenders who also lease out land (in West Bengal it is 9.1 percent, in Bihar it is 36 percent, and East UP, it is 26 percent). It is also interesting to note that the majority of villages where professional moneylenders lease out land happen to be villages which may be regarded as technologically advanced. Out of 36 *such* sample villages in Bihar, 9 are advanced villages, 18 are moderately advanced, and only 9 are backward villages by our earlier definition. Out of 17 *such* sample villages in East UP, 2 are advanced villages, 8 are moderately advanced, and 7 are backward villages.

Apart from professional moneylenders, there are rich farmers who practise money-lending in most of the villages, but this practice is not mainly confined to backward villages. Out of 106 sample villages in West Bengal where rich farmers indulge in moneylending, 93 villages are advanced or moderately advanced by our definition. Out of 67 sample villages in Bihar, where rich farmers indulge in money-lending, 51 villages are advanced or moderately advanced. Out of 57 sample villages in East UP, where rich farmers indulge in moneylending, 35 villages are advanced or moderately advanced. Needless to say, in the majority of these cases (80 percent in West Bengal, 66 percent in Bihar, and 48 percent in East UP) the main occupa-

Table 18.4
Principal occupation of landlords of tenants

Level of Development	States	Percentage of Landlords of Tenants					
		Self-Cultivation as Principal Occupation	Trade as Principal Occupation	Money Lending as Principal Occupation	Other Activities as Principal Occupation	Using HYV Seeds on Self-Cultivated Land	Using Chemical Fertilisers on Self-Cultivated Land
Highly Advanced Areas	West Bengal	67	5.1	–	22	66	66
	Bihar	93	5.9	–	1.5	88	90
	East UP	75	–	17	8.3	75	83
	East India	79	5.0	1.3	12	75	77
Moderately Advanced Areas	West Bengal	62	11	–	24	60	66
	Bihar	81	12	–	6.9	67	79
	East UP	69	–	14	12	71	68
	East India	69	8.3	3.5	17	65	70
Not Advanced Areas	West Bengal	50	15	–	35	31	31
	Bihar	30	9.7	7.6	26	19	22
	East UP	76	–	9.0	15	58	73
	East India	50	8.1	6.2	25	34	40
All Areas	West Bengal	62	0.9	–	25	59	62
	Bihar	72	9.0	2.0	9.9	63	68
	East UP	72	–	12	2	66	71
	East India	68	7.2	3.4	17	62	66

Table 18.5

Importance of professional moneylenders and moneylending rich farmers, importance of land-leasing among professional moneylenders and importance of cultivation with laborers among moneylending rich farmers (in villages grouped according to level of development)

Level of Development	States	Percentages of Villages					Total Number of Villages
		With Money-lenders	With Money-lenders Leasing Out Land	With Money-lending Rich Farmers	With Such Farmers Cultivating With Hired Laborers	With Such Farmers Leasing Out Land	
Highly Advanced Areas	West Bengal	20	5	95	94	22	40
	Bihar	42	24	74	74	–	38
	East UP	50	33	83	67	67	6
	East India	32	15	85	83	15	84
Moderately Advanced Areas	West Bengal	36	9	98	98	16	56
	Bihar	72	56	72	72	–	32
	East UP	53	22	83	83	36	36
	East India	50	25	87	87	18	124
Not Advanced Areas	West Bengal	36	21	93	93	–	14
	Bihar	48	29	52	52	–	31
	East UP	65	30	96	96	35	23
	East India	51	28	75	75	12	68
All Areas	West Bengal	30	9	96	96	16	110
	Bihar	53	36	66	66	–	101
	East UP	57	26	88	86	38	65
	East India	45	23	83	83	16	276

Table 18.6
Incidence of landlord giving production loan to tenants with and without interest

Level of Development	States	Proportion of Tenants Taking Production Loan from Landlords		
		With Interest	Without Interest	Total
Advanced Areas	West Bengal	34	19	53
	Bihar	31	18	49
	UP (East)	17	–	17
	East India	31	17	48
Moderately Advanced Areas	West Bengal	16	30	46
	Bihar	32	14	46
	UP (East)	40	2	42
	East India	26	19	45
Not Advanced Areas	West Bengal	8	4	12
	Bihar	12	13	25
	UP (East)	49	3	52
	East India	22	7.6	30
All Areas	West Bengal	21	23	44
	Bihar	26	15	41
	UP (East)	40	2	42
	East India	27	16	43

tion of these moneylending rich farmers is to cultivate land with the help of hired laborers.

Going back to our respondent tenants who take loans from their landlords, we find that, in West Bengal, in 45 percent of cases of the tenant taking consumption loans from his landlord, the loans do not involve any interest. The cases of interest-free consumption loans from landlord are much less frequent for tenants in Bihar and East UP (Table 18.3). But what is more important to note for our present purpose is that, in 44 percent of cases of reporting tenants in West Bengal, the landowner gave advances to the tenant to meet his production needs of seeds, fertilizers, etc., and in 23 percent cases such advances were given free of interest (Table 18.6). In 41 percent of cases of reporting tenants in Bihar the landowner gave advances to the tenant to meet his production needs and in 15 percent of cases such advances were given free of interest. In 42 percent of reporting villages in East UP, the landowner gave advances to the tenant to meet his production needs, and in 2 percent of cases such advances were interest-free. As Table 18.6 shows, the incidence of production loans by the landlord is obviously much more important in advanced than in backward villages.

Apart from providing production loans, in a majority of the cases the landlord himself bears part of the production costs (seeds, fertilizers, etc.). In 64 percent of cases in West Bengal, the landlord shares in some costs; in Bihar it is in 53 percent

Table 18.7(A)
Proportion of tenancy contracts with cost sharing-states

State	Cost Sharing		
	Exists	Does Not Exist	Total
West Bengal	227	127	354
	(64.12)	(35.88)	(100.00)
Bihar	116	103	219
	(52.97)	(47.03)	(100.00)
UP (East)	73	53	126
	(57.94)	(42.06)	(100.00)
East India	416	283	699
	(59.51)	(40.49)	(100.00)

Table 18.7(B)
Proportion of tenancy contract; with cost sharing more and less advanced areas

Level of Development	Cost Sharing		
	Exists	Does Not Exist	Total
Advanced Areas	164	65	229
	(71.62)	(28.38)	(100.00)
Moderately Advanced Areas	175	152	327
	(53.52)	(46.48)	(100.00)
Not Advanced Areas	77	66	143
	(53.85)	(46.15)	(100.00)
All Areas	416	283	699
	(59.51)	(40.49)	(100.00)

of cases; and in East UP, it is in 58 percent of cases (Table 18.7A). One also observes a strong association between cost sharing and giving of production loans by the landlord (Table 18.8). Production loans as well as cost-sharing obviously indicate a strong interest on the part of the landlord in productive investment on the tenant farm. It is also observed that, in a majority of cases (in about 56 percent of the cases in West Bengal, and 96 percent of the cases in East UP), the landowner either himself or jointly with the tenant decides about the use of seeds, fertilizers, etc., on the tenant farm; in Bihar, this is observed in about 29 percent of cases (Table 18.9). This phenomenon is clearly more important in the advanced villages than in the backward villages in our definition. It is also worth noting that, in 60 to 70 percent of the cases in West Bengal, Bihar, and East UP, the respondent tenant reported that his landlord uses HYV seeds and chemical fertilizers on the latter's self-cultivated land (Table 18.4). All this is a far cry from usurious landlords uninterested in productive investment.

Table 18.8

Association between landlords giving production loans to tenants and landlords sharing in the cost of cultivation

	Advanced Tenant's Share of Cost			Moderately Advanced Tenant's Share of Cost			Not Advanced Tenant's Share of Cost		
	Less than 100 Percent	100 Percent	Total	Less than 100 Percent	100 Percent	Total	Less than 100 Percent	100 Percent	Total
West Bengal									
Advance Given	62	11	73	63	21	84	3	–	3
	84.93	15.07	100.00	75.00	25.00	100.00	100.00		100.00
Advance Not Given	44	19	63	47	58	105	8	18	26
	69.84	30.16	100.00	44.76	55.24	100.00	30.77	69.23	100.00
Total	106	30	136	110	79	189	11	18	29
	77.94	22.06	100.00	58.20	41.80	100.00	37.93	62.07	100.00
Bihar									
Advance Given	29	13	42	22	6	28	16	6	22
	69.04	30.96	100.00	78.57	21.43	100.00	72.73	27.27	100.00
Advance Not Given	19	20	39	7	33	40	23	25	48
	48.72	51.28	100.00	17.50	82.50	100.00	47.92	52.08	100.00
Total	48	33	81	29	39	68	39	31	70
	59.26	40.74	100.00	42.65	57.35	100.00	55.71	44.29	100.00
Uttar Pradesh (East)									
Advance Given	2	–	2	17	15	32	14	11	25
	100.00		100.00	53.12	46.88	100.00	56.00	44.00	100.00
Advance Not Given	8	2	10	18	20	38	13	6	19
	80.00	20.00	100.00	47.37	52.63	100.00	68.42	31.58	100.00
Total	10	2	12	35	35	70	27	17	44
	83.33	16.67	100.00	50.00	50.00	100.00	61.36	38.64	100.00

Table 18.9
Landlords taking production decisions singly or jointly with tenants

Level of Development	States	Percentage of Tenants	
		Whose Owner Takes Crop Decisions Singly or Jointly with the Tenant	Whose Owner Takes Decisions about Inputs Singly or Jointly with the Tenant
Highly Advanced Areas	West Bengal	77	77
	Bihar	35	40
	East UP	100	83
	East India	61	61
Moderately Advanced Areas	West Bengal	40	38
	Bihar	21	24
	East UP	95	91
	East India	49	49
Not Advanced Areas	West Bengal	54	54
	Bihar	28	24
	East UP	97	97
	East India	56	54
All Areas	West Bengal	56	54
	Bihar	29	30
	East UP	96	92
	East India	54	54

On the inter-relationship between tenancy contracts and obligatory labor on the part of the tenant on the landlord's farm or non-farm activities, we have the following information from the survey (Table 18.10). Fifty-two percent of the landless tenants interviewed in West Bengal reported rendering certain services for the landlord and the percentage for the landed tenants was 9.9. However, among those rendering services 92 percent of the landed tenants and 58 percent of the landless tenants reported being "properly" paid. Corresponding figures for Bihar and East UP may be seen in Table 18.10. It is clear that rendering unpaid or underpaid services by the tenant for the landlord is far from being the prevalent general pattern. It is, however, interesting to note that such incidence of unpaid or underpaid work for the landlord is *not* mainly in backward villages.

The tenancy contract may sometimes bind the tenant to a particular landlord (and may in that case make it difficult to distinguish the tenant from an attached laborer). But in our sample of tenants for West Bengal, Bihar, or East UP, there are very few cases where the tenant reports that the tenancy contract prohibits his leasing in land from more than one landlord (Table 18.11).

Sometimes the tenant's dependence on the landlord is associated with or reinforced by other members of his family working for the same landlord. In the sample

Table 18.10(A)
Incidence of tenants rendering labor services to landlords (Separately for landed and landless tenants)

Level of Development	Does Tenant do any Work for Landlords					
	With Land			Without Land		
	Yes	No	Total	Yes	No	Total
West Bengal						
Advanced Areas	5	37	42	23	12	35
	11.90	88.10	100.00	65.71	34.29	100.00
Moderately	4	60	64	20	26	46
Advanced Areas	6.25	93.75	100.00	43.48	56.52	100.00
Not Advanced	3	12	15	5	6	11
Areas	20.00	80.00	100.00	45.45	54.55	100.00
All Areas	12	109	121	48	44	92
	9.92	90.08	100.00	52.17	47.83	100.00
Bihar						
Advanced Areas	9	43	52	10	6	16
	17.31	82.69	100.00	62.50	37.50	100.00
Moderately	7	41	48	6	4	10
Advanced Areas	14.58	85.42	100.00	60.00	40.00	100.00
Not Advanced	3	37	40	1	4	5
Areas	7.50	92.50	100.00	20.00	80.00	100.00
All Areas	19	121	140	17	14	31
	13.57	86.43	100.00	54.84	45.16	100.00
Uttar Pradesh (East)						
Advanced Areas	–	8	8	2	2	4
		100.00	100.00	50.00	50.00	100.00
Moderately	3	26	29	10	20	30
Advanced Areas	10.34	89.66	100.00	33.33	66.67	100.00
Not Advanced	3	13	16	2	14	16
Areas	18.75	81.25	100.00	12.50	87.50	100.00
All Areas	6	47	53	14	36	50
	11.32	88.68	100.00	28.00	72.00	100.00

villages in West Bengal, 32 percent of reporting tenants reported some member in his family working as a casual laborer or farm servant for the landlord. The same phenomenon was observed in 32 percent of cases in Bihar. In East UP, it is much less frequent. It may however, be noted that the overwhelming majority of these cases in West Bengal or Bihar are in advanced or moderately advanced villages (Table 18.12).

Now, moving away from tenancy contracts, let us note the cases of obligatory labor that credit contracts sometimes impose on casual laborers or farm servants. Let

Table 18.10(B)
Incidence of underpaid and unpaid services by tenants to landlords out of cases where
the tenant works for the landlord (Separately for landed and landless tenants)

Level of Development	With Land				Without Land			
	Properly Paid	Under-paid	Unpaid	Total	Properly Paid	Under-paid	Unpaid	Total
West Bengal								
Advanced	8	–	–	8	14	4	5	23
Areas	100.00			100.00	60.87	17.39	21.74	100.00
Moderately	3	1	–	4	10	5	5	20
Advanced Areas	75.00	25.00		100.00	50.00	25.00	25.00	100.00
Not Advanced	3	–	–	3	4	1	–	5
Areas	100.00			100.00	80.00	20.00		100.00
All Areas	11	1	–	12	28	10	10	48
	91.67	8.33		100.00	58.34	20.83	20.83	100.00
Bihar								
Advanced	2	3	4	9	10	–	–	10
Areas	22.22	33.33	44.45	100.00	100.00			100.00
Moderately	2	2	3	7	3	2	1	6
Advanced Areas	28.57	28.57	42.86	100.00	50.00	33.33	16.67	100.00
Not Advanced	–	2	1	3	–	1	–	1
Areas		66.67	33.33	100.00		100.00		100.00
All Areas	4	7	8	19	13	3	1	17
	21.05	36.84	42.11	100.00	76.47	17.65	5.88	100.00
Uttar Pradesh (East)								
Advanced Areas	–	–	–	–			2	2
					–	–	100.00	100.00
Moderately			3	3			10	10
Advanced Areas	–	–	100.00	100.00	–	–	100.00	100.00
Not Advanced			3	3			2	2
Areas	–	–	100.00	100.00	–	–	100.00	100.00
All Areas	–	–	6	6			14	14
			100.00	100.00	–	–	100.00	100.00
East India								
Advanced	7	3	4	14	24	4	7	35
Areas	50.00	21.43	28.57	100.00	68.57	11.43	20.00	100.00
Moderately	5	3	6	14	13	7	16	36
Advanced Areas	35.71	21.43	42.86	100.00	36.11	19.44	44.45	100.00
Not Advanced	3	2	4	9	4	2	2	8
Areas	33.33	22.22	44.45	100.00	50.00	25.00	25.00	100.00
All Areas	15	8	14	37	41	13	25	79
	40.54	21.62	37.84	100.00	51.89	16.46	31.65	100.00

Table 18.11
Proportion of tenancy contract where tenant can lease in land from more
than one landlord

States	Advanced Areas	Moderately Advanced Areas	Not Advanced Areas	All Areas
West Bengal	97	95	92	96
Bihar	100	100	93	98
East UP	92	95	100	96
East India	98	96	95	97

Table 18.12
Dependence of family members of tenants on landlords

Level of Development	States	Percentage of Tenants	
		With Other Members of the Family working as Casual Labor or Farm Servant	With Other Members of the Family Working as Casual Labor or Farm Servant for the Landlord
Highly Advanced Areas	West Bengal	53	34
	Bihar	46	25
	East UP	–	–
	East India	46	28
Moderately Advanced Areas	West Bengal	62	34
	Bihar	43	26
	East UP	19	3
	East India	46	24
Not Advanced Areas	West Bengal	46	15
	Bihar	52	11
	East UP	12	6
	East India	38	10
All Areas	West Bengal	57	32
	Bihar	47	22
	East UP	14	4
	East India	44	22

us first discuss the incidence of "bonded labor" in the sense that a laborer is tied to a particular creditor as a laborer for an indefinite period until some loan taken in the past is repaid. In West Bengal, only 2.4 percent of cases reported such a case of bonded labor. In Bihar, 14 percent out of 101 sample villages reported any bonded labor (mostly in the districts of Monghyr, Darbhanga, Bhagalpur and Saharsa). In

Table 18.13(A)
Duration of contract of attached laborers (†Percentage of cases)

States	Year	Less than One Year	Indefinite Period (Debt Bondage)
West Bengal	92.0	20.8	2.4
Bihar	81.7	4.2	14.0
East UP	88.5	7.6	3.8
East India	87.3	11.1	7.0

Note: †Due to double coding total percentage share has dometimes exceeded 100.

Table 18.13(B)
Actual duration of attachment of attached laborers (Percentage of cases)

States	One Year	Up to 5 Years	More than 5 Years
West Bengal	20.0	71.8	8.0
Bihar	11.0	67.0	22.0
East UP	0.7	32.0	67.9
East India	11.1	58.5	30.1

East UP, 3.8 percent of the 65 sample villages reported any bonded labor (Table 18.13). Contrary to the repeated assertions of the theorists of "semi-feudalism", bonded labor seems to be a relatively unimportant phenomenon in the agrarian economy of Eastern India. To assert the prevalence of bonded labor on the empirical evidence of *any* kind of indebtedness in agricultural labor households, as Prasad has done, is highly illegitimate, to say the least.

Indebtedness of the laborer to his employer is, of course, not uncommon. In 68 percent of cases in West Bengal and 33 percent of cases in Bihar, the casual laborer takes advances from his employer against future commitment of labor (in East UP, the relevant percentage of villages is very small). In more than 80 percent of such cases in West Bengal and nearly half of such cases in Bihar, where the casual laborer takes advances from his employer, he works at lower than market wage rate at the time of repayment. The payment of interest thus takes the form of wage cut and the employer also ensures thus a steady supply of labor when he needs it. It is worth noting that nearly 90 percent of the cases of casual laborer taking advances against future commitment of labor in West Bengal are in advanced or moderately advanced villages; in Bihar nearly 60 percent of such cases are in advanced or moderately advanced villages (Table 18.14).

Farm servants taking consumption loans from the employer is, of course, also quite common. In 61 percent of cases of reporting farm servants in West Bengal, 70 percent of cases in Bihar and 92 percent of cases in East UP, farm servants take consumption loans from the employer. More than 85 percent of such cases of consumption loans in West Bengal are interest-free; in Bihar about one-third cases of such consumption loans for farm servants are interest-free, but in East UP interest-free

Table 18.14
Incidence of casual laborers taking loans against future commitment of labor

Level of Development	States	Percentage of Casual Laborers		
		Taking Advance Against Future Commitments of Labor	Working at Lower than Market Wage Rate for Repayment	Rendering Other Services to the Employer Against the Advance
Highly Advanced Areas	West Bengal	65	49	–
	Bihar	24	–	10
	East UP	17	17	–
	East India	44	31	4.4
Moderately Advanced Areas	West Bengal	73	65	–
	Bihar	33	20	3.3
	East UP	5.6	5.6	2.8
	East India	43	36	1.6
Not Advanced Areas	West Bengal	57	46	–
	Bihar	43	30	8.3
	East UP	2.1	2.1	–
	East India	32	24	3.7
All Areas	West Bengal	68	60	–
	Bihar	33	16	7.4
	East UP	5.3	5.3	1.5
	East India	41	31	3.0

loans for farm servants are rare[7] (Table 18.15). Again, the overwhelming majority of the cases of farm servants taking consumption loans from the employer in West Bengal and Bihar are in advanced and moderately advanced villages. It may also be worth noting that, in spite of dependence on the employer for consumption loans, only in 8 percent of cases in West Bengal the respondent farm servant has been attached to the same employer for more than 5 years; in Bihar, this is in 22 percent of cases; in East UP it is, however, in a much larger percentage of cases (Table 18.13B). Apart from credit, sometimes the homestead provided by the employer ties a laborer to him. But cases of the farm servant living in homestead provided by the employer are relatively unimportant in Eastern India (they are observed only in about 20 percent of cases in our sample for West Bengal and Bihar and almost non-existent in our sample of East UP) (Table 18.16). Cases of land temporarily allotted to the farm servant by the employer are rare in West Bengal, but are significant in Bihar (41 percent of cases) and East UP (89 percent of cases) (Table 18.17).

For understanding the nature of the employers of farm servants, it is worth noting that his principal occupation is reported (by the farm servant) to be self-cultivation

Table 18.15

Incidence of attached laborers taking consumption loans from employers
with and without interest

Level of Development	States	Percentage of Attached Laborers	
		Taking Consumption Loan from the Employer	Taking Such Loan Without Interest
Highly Advanced Areas	West Bengal	60	55
	Bihar	53	20
	East UP	100	9.1
	East India	60	36
Moderately Advanced Areas	West Bengal	70	59
	Bihar	90	22
	East UP	89	8.5
	East India	82	30
Not Advanced Areas	West Bengal	20	20
	Bihar	66	37
	East UP	95	9.1
	East India	72	22
All Areas	West Bengal	61	53
	Bihar	70	24
	East UP	97	8.7
	East India	73	30

Table 18.16

Incidence (in percentage) of attached laborers living in homestead provided by employer

States	Advanced Areas	Moderately Advanced Areas	Not Advanced Areas	All Areas
West Bengal	21	21	13	20
Bihar	32	12	5.3	18
East UP	–	1.4	–	0.8
East India	24	11	4.1	14

in about 74 percent of cases in our sample for West Bengal and in about 84 percent of cases in Bihar. The employer uses HYV seeds in his self-cultivated land in 85 percent of cases in West Bengal, 83 percent of cases in East UP, and 74 percent of cases in Bihar (Table 18.18). If one takes the set of cases of farm servants attached to the same employer for more than 5 years, in *all* of 86 such cases in our sample for East UP, the employer uses HYV seeds and/or chemical fertilizers on his self-cultivated land; in Bihar this is so in 31 out of 36 of such cases. In almost all cases

Table 18.17
Proportion of attached laborers receiving allotment of land for cultivation

States	Advanced Areas	Moderately Advanced Areas	Not Advanced Areas	All Areas
West Bengal	1.3	5.5	–	3.1
Bihar	47	48	21	41
East UP	82	94	82	89
East India	27	49	45	41

Table 18.18
Charateristics of employers of attached laborers

Level of Development	States	Percentage of Attached Laborers with Employers			
		Whose Main Occupation Is Self-Cultivation	Whose Main Occupation Is in Other Fields	Using HYV Seeds	Using Chemical Fertilizers
Highly Advanced Areas	West Bengal	74	15	97	100
	Bihar	85	4.5	94	94
	East UP	–	–	100	100
	East India	73	9.5	96	97
Moderately Advanced	West Bengal	71	18	78	93
	Bihar	88	5.0	77	93
	East UP	–	–	86	94
	East India	51	8.1	80	94
Not Advanced Areas	West Bengal	87	13	53	47
	Bihar	76	24	37	68
	East UP	–	–	73	95
	East India	43	11	56	77
All Areas	West Bengal	74	17	85	92
	Bihar	84	9.1	74	88
	East UP	–	–	83	95
	East India	57	9.3	80	91

of long-term attachment of the farm servant the employer thus seems to be techno-logically progressive.

In 54 percent of the cases in West Bengal casual laborers with some amount of land reported having lost leased land through evictions; the corresponding propor-tion for Bihar and East UP are 40 and 42, respectively. The corresponding propor-tion for casual laborers without land are 19, 19 and 51, respectively (Table 18.19). Eviction of tenants is reported to be increasing in 59 percent of villages in West

Table 18.19

Incidence of casual laborers losing land through eviction from leased land
(separately for landed and landless casual laborers)

| | Areas | | | | | | | |
| | Advanced | | Moderately Advanced | | Not Advanced | | All | |
States	With Land	Without Land	With Land	Without Land	With Land	Without Land	With Land	Without Land
West Bengal	23	6	36	13	5	–	64	19
	(56.10)	(15.38)	(56.25)	(27.08)	(35.71)	–	(53.78)	(18.81)
Bihar	16	10	19	4	10	–	45	14
	(50.00)	(28.57)	(50.00)	(17.39)	(23.26)	–	(39.82)	(18.67)
East UP	2	2	13	9	20	24	35	35
	(33.33)	(33.33)	(26.53)	(32.14)	(71.43)	(70.59)	(42.17)	(51.47)
East India	41	18	68	26	35	24	144	68
	(51.90)	(22.50)	(45.03)	(26.26)	(41.18)	(36.92)	(45.71)	(27.87)

Bengal, 51 percent of villages in East UP, and 34 percent of villages in Bihar. The overwhelming majority of villages where tenant eviction is reported to be increasing are advanced or highly advanced. Apart from increased profitability of self-cultivation preventive action in the face of protective tenancy legislation has obviously motivated increased tenant eviction on the part of landlords. It is not surprising, therefore, that in our survey the institution of tenancy is reported to be on the decline in 76 percent of sample villages in West Bengal, 56 percent of sample villages in Bihar and 66 percent of sample villages in East UP (Table 18.20). Of the backward villages 36 percent in West Bengal, 42 percent in Bihar, and 77 percent in East UP, report declining tenancy; of the moderately advanced villages 82 percent in West Bengal, 68 percent in Bihar, and 55 percent in East UP report declining tenancy; of the advanced villages 82 percent in West Bengal, 58 percent in Bihar, and 83 percent in East UP report declining tenancy.

In 88 out of 110 sample villages in West Bengal, 55 out of 101 sample villages in Bihar and in 24 out of 65 sample villages in East UP self-cultivation with the use of casual laborers is on the increase. Employment of farm servants is also reported to be increasing in 45 out of 105 reporting villages in West Bengal, 22 out of 97 reporting villages in Bihar and 39 out of 65 villages in East UP. The overwhelming majority of cases of increasing employment of farm servants is in moderately advanced or advanced villages.

To summarise briefly, the landlord or the employer is an important source of credit to the tenant or wage laborer, but the evidence in Eastern India strongly suggests that incidence of usury as the main mode of exploitation or of bonded labor is very rare. The landlord quite often gives production loans to the tenant,

Table 18.20
Trends in employment of casual laborers and farm servants and cultivation by tenants

Level of Development	States	Percentages of Villages where							Total Number of Villages
		Tenancy Is Decreasing	Use of Casual Labor Is Increasing	Use of Farm Servant Is Increasing	Tenancy Decreasing and Casual Labor Increasing	Tenancy Decreasing and Farm Servant Increasing	Casual Labor and Farm Servant Is Increasing	Tenant Eviction Increasing	
Highly Advanced Areas	West Bengal	82	85	59	80	55	58	81	40
	Bihar	58	68	29	58	24	29	44	38
	East UP	83	50	50	33	50	17	50	6
	East India	71	75	45	67	40	42	63	84
Moderately Advanced Areas	West Bengal	82	84	38	71	29	34	52	56
	Bihar	68	69	35	59	31	31	36	32
	East UP	55	39	58	28	31	28	51	36
	East India	71	67	44	56	30	31	48	124
Not Advanced Areas	West Bengal	36	50	–	43	7.1	7.1	19	14
	Bihar	42	23	–	9.7	–	–	15	31
	East UP	77	30	65	26	52	8.7	52	23
	East India	52	31	26	22	19	4.4	28	68
All Areas	West Bengal	76	80	43	71	35	39	59	110
	Bihar	56	54	23	44	19	21	34	101
	East UP	66	37	60	28	40	20	51	65
	East India	66	61	40	51	30	28	48	276

shares in costs of seeds, fertilizers, etc., participates in decision-taking about the use of these inputs and in general takes a lot of interest in productive investment on the tenant farm. Consumption loans to tenants and wage laborers are occasionally interest-free; sometimes interest is charged in the form of a wage cut for the casual laborer. But loans taken by the laborer, usually repaid in harvest time in grains and in labor, do not in general lead to long-term bondage relationships. The majority of loan-giving employers are self-cultivators using HYV seeds, chemical fertilizers, pumps and tubewells. Tenancy is on the decline and self-cultivation with the help of casual laborers and sometimes also attached laborers is increasing.

Much too often in the literature on production relations, tenancy or the institution of attached labor has been equated with feudalism and indebtedness by poor peasants to their landlords or employers with debt-bondage. This has been a source of considerable confusion in the recent discussion on agrarian modes of production. The essential features of a feudal mode are associated with the appropriation of surplus in the form of ground rent and unpaid labor services by primarily non-cultivating landlords through extra-economic coercion or social and legal compulsion. Our survey in Eastern India suggests that the overwhelming majority of tenancy and attached labor contracts do not display such feudalistic features. The institution of share-cropping tenancy has been largely adapted to the needs of increasing production and profit by enterprising farmers, both owners and tenants. Unpaid and obligatory service by the tenant for the landlord is rather uncommon. Desperate conditions of poverty and unemployment afflict the peasant in the labor market, but not so much *extra-economic* coercion. The attached laborer has a longer-duration contract with his employer than the casual laborer, but this does not usually imply serfdom to any significant extent more than the case of tenured and salaried employees in the organized labor markets. The employee's need for job security and the employer's need for a dependable and readily available source of labor supply – and not feudal subordination – provide the major motivation of attached labor contracts. Indebtedness to one's employer does not necessarily make one a bonded laborer, just as an office worker borrowing from his provident fund account is not an unfree laborer, even though he may not be in a position to easily switch jobs for *economic* reasons. Needless to say, the economic constraints faced by the small share-cropper or the attached laborer are much more severe and they frequently push him into unequal relationships of mutual dependence with the landlord-creditor-employer. But, surely, unequal contracts and economic exploitation are not distinguishing features of feudalism as opposed to other modes of production.

Notes

[The authors are grateful to the Indian Council of Social Science Research for financing the collection and preliminary processing of the survey data used in this paper.]
1. A Bhaduri, "A Study in Agricultural Backwardness under Semi-feudalism", *Economic Journal*, March 1973.

2. P. H. Prasad, "Reactionary Role of Usurers' Capital in Rural India", *Economic and Political Weekly*, Special Number, August 1974; "Production Relations: Achilles Heel of Indian Planning", *Economic and Political Weekly*, May 12, 1973.
3. A similar survey in Punjab and West UP has also been completed. The study will be reported in a subsequent article.
4. It was decided to take about 100 villages in each state. The villages were allocated to the districts in proportion to the agricultural population of the districts; and, within each district, villages were selected randomly with probability proportional to the village population. The numbers allocated to West Bengal, Bihar and the districts of East UP, were 110, 101 and 65, respectively.
5. These and subsequent average percentage figures based on answers of respondents about themselves or about their particular landlord or employer refer to averages over *cases* of respondents, not exactly villages. When percentage figures refer to villages, on the basis of answers on general questions regarding the village, we have explicitly called them village percentages.
6. If a tenant has leased in land from more than one landlord, the relevant characteristics reported here (and subsequently) are presumably those of the principal landlord.
7. In 20 sample villages in Bihar (mostly in Darbhanga, Gaya, Muzaffarpur and Patna) the farm servant reports repaying consumption loans by doing extra days of work. Of these 20 villages, 12 are advanced and 4 moderately advanced. In West Bengal and East UP, this practice is less frequent.

Index

Printed and bound by CPI Group (UK) Ltd, Croydon, CR0 4YY

23/04/2025

14660951-0001